Cloud of Witnesses

REVISED EDITION

Edited by
Jim Wallis and Joyce Hollyday

ORBIS BOOKS
Maryknoll, NY 10545

SOJOURNERS
Washington, DC

Twelfth Printing, September 2012

Founded in 1970, Orbis Books endeavors to publish works that enlighten the mind, nourish the spirit, and challenge the conscience. The publishing arm of the Maryknoll Fathers and Brothers, Orbis seeks to explore the global dimensions of the Christian faith and mission, to invite dialogue with diverse cultures and religious traditions, and to serve the cause of reconciliation and peace. The books published reflect the views of their authors and do not represent the official position of the Maryknoll Society. To learn more about Maryknoll and Orbis Books, please visit our website at www.maryknollsociety.org.

Published by Orbis Books, Maryknoll, NY 10545-0308 and *Sojourners*, 2401 15th Street NW, Washington DC 20009.

Manufactured in the United States of America

Library of Congress Cataloging-in-Publication Data

Cloud of witnesses / edited by Jim Wallis and Joyce Hollyday.—Rev. ed.
    p. cm
    "The articles and interviews in this book have been adapted from
material originally published in Sojourners magazine"—T.p. verso.
    ISBN 1-57075-571-X (pbk.)
    1. Christianity and justice. 2. Christians. I. Wallis, Jim. II. Hollyday, Joyce. III. Sojourners.

BR115.J8C56 2005
270′.092′2—dc22

                              2004050104

To all sojourners through the ages

Blessed are the poor in spirit, for theirs is the kingdom of heaven.

Blessed are those who mourn, for they shall be comforted.

Blessed are the meek, for they shall inherit the earth.

Blessed are those who hunger and thirst for righteousness, for they shall be satisfied.

Blessed are the merciful, for they shall obtain mercy.

Blessed are the pure in heart, for they shall see God.

Blessed are the peacemakers, for they shall be called sons and daughters of God.

Blessed are those who are persecuted for righteousness' sake, for theirs is the kingdom of heaven.

— Matthew 5:3-10

Contents

Foreword to the Revised Edition

To be a Christian is to walk with Jesus—to share in his hope, his love, his destination. But those who try to walk that path discover quickly that they are not alone. As Scripture notes, we are surrounded by a great "cloud of witnesses" who strengthen and encourage us on our journey.

For a long time I have believed that one of the greatest responsibilities of the church is to publicize and remember the stories of these saints, prophets, and witnesses—both those of ancient times and those alive in our midst. The purpose is not simply to honor those who were often overlooked or even scorned by their contemporaries, but to enlarge our own moral imagination. Those who have learned the stories of Dietrich Bonhoeffer, Fannie Lou Hamer, Oscar Romero, and Dorothy Day inhabit a wider universe. New options—and new challenges—become available.

For those who question the meaning of discipleship in our time, the stories and interviews assembled in this book present an excellent starting point. Here is a collection of peacemakers, prophets, martyrs, servants of the poor, holy misfits, and other disturbers of the false peace—in short, people of the Beatitudes—who expand the common definition of human love and courage. Some of them are famous; others obscure. All of them have given proof that the gospel can be lived.

As the person who first proposed this book some fifteen years ago, it gives me particular pleasure to welcome this revised edition. Out of print for some years, *Cloud of Witnesses* is now back—quite literally—"by popular demand." Particular credit for this goes to JustFaith, a church-based program for justice education and formation, whose strong interest provided an incentive to make this book available once more.

The collaboration of Orbis Books and *Sojourners* on this project deserves some comment. Both founded in the early 1970s, Orbis and *Sojourners* have each struggled in parallel ways to address the meaning of the gospel in a world marked by violence and injustice. In doing so we have each highlighted the work of prophets and witnesses whose lives have incarnated the gospel message. It is a mark of our kinship that we have tended to draw inspiration from the same cast of characters. (Almost all of the figures featured in this book have appeared as well in the Orbis catalog, either as authors or as subjects of books.)

In the case of *Sojourners* this appeal to an ever-widening circle of heroes and fellow travelers has served to characterize the magazine in its journey over the past thirty years. With its prophetic integration of evangelical faith and commitment to social justice, there is no doubt that *Sojourners'* appearance represented something new on the American religious landscape. But its early years were constantly marked by the happy discovery of forerunners and companions on the way: from the Confessing Church in Germany to the Black freedom struggle in the South; from the Catholic peace movement of the 1960s to the radical spirit of St. Francis; from the abolitionist struggle against slavery to the persecuted Anabaptists of the sixteenth century. Connections were discovered with the Bruderhof, and Koinonia Farm, and above all with the witness of Dorothy Day, founder of the Catholic Worker, who had set out with the same kind of creative spirit forty years before to invent her own brand of Catholic radicalism.

New links were forged with the struggle against apartheid in South Africa, with the base communities in Central America, and with faith-based struggles for peace and human rights around the globe. Increasingly, *Sojourners* became a meeting place for people of many traditions who found a common kinship in the radical message of Jesus and the promise of the Kingdom. For those who found a home in this magazine, and the spirit it represented, each issue was an exhilarating reminder that we are not alone—that we are part of a community across the centuries and around the globe.

More than a decade since the first edition of this book, the journey continues. But the essential challenge remains unchanged. As Jon Sobrino observes in his interview: "To be a Christian today in our world is to look a little bit like Jesus. It is to take seriously the reality of creation, to make this so-called option for the poor, to be really compassionate and merciful and to make something ultimate out of that mercy and compassion."

Or as Beyers Naudé suggests, after urging Christians to open their eyes to the suffering around them: "Then begin to share, in the deep and meaningful sense of the word, by going out to Christians and others saying, 'We are with you. We are one in the realization of our weakness. But we are also one in the realization of the tremendous potential for change that God has given to all of us. Let us build together so that we may truly make this world God's Kingdom.' "

One finishes this book with gratitude for these lives, and a sense of responsibility for the tasks before us. Drawing on the wisdom, courage, and energy of this cloud of witnesses, it becomes possible for each of us to take up the words of the late Chuck Matthei, one of the peacemakers profiled in this volume: "Here I am. Let's get moving."

ROBERT ELLSBERG
Editor-in-Chief, Orbis Books
June 2004

Acknowledgments

Our first thanks for this project go to Robert Ellsberg, who conceived the idea of the book and searched through years' worth of *Sojourners* magazines to begin to pull it together. He and his colleagues at Orbis Books have been competent and committed in seeing the project through.

We also wish to thank the editors of *Sojourners* who offered invaluable help. And we thank all those saints who went before us, both those mentioned in these pages and those unnamed, for crossing lines, lighting candles in the dark, and being persistently courageous as they have faithfully showed us the way.

This book is dedicated, with profound gratitude, to all those who have been part of Sojourners for more than three decades, some sharing the journey for a few steps and some for many miles. It is especially offered for those with whom we walk hand in hand today, discerning the way as we step forward, carrying Sojourners into the future.

Introduction to the 1991 Edition

Now faith is the assurance of things hoped for, the conviction of things not seen. For by it men and women of old received divine approval. . . . These all died in faith, not having received what was promised, but having seen it and greeted it from afar, and having acknowledged that they were strangers and exiles on earth.

(Hebrews 11:1–2, 13)

One afternoon, in the fall of 1978, a woman from the apartment building across the street knocked on the door of our Sojourners Community household, asking for help. Two real estate speculators had bought the building where Katherine lived with her two young sons. Five other families had also lived there, but they had all been evicted. The new owners stood to make a 100 percent profit on resale of the building to a wealthy couple.

Katherine had decided to stay and fight for her home. She was up against a force that was sweeping the inner city of Washington and other cities around the country. It was named "gentrification," and it meant that the poor were being put out of their homes in record numbers.

Sojourners Community raised money to buy the building in a non-profit sale. The new owners scoffed at the offer. Ignoring the owners' response, we put the money in an escrow account, and on a Friday afternoon we celebrated neighborhood ownership of Katherine's home, in the name of justice. Katherine broke a bottle of sparkling water on the side of the building, decorated brightly with balloons, while the children from the Sojourners Daycare Center, where Katherine's son Ofon was a student, planted a tree and marched around with signs that read "Let Ofon Keep His Home."

Three of us from Sojourners Community moved in with sleeping bags and toothbrushes to wait with Katherine. At 8 o'clock the next morning, long after the crowd had left, the police came and hauled us off to jail.

We were arraigned on Monday morning. A sincere, but very young, public defender offered to take on our case. We gently refused his help. But he was persistent. Finally he said, "Just tell me what you did." We explained it to him.

His eyes grew big, and finally he said with utter seriousness, "I think you should plead insanity. Because anyone who thinks they can stop real estate gentrification in Washington, D.C., is crazy."

This year, 1991, marks the 20th anniversary of Sojourners Community and magazine. In the summer of 1971, seven students from Trinity Evangelical Divinity School outside Chicago published the first issue of a tabloid we called then *The Post-American*. The $700 we had scraped together bought us 30,000 copies. Some of us traveled east, and some west, taking *The Post-American* to colleges, seminaries, churches, and people we met along the way.

We were thoroughly unprepared for the amount of mail we received in response. Before long, the shoebox we had set aside for keeping track of subscriptions couldn't contain all the names, and we were deluged with phone calls, visits, and invitations.

The publication of *The Post-American* had sparked something, and from the beginning it began to draw people together, creating an ecumenical spirit among Christians and reaching members of secular movements for justice and peace searching for faith and meaning in their lives. The brutality of the war in Vietnam, the persistence of white racism, and the grinding oppression of the poor were the issues *The Post-American* first addressed—from the perspective of the prophetic biblical tradition and the gospel that is good news to the poor.

In the fall of 1975, *The Post-American* became *Sojourners*, and the community attached to the magazine moved into inner-city Washington, D.C., where it remains today. The name change reflected a deepening of our identity as a Christian community and our commitment to rebuilding the church. Our understanding of the prophetic tradition grew from simply attacking the cruel manifestations of America's civil religion to offering a new vision for the church's life, with the seeds of new possibilities for the wider society.

The name *Sojourners* came from the passage quoted above, from the Letter to the Hebrews, in which the people of God are seen as pilgrims and strangers in this world because of their loyalty, not to the values of the world, but to God's way of justice and peace.

In two decades, the heady days of a new beginning have given way to bitter realities. Thirteen years after our experience with Katherine's home, we know only too well the truth of the words of that young public defender. Many more of our friends have been evicted. Families now swell the ranks of the homeless "urban refugees." And some of those children from our daycare center have lost their lives as teenagers in the drug-related violence born of desperation that has earned Washington, D.C., the title "murder capital" of the United States. (The federal Centers for Disease Control recently reported that it is now more likely for a young black male in our nation's inner cities to lose his life to homicide than it was for a soldier to be killed on a tour of duty in Vietnam.)

The United States has just been through another war, this one leaving tens of thousands of Iraqis dead in the sands of the Middle East. White racism is more entrenched than ever, evident in economic indicators and a rise in "hate crimes." And the poor face grinding oppression in ever more deadly and sophisticated ways.

The "quick success" of the Persian Gulf war, which drove the nation to unprecedented pride and euphoria, is likely to set into motion calls for more and more military spending, while schools and hospitals and drug rehabilitation centers close for lack of funds. We live in a time begging for prophets, for people of compassion who can call the nation to repentance and justice.

In days such as these, we are driven back to that scripture that first touched us in the beginning, the one that speaks about faith and the "conviction of things not seen." We draw hope and courage from the "heroes of the faith" who are listed there, the ones who remained faithful in spite of the fact that they did not see the promise fulfilled in their lifetimes.

Hebrews 11:4 begins the "roll call of faith," mentioning by name Noah, Abraham, Sarah, Isaac, Moses, Rahab, and others. This is not a gallery of success and accomplishment; these are not winners and world shakers. Most of them wouldn't be called successful by any standard. But they kept the faith. And so they are remembered.

This passage is our family tree. Here are listed the men and women who have gone before and blazed the trail for us. Here are our foremothers and forefathers, the ones on whose shoulders we now stand.

Their faithfulness has given birth to other children of the faith. If anything has encouraged us in the twenty years that we have attempted to live faithfully in community and in the inner city, it has been the companionship of others on this journey—some close by and some far away, some contemporaries and some from the pages of history—but all sisters and brothers united by a common hope, a "communion of saints."

This book is a collection of their stories, a tribute to the people and the movements they spawned, which have inspired and sustained us at Sojourners through the years. Some of the stories first appeared in our annual December "incarnation" issues of *Sojourners*, as each year we have maintained a tradition of focusing on an individual who incarnates the love and witness of Christ. Others appeared in *Sojourners* spread over the years and seasons.

Although in some instances the historical situations in which they witnessed have changed, each person in these pages has spoken as a prophet, proclaiming the gospel in a concrete reality, in a manner that will never be outdated. Ephemeral events have inspired lasting testimony, upon which the community of faith will draw for generations to come.

This collection is not an exhaustive one. We had to pare down the book by almost half, often making painful choices about whom to include and whom to leave out. So the individuals included here stand for many others who must remain unnamed.

We have chosen to organize their stories according to the Beatitudes. While many stories could have fit into several categories, each seemed to have a most compelling aspect to it—a life marked by humility or compassion, a strength born out of grieving or persecution, a courage rooted in conviction.

Each person here has made the path just a bit easier for the rest of us. As Cleo Fields, the 25-year-old state senator from Louisiana, put it at the Democratic National Convention in 1988: "Booker T. Washington started to teach so Rosa Parks could take her seat. Rosa Parks took her seat so Fannie Lou Hamer could take her stand. Fannie Lou Hamer took her stand so Martin Luther King, Jr., could march. Martin Luther King marched so Jesse Jackson could run."

We have been granted a rich legacy by the strength and courage of these and many other heroes of the faith. But they do not ask us to enshrine them; they invite us to follow them. The Hebrews passage continues: "And all these, though well attested by their faith, did not receive what was promised, since God had foreseen something better for us, that apart from us they should not be made perfect" (Hebrews 11:39–40).

These verses remind us that, though we may never see the results we hoped for, our disappointment simply puts us in good company. But most important of all, they place the responsibility on each of us to carry on—because "apart from us they should not be made perfect."

We act in faith for the sake of the faithful ones who went before us, trusting that we would follow—and for those who will come after us on this journey. Those who have gone before—and those who will follow—are invested in our struggle for faithfulness.

In the closing words of her last book, Penny Lernoux quoted a young Guatemalan peasant woman. The words were a reflection on the gospel mandate to lay down our lives, offered a few months before this woman was killed by the Guatemalan military. "What good is life," she said, "unless you give it away?—unless you can give it for a better world, even if you never see that world but have only carried your grain of sand to the building site. Then you're fulfilled as a person."

In the words of our good friend Vincent Harding, "Living in faith is knowing that even though our little work, our little seed, our little brick may not make the whole thing, the whole thing exists in the mind of God, and that whether or not we are there to see the whole thing is not the most important matter. The most important thing is whether we have entered the process."

But what about when we get tired? What about those days when it is difficult to hang on to hope, when we are more aware of our weaknesses and failures than our successes, when it seems that nothing we do makes any difference and, despite our efforts, things seem to go from bad to worse?

Hebrews beckons to us again, with an invitation and a challenge: "Therefore, since we are surrounded by so great a cloud of witnesses, let us also lay aside every weight, and sin which clings so closely, and let us run with perseverance the race that is set before us, looking to Jesus the pioneer and perfecter of our faith, who for the joy that was set before him endured the cross, despising the shame, and is seated at the right hand of the throne of God" (Hebrews 12:1–2).

Vincent Harding likens these witnesses to "a great cheering squad for us. In the midst of everything that seems so difficult, that seems so powerful, that seems so overwhelming, they are saying to us: 'We are with you,' and 'There is a way through; there is a way to stand; there is a way to move; there is a way to hope; there is a way to believe. Don't give up!'"

There is nothing—no emotion or struggle or obstacle—that we face that these witnesses haven't already faced. And surely, some day, we will all meet around the table of faithfulness, to share a banquet of joy. Vincent Harding describes the scene:

"Well, here we are, all present and accounted for. What a gang! What a table! What a host! What a chance for holding and being held, for feeding and being fed, for giving, receiving, and being the light.

"No excuse for drooping—-at least not for long. No excuse for not running—or at least walking strong. No excuse for staying down. 'Cause we are surrounded, folks. So, let's straighten up; let's get refreshed at the table, and then get down with some real long-distance walking and running—and maybe even some flying, like eagles, in due time. That's our tradition. That's our destiny. That's our hope. So go right on, sisters and brothers, people of the tents: walk in the light, run with the cloud, mount up on wings, follow the Pioneer. There is a city to build."

Indeed, there is a city to build. It is our hope that this book will be a worthy tool for the work. We offer it as an invitation to toil with joy, and as a reminder that we are never—no, never—alone.

JOYCE HOLLYDAY AND JIM WALLIS
March 1991

I

Blessed Are the Poor in Spirit

St. Francis of Assisi

Consumed with the Gospel

by Jim Wallis

The following article appeared in the December 1981 issue of S*ojourners,*** **in celebration of the 800th birthday of St. Francis.**

I suppose my knowledge of St. Francis was like most people's. If someone had asked me, a midwestern evangelical kid from Detroit, "Who was the most famous saint?" I would have puzzled for a moment and probably ended up by saying, "Oh, yes, St. Francis." If that person had then asked me what I knew about the famous saint, I would certainly have been stumped and, at best, come up with something about him loving birds and nature. St. Francis of the birdbath endures as one of the worst caricatures of history.

Years of university and seminary education did little to correct my shallow impression of the little poor man of Assisi. (Protestant seminaries generally don't do very well with the lives of saints.) It wasn't until a few years ago, when I had the rare commodity of a free evening, that I had my first real exposure to Francis. *Brother Sun, Sister Moon,* the movie directed by Franco Zeffirelli, was playing for a dollar at our local cheap movie theater, on a double bill with *Romeo and Juliet.*

I was completely unprepared for my first meeting with the saint. It was the beginning of an intense and often painful friendship, one that has affected me profoundly.

Now, after studying the life of Francis, the movie seems quite inadequate, with an unnecessarily romantic and ethereal quality. The real Francis, I think, was much more human and powerful than Zeffirelli's fragile and otherworldly character. But despite the film's limitations, this introduction to Francis left me overwhelmed with emotion.

I left the theater stunned and speechless. On the way home in the dark car, I quietly began to weep. Never before had I encountered a life so consumed with the gospel, a man so on fire with the love of God, a disciple so single-mindedly focused on following after Jesus, a spirit so joyful in abandoning everything to serve his Lord. The evangelical poverty of Francis had evangelized me to the depths of my soul.

I immediately began to question everything about my life. His utter obedience to Christ was radiant in exposing the places where my commitment was still compromised. His intimacy with God created in me what the monks call "a holy jealousy." His wholehearted love for Jesus Christ made me love our Master more than I ever had before. Francis was converting me again to Jesus. I cried that night because my faith seemed so small and weak when compared to his. I wondered what my life was counting for.

It's so easy to be a "radical Christian" in America. Here the church is so affluent, so comfortable, so lukewarm, that the most basic kind of discipleship or the simplest acts of justice, mercy, and peace seem extraordinary by comparison. Living what should be just an ordinary Christian life is enough to be designated radical by a spiritually impoverished church.

It is a constant temptation to accept the designation and, worse yet, to allow the American church to become the standard by which we measure ourselves. For Francis, the standard was always Christ and Christ alone, not the thirteenth-century church, nor even the movement of renewal that he founded.

G. K. Chesterton wrote of him, "So soon as he certainly has followers, he does not compare himself with his followers, towards whom he might appear as a master; he compares himself more and more with his Master, towards whom he appears only as a servant."

That simple insight articulated by Chesterton struck deep within me that night. What is the measure of my life? How have I let the standard of others make me complacent to the standard of Christ? I felt a hunger in me for what I saw in this little man from Assisi.

What I saw was Christ vividly incarnate in the life of Francis. It was like meeting Jesus afresh.

Three years have passed, and my struggle with the testimony of Francis has grown. On a retreat, I read his biographies. Again I felt drawn closer to Jesus than at any time since my conversion and the founding of Sojourners. I came home with a deepening love for the humble saint and a growing desire for a closer walk with Christ.

Since then, Francis has been the subject of more reading, the cause of much reflection, the catalyst for prayer, the push, for deeper self-examination.

Francis did not merely accept poverty, he pursued it. Some want to be poor for reasons of philosophy, ideology, or asceticism. Francis wanted to be poor because Jesus was poor and because his beloved Master so loved the poor. In other words, Francis stressed poverty so strongly, not for its own sake, but in order to become closer to God and nearer to the forgotten and suffering ones of the earth.

"Love for the poor was born in him," wrote St. Bonaventure. He virtually reveled in poverty and took the greatest joy in destitution. The great love affair between Francis and his "Lady Poverty" rivals all of the most famous romances of history.

For Francis, poverty without humility was no gain. "What is the use of renouncing the riches of the earth, if you intend to keep those of self-love?" he used to say to his friars, according to Omer Englebert.

He called his brothers Friars Minor, which means the little, unimportant ones. But for Francis humility was not a virtue to be sought after; rather, it was the natural result of a heart overflowing with the worship of God and the most profound respect and affection for every creature God had made.

Never has God been so freely praised nor ordinary men and women so highly regarded as in the life of Francis. His was a spiritual populism rooted in the love of God.

Chesterton reflects on this point:

I have said that St. Francis deliberately did not see the wood for the trees. It is even more true that he deliberately did not see the mob for the men. What distinguishes this very genuine democrat from any mere demagogue is that he never either deceived or was deceived by the illusion of mass-suggestion. Whatever his taste in monsters, he never saw before him a many-headed beast. He saw only the image of God multiplied but never monotonous. To him a man was always a man and did not disappear in a dense crowd any more than in a desert. He honoured all men; that is, he not only loved but respected them all. What gave him his extraordinary personal power was this: that from the Pope to the beggar, from the sultan of Syria in his pavilion to the ragged robbers crawling out of the wood, there was never a man who looked into those brown burning eyes without being certain that Francis Bernadone was really interested in him; in his own inner individual life from the cradle to the grave; that he himself was being valued and taken seriously, and not merely added to the spoils of some social policy or the names in some clerical document.

Francis received his vocation before the wooden crucifix of the abandoned church at San Damiano: "Francis, go repair my house, which is falling into ruins." To see the church restored to Christ was his driving passion and the heart of his calling. Like every authentic renewal movement in the history of the church, the Franciscan revolution was simply a return to the gospel, and Francis of Assisi returned to the gospel with such force that it shook the entire world.

The church always wanted Francis to write a rule for his order, as the leaders of all the other orders had done. But he always felt the gospel was enough:

> At daybreak they set out for the Church of San Nicolo to hear Mass, taking with them Peter of Catanii, who had likewise resolved to leave the world. They opened the missal three times at random. The first time, their eyes fell on these words: "If you will be perfect, go, sell what you have, and give to the poor." The second time, they read: "Take nothing for your journey"; and the third time: "If anyone wishes to come after Me, let him deny himself, and take up his cross, and follow Me."
>
> "Here," said Francis, "is what we are going to do, and all those who shall afterwards join us."
>
> (*St. Francis of Assisi*, Englebert)

Those simple gospel imperatives became the basis for the Franciscan way of life and the foundation for the first Rule of 1209. Francis' rules were simply the repetition of gospel texts with some commentary and guidelines for regulating the life of the friars. The Sermon on the Mount would have sufficed as Francis' rule, if he had had his way.

The Rule of 1221, written near the end of his life and under increasing pressure from the church, merely reiterated the way of life that the friars had lived since the beginning, and beautifully expressed the behavior and spirit that Francis hoped would always characterize the movement he had begun. However, Francis' great rule was never officially accepted. The Rule of 1223 used more legal and traditional language in revising and adding to the words of Francis.

The desire of Francis and his brothers to live without property and security was always resisted by the church. The story of their first trip to Rome to gain acceptance of their order raised the central problem:

> Thus all were of the opinion that so literal an interpretation of the Gospel went beyond human strength, and the Pope himself declared, "Although your zeal, my dear sons, reassures Us, We must nevertheless think of your successors, who may find the path you wish to follow too austere."

But the Cardinal of St. Paul replied, "If we reject this poor man's request on such a pretext, would not this be to declare that the Gospel cannot be practiced, and so to blaspheme Christ, its Author?"

(Englebert)

Francis lived and spoke directly to the confusion most of us still have between success and obedience, a particularly American affliction. One of his greatest masterpieces is the dialogue he had with Brother Leo about the meaning of "perfect joy":

"Brother Leo, God's Little Sheep, take your pen, I am going to dictate something to you," declared Francis.

"I am ready, Father."

"You are going to write what perfect joy is."

"Gladly, Father!"

"Well, then, supposing a messenger comes and tells us that all the doctors of Paris have entered the Order. Write that this would not give us perfect joy. And supposing that the same messenger were to tell us that all the bishops, archbishops, and prelates of the whole world, and likewise the kings of France and England, have become Friars Minor, that would still be no reason for having perfect joy. And supposing that my friars had gone to the infidels and converted them to the last man. . . ."

"Yes, Father?"

"Even then, Brother Leo, this would still not be perfect joy."

(Englebert)

Francis enumerated, and then dismissed, several other marks of success. Then he described to his astounded brother what perfect joy really is. He detailed a scene in which the two of them would arrive at the friary "soaked by the rain and frozen by the cold, all soiled with mud and suffering from hunger" and be driven away with "curses and hard blows." Francis said, " . . . and if we bear it patiently and take the insults with joy and love in our hearts . . . that is perfect joy!" He concluded, "Above all the graces and gifts of the Holy Spirit which Christ gives to his friends is that of conquering oneself and willingly enduring sufferings, insults, humiliations, and hardships for the love of Christ."

At the heart of Christian faith is the incarnation. I don't know what I would do without Jesus; abstract talk about God has always left me empty and longing for more. I need God made flesh, human like us, walking our streets, even in our shoes, teaching us the way of God. I also need people who teach me again the reality of the incarnation in their own lives and history. We all need that.

Francis is perhaps our greatest teacher. He has been called both "the first Christian" and "the last Christian." My struggle is just that; his life presents the gospel in such stark contrast to the world, to the church, and to my own life. Sometimes his example convinces me that it is indeed possible, with God's abundant grace, to live the gospel life. Other times his star shines so bright that it only exposes my own darkness. Francis converts me over and over to Jesus, but he also makes me sometimes wonder if I really am or want to be a Christian. He both points to the great possibility and shows me how much further I have to go to see what he saw.

This year the church celebrates the 800th birthday of the greatest saint. Many Christians will have a fresh opportunity to meet him, to come to know him, to let themselves be touched by the little poor man. I must warn you that if you begin to follow after him as he dances through the world, he will certainly turn your life upside down, as he has mine. To walk with Francis, even a little way, is a great adventure, but also a painful one. It is a journey that I still find myself very much in the middle of.

I don't know where the journey will end, either for me or for you. But I do know that I want to commend him to you. Once you have looked into his eyes, you will never see the same way again.

Dorothy Day

A Radical Simplicity

by Jim Forest

"Who was Brezhnev?" a Russian child of the future asks his grandfather in a contemporary Soviet joke. And he responds, "A minor politician of the Solzhenitsyn and Sakharov period."

Perhaps the day will come when a child will ask, "Who was Billy Graham? Who was Pope Paul?" And the answer may be, "Minor religious figures of the Dorothy Day period."

Dorothy Day wouldn't approve of the joke, of course. For one thing, she has great appreciation for Pope Paul. For another, she doesn't want to be burdened with admiration. "Don't call me a saint," she fired back at one starry-eyed soul, "I don't want to be dismissed so easily."

Nor would she appreciate being torn from her context, the Catholic Worker movement. For others, that movement is incarnated in her; in her own vision it is nothing more than an awkward but necessary expression of the practical life (and the hard sayings) of Jesus. She would emphasize, without a trace of false modesty, the founding role played by a wandering scholar from France, Peter Maurin. She would

Jim Forest was an editor of *The Catholic Worker* in the early 1960s. This article appeared in a special issue of *Sojourners* devoted to Dorothy Day and the Catholic Worker in December 1976. Dorothy Day died four years later at the age of 83.

talk of all those who have come into the Worker community over its forty-three long years.

And yet her friends and co-workers know, in both love and bruises, the Catholic Worker movement would be a very different thing, if it existed at all, were it not for the volcanic stubbornness of Dorothy Day.

Apart from that religious stubbornness that has become such a signature of the Catholic Worker movement, it is unlikely that contemporary Christianity would be dotted with so many occasions of hope, so many communities dedicated to the works of mercy and of peace, as many lives so closely centered on the simplicity, poverty, and vulnerability of Jesus.

To look at recent history with a biblical consciousness is to see in the Catholic Worker movement, and in Dorothy Day and others who have been its parents and guardians, one of the main vehicles of God's presence in recent history, transforming individual lives and even reviving the conscience of religious institutions. Had there been no Catholic Worker, no Christian body would be quite as respectful of the sacredness of conscience and of life.

Yet the recognition of this is rather new. If Dorothy Day is prominently featured in the latest *Who's Who* and has a full page of four-color presence in *Life's* recent special issue on women, only a few years ago she, with the Catholic Worker movement, was often viewed as a borderline heretic who rightly belonged in the prison cells she so often inhabited. Catholic theologians and bishops (but it could have been Niebuhr or Tillich) denounced the Catholic Worker pacifism—even while grudgingly admiring the Worker's houses of hospitality (which were nothing more than the Worker's witness to that absolute reverence for life which the theologians condemned).

Dorothy was viewed with intense suspicion. After all, as she herself sometimes puts it, "the bottle always smells of the liquor it once held." And Dorothy used to be a communist, if never a docile pupil of party line. She was a militantly radical secular journalist (first jailed in a feminist demonstration in front of Woodrow Wilson's White House). She was the common-law wife of an anarchist—and mother of a daughter out of wedlock. She used to drink into the small hours of the morning with Eugene O'Neill and many other Greenwich Village visionaries who were only too willing to agree with Marx that religion is the opiate of the people. "Convert" though she might be, she would never be cleansed of her absurd and dangerous notions. Why, she calls herself an "anarchist" and recommends books by Kropotkin! In a "Catholic" newspaper!

But there was, in Dorothy, no wolf in sheep's wraps. In 1927, in a conversion process brought on by her pregnancy and the birth of Tamar, she had been slowly drawn to the end of her "long loneliness," intoxicated with an ardor not only for the life taking root within herself, but for that mystery in which all life is rooted. "How can there be no God, when there are all these beautiful things?"

She became, to the scandal of most of her friends, not merely religious, not just Christian, but a Catholic—so often seen as the worst, the most reactionary, the least free, the least tolerant of all the major religious bodies. A *Catholic.*

But for Dorothy Catholicism was something altogether different from what her friends perceived. It was that immense net that had caught, not only scoundrels, but saints beyond counting. It was the church of the Mass: the persistently present Jesus waiting in bread and wine on the altar. A church of respect for those who have died, a church which, in G.K. Chesterton's words, thought of tradition as being "democracy extended through time . . . the universal suffrage of giving the vote to one's ancestors." It was a church in which there was not only the thanksgiving sacrament on the altar, but the healing sacrament of forgiveness in the confessional. It was a church insistent about the demands and discipline of faith. And it was the church of the working masses of the poor. So she saw it. Such was her experience. And she could not resist saying yes to a longing to be in it rather than at its edges.

Yet in December 1932, a freelance journalist watching a "hunger march" parading past heavily armed police into the city of Washington, she was filled with grief that, however spiritually fulfilling the church had become for her, it offered her no adequate vehicle to respond to injustice and suffering. The march she was reporting for a Catholic journal had been inspired and led by Communists, not Christians. She ached with the realization that there were so many "comfortable churchgoers" who gave "little heed to the misery of the needy and the groaning of the poor."

She went from the march route to the crypt of the National Shrine of the Immaculate Conception. It was the feast day for which the Shrine was named. "There I offered up a special prayer, a prayer which came with tears and with anguish, that some way would open for me to use what talent I possessed for my fellow workers, for the poor."

One has to watch out about prayers, particularly those of the heart. There is always the danger they will be answered.

When Dorothy returned from Washington to her New York tenement apartment, Peter Maurin was waiting for her: a rumpled, tramp-like man in his fifties who spoke with a thick French accent. He came because, having read her articles, he had decided she alone could start a unique newspaper, to be the voice of a major movement. He wanted to call it *The Catholic Radical.*

Not everyone could stand Peter. He was a better talker than a listener. He had an intense vision of what needed to be done, and he pushed his ideas with seldom a pause. But Dorothy, though not a bad talker herself, was fascinated. Peter had a plan for a movement that would help produce a society "in which it is easier for people to be good," and the vision struck a chord in Dorothy that has never stopped resonating.

By May 1, 1933, the first issue of the paper minted from their friendship appeared. Its name had evolved into *The Catholic Worker* and it was distributed first at a communist rally at Union Square.

From the first, the paper stood for certain rather definite programs. What made the *Worker* different, however, from numerous publications was that the editors felt it a duty to carry out their own ideas and not just write about them. Thus, the *Catholic Worker's* proposal that every parish have a house of hospitality translated itself into the Catholic Worker's first house of hospitality: a place of welcome and sustenance for those who had no food or welcome.

The *Catholic Worker* advocated communities on the land, and soon they had such a community. The *Worker* saw scant hope for a more human society within the industrial system, whether capitalist or Marxist in sponsorship—nor did it see cities as having much reason apart from industry. The *Worker* stood instead for a culture founded in faith, agriculture and decentralism—the sort of thing that Gandhi was already saying, half the world away, and E.F. Schumacher and the ecology movement have said more recently. While the urban houses of hospitality responded to devastating needs and sufferings in practical ways, its rural communities were the seeds of "a new society within the shell of the old."

The editors advocated, but, more significantly, they practiced "voluntary poverty," a way of life resting on the New Testament admonition, "Let the person with two coats give to the one who has none." When some have nothing, let no one have too much. Nor let anyone imagine that owning and controlling make life more meaningful or secure—rather, more hemmed in by fears and less secure. They yield more days, perhaps, but less love, less sense of dependence on God's providence, less need for community and human caring.

But the Worker's most dangerous and alarming affirmation was of nonviolence. They found in Jesus no closet general. He was the one who not only ordered his disciples to "put away the sword" but who made himself a victim of the sword—who submitted to the electric chair of his day, and made it a passage—way to life, a sign of freedom from bondage to those who would, in the name of law or idolatry to flags and borders, make murderers of us.

The *Catholic Worker's* oft-tested pacifism was given its first trial in the Spanish Civil War. The *Worker* was one of three Catholic papers in the U.S. that refused to sanction Franco's war against the Republic. Nor did the Worker offer its blessing to the Republican side. It published articles decrying the violence of both sides—for which it was excommunicated from the Catholic Press Association and shorn of the bundle orders, nearly 100,000 copies in all, which went into parish newspaper racks.

During World War II, the Korean War, and the Indochina War, it continued to stand for "peace without victory." Despite a controversy within the Worker movement in the early 1940s Dorothy's conviction prevailed that the way of Jesus had nothing to do with "just wars," or killing of any kind. The Worker would instead continue with "the works of mercy," a way that answered to hunger, thirst, illness, homelessness, rejection and grief—and which would add nothing to those forces (such as war) which create hunger, thirst, illness, homelessness, rejection and grief.

Amazingly, the Catholic Worker community lived its dissenting life in a joyful spirit. "All the way to heaven is heaven," Dorothy would say over and over, quoting from one of the saints, "because Jesus said, 'I am the way.'" In the *Worker's* pages one would often find a sentence of Leon Bloy's, "Joy is the most infallible sign of the presence of God."

The Worker witness has often been marked, however, with sacrifices, not only of material comforts, but of freedom. No one has counted how many in the Catholic Worker movement have gone to prison for work against war and racism and various other injustices, but it has been the norm rather than the exception. Dorothy herself was arrested repeatedly for her unwillingness, in the '50s and early '60s to join in New York City's annual war game: Citizens were required to obey a siren's wail and hurry into basements and subways—"shelters," it was advertised, from a potential nuclear blast. (Finally, as the number of resisters to the war ritual grew, the city gave up the annual drill.)

The Worker's history is full of such episodes. They all offer evidence to sustain a conviction that this is a witness transcending any particular religious tradition or non-tradition. The Worker is less a body of doctrine than a way of life founded in compassion, a compassion so genuine—and thus so practical—that it has kept its adherents in day-to-day community with those most scarred by what Dorothy calls, in her usual plain speech, "this filthy, rotten system."

The spirit of the Worker is of love, but of a love willing to resist, and of conversation, but conversation ready for action and argument. Yet love, resistance, and action are all in the spirit of conversation—of friends sitting around a table late into the night, drinking tea or coffee and eating stale scavenged bread. Thus I often recall the words in which Dorothy ended her autobiography, *The Long Loneliness*:

> We were just sitting there talking when Peter Maurin came in.
>
> We were just sitting there talking when lines of people began to form, saying, "We need bread." We could not say, "Go, be thou filled." If there were six small loaves and a few fishes, we had to divide them. There was always bread.
>
> We were just sitting there talking and people moved in on us. Let those who can take it, take it. Some moved out and that made room for more. And somehow the walls expanded.
>
> We were just sitting there talking and someone said, "Let's all go live on a farm."

It was as casual as that, I often think. It just came about. It just happened.

I found myself, a barren woman, the joyful mother of children. It is not easy always to be joyful, to keep in mind the duty of delight.

The most significant thing about the Catholic Worker is poverty, some say.

The most significant thing is community, others say. We are not alone anymore.

But the final word is love. At times it has been, in the words of Father Zossima [in *The Brothers Karamazov*], a harsh and dreadful thing, and our very faith in love has been tried through fire.

We cannot love God unless we love each other, and to love we must know each other. We know Him in the breaking of the bread, and we know each other in the breaking of bread, and we are not alone anymore. Heaven is a banquet and life is a banquet, too, even with a crust, where there is companionship.

We have all known the long loneliness and we have learned the only solution is love and that love comes with community.

It all happened while we sat there talking, and it is still going on.

Chuck Matthei

The Duty of Delight

by Robert Ellsberg

Chuck Matthei was an innovative thinker who helped pioneer community land trusts and other alternative economic models, and a longtime friend and supporter of Sojourners. From his earliest activism for civil rights and against the Vietnam War to his final work as founder and director of Equity Trust Inc., Chuck led a life of protest, service, and solution-seeking, fed by a deep understanding of the connections between nonviolence, economics, and justice. Chuck was 54 when he died of pneumonia as a complication of thyroid cancer on October 1, 2002.

After receiving the news that Chuck Matthei—friend, brother, mentor—had returned home to Voluntown, Connecticut, to die, I left a message to see whether I might visit one last time. His sister called and said that Chuck would be delighted to see me. I knew he could not speak. But evidently with the help of his laptop computer he was able to dictate requests. "Bring prints of Fritz Eichenberg for me to look at," he

Robert Ellsberg, editor-in-chief of Orbis Books, is the author of *The Saints' Guide to Happiness*.

said. "Bring photos of your children—to illustrate the stories you will tell." I promised to come the next day.

I didn't know quite what to expect. I was conducted into his office, where he sat on a wheelchair with the computer poised on his lap. He looked very old and frail. As usual, though, he was able to communicate a lot through his eyes.

I was amazed by how well he could carry on a conversation by typing away on his laptop—almost as fast as he could talk, stopping occasionally to backspace and correct a spelling or reconsider a word or phrase.

I described the book I am working on. I said I was trying to reflect, through the lives of holy people, on what makes for a happy and whole life. He said, "I have a lot of thoughts about this." He began typing, words to this effect:

"Since I got sick, many people have asked whether I am angry, frustrated, bitter. And I say, Never. When people receive the diagnosis of a terminal illness, they are first of all afraid of being alone, and they wonder about how they might have lived differently. But I have never been alone. I have been surrounded by good friends and community, and blessed with meaningful work. I have never had to make decisions on the basis of money or peer pressure. Of course there are things I would do differently. If it were otherwise it would mean that I had not learned from life."

He did have a concern: "There are things I have learned that I wish I could pass on to my nephews and niece. I wouldn't want to tell them what to do with their lives. But there are things I have learned from people and experiences."

By this time theologian and activist Bill Wylie-Kellermann had joined us. Chuck suggested that we just talk as friends—as we always had in the past—and he would chime in. And so we talked. He would type and I, sitting next to him, would read the words off his monitor.

Bill asked him whether he felt "finished" with his work. "Never," Chuck typed. He said it was tempting to be discouraged sometimes. "You know how Dorothy Day wrote in the postscript to *The Long Loneliness* about how hard it is to remember 'the duty of delight.' But I have said to friends, as I contemplate the life I've had and the end that is coming, 'It's not so hard, either, when one has been graced by such good work and good friends.' To me it is the recognition that we are never without a meaningful choice. This is a culture that nearly drowns people with meaningless consumer choices, yet leaves most of them feeling that they are powerless in the most important affairs of life— but that's not true.

"We may not be able to choose the moment of our entry into the world, the circumstances that confront us, the choices available, or the consequences that face us for making those choices. But we can always decide *how* we will respond. We can keep hold of the only 'possession' that cannot be taken from us: our dignity, integrity, soul, call-it-what-you-will. That is the decision that defines us, the first important 'life lesson' we should teach our children. This is the decision I have to make every morning: I can rise and think about what has been done to me, what I have lost . . . or I can rise and say to myself, 'Here I am. Let's get moving!'

"With gratitude for good work, good friends, and a wonderful family, it's not a hard choice to make. . . . It's not hard to remember the 'duty of delight.'"

I had first heard Chuck speak about this freedom to choose our attitude when I was 18 and a freshman at Harvard; I had written to the Selective Service System telling them that I would refuse to register for the draft. All my life I had been awaiting this fork in the road, inspired by the example of other draft resisters I had met. But by the time this day came in 1973, the draft was over, most people had moved on, and I found little support or understanding among my friends. I felt terribly alone.

Then late one night I came home to find a stranger waiting for me in my dorm room. One of my roommates had let him in. I never really did find out how Chuck had heard about me, but evidently he had hitchhiked across the state to come see me.

I later discovered how characteristic this was of Chuck Matthei. He believed that the kind of struggle I was going through was the most important question anyone could face (not the question of the draft, per se, but whatever occasion causes a young person to ask what life is ultimately about). Like a magnet, he was drawn to people in that situation—not to tell them what to do, but to offer support and the wisdom of his own experience.

With his long beard and balding head, he seemed like a real old guy to me (he was in his mid-20s). He recounted his own experiences with the draft, how he was arrested and almost died as a result of his non-cooperation in jail. He talked about Dorothy Day, Gandhi, Tolstoy, and other heroes. And he told me about Victor Frankl and his book *Man's Search for Meaning*. From his experience in a Nazi concentration camp Frankl had devised a theory of psychotherapy based on the idea that the primary drive for human beings is the need for meaning. Frankl believed it was possible to find that meaning under all circumstances; we have the power, under all circumstances, to shape our attitude. This was the first of Chuck's many lessons.

I took away from my first encounter with Chuck that there wasn't really a right or wrong answer to my dilemma with the draft. But I did have a choice to respond to the big questions of life, and to find my own answers. I ended up registering. But I also ended up dropping out of college the next year and making my way to the Catholic Worker—a community where it no longer seemed strange at all but simply obvious why one should struggle over such questions.

By this time Chuck's mother and sister and some other friends had joined us. From the table that was covered with books and pictures, Chuck asked someone to hand him a copy of *The Family of Man*, Edward Steichen's classic book of photographs. He paged through until he found his favorite picture: a crowd of African children surrounding an older man who was in the middle of saying something amazing. There was no caption, and at first I was confused. Then I said, "Aha, the story-teller!" Chuck replied, "He is my hero."

We talked about the importance of preserving a memory, a connection with the stories and the wisdom of those who came before us. This was another lesson that Chuck had always imparted, and that he wanted his niece and nephews to understand: the importance of listening to the wisdom of our elders, not to think that we have to start from scratch.

I said he reminded me of Socrates—someone who had no official title or office, but who simply hung out in the public square asking people questions, making them examine their lives, their assumptions about what it meant to live well. Socrates was convicted by the authorities for "corrupting the youth."

I was struck by how much our conversation circled back to the beginning of our acquaintance, twenty-eight years before. What he had to say now was exactly the same message he had shared with me then. On the one hand that just showed how consistently he had lived by his personal code. It had guided him through life and remained his support up to the end.

I told him I was sure that he had successfully communicated this wisdom to his niece and nephews—and countless other people over his life—even if he never wrote any of it down.

Eventually it was time for me to leave. I kissed him on the top of his bald head and thanked him for *everything*. And said goodbye. As I walked out of this sacred space into the cold autumn air of New England that he loved, I felt that I was leaving the best and bravest man I ever met. Chuck would have dismissed such sentiments. He never wanted people to be like him—just to find their own inner light, and to follow as faithfully as they could. As he had remarked in our last conversation, four days before he died, "Every age has need of a few fools."

If ever I am prone to discouragement, I will try to remember my last sight of him in his wheel chair, so close to death, typing away on his laptop computer: "Here I am! Let's get moving!"

II

BLESSED ARE THOSE WHO MOURN

Jon Sobrino

Touching the Idols

On November 16, 1989, six Jesuit priests, their cook, and her teenaged daughter were murdered in their residence at the University of Central America in San Salvador, El Salvador. Jon Sobrino, S.J., a renowned theologian whose absence when the attack came surely saved his life, had been a member of that community for more than fifteen years.

Sobrino's theology grows out of the experience of the people. His life is a testimony to the words of liberation theologian Gustavo Gutiérrez: "One act of solidarity or love means more than a thousand books of theology." He was interviewed by Jim Wallis three weeks after the killings.

This is a difficult place to begin, but I'd like to ask you to reflect on the meaning of the sacrifice of your brothers, the martyred Jesuits.

Well, I could say so many things, but I will start by saying this: The killings of the six Jesuits—and of so many other people—is a revelation of something which is usually hidden. What they reveal is the truth of El Salvador, of the Third World, and of the whole world.

In general, the First World—and all those who have power—try very consciously to hide the truth. But as we all know, the killings of six

Jesuits makes news. The assassinations of 75,000 people in El Salvador unfortunately doesn't make news. And the 30 million people around the world who die yearly due to hunger or diseases related to hunger make absolutely no news.

What is the truth of our world? The truth is that God's creation is in very poor shape. Lots of human beings do not live with the minimum of life and dignity that God wants for them. Poverty in our country, and in the Third World—maybe in the place where you live—means that people are closer to death. Poverty is not just lacking opportunity; it is much more than that. Poverty means that maybe 60, 70, 80 percent of the population has survival as their daily task.

The main reason why so many people have been assassinated in El Salvador is because, in the last twelve years, they have wanted to organize themselves to exercise their right to survival. And when other people who are not poor—like the Jesuits who were killed, or myself, or the four North American sisters [Maura Clarke, Ita Ford, Dorothy Kazel, and Jean Donovan]—try to help the poor so that they can live, they also get killed.

We live in a world of death which goes beyond Western or Eastern, Marxist or democratic categories. This world wants to cover up death.

In the biblical writings of John, the Evil One is described as both assassin and as liar. Sin has a tendency to hide itself; whenever there is a scandal, automatically it's covered up. This world which gives death to so many millions of people also lies about it. It tries to ignore death very consciously; even worse, its uses euphemisms to cover death up.

For example, we hear El Salvador referred to as a country on its way to development. That's a euphemism. We have to analyze whether El Salvador is really on the way to development or to more underdevelopment. Another euphemism is the word "democracy." I favor democracy, you understand. But you have to realize what is meant by democracy. President Reagan said he was so happy now that in the Americas "almost all countries are democratic countries." Well, that was a euphemism used to cover up basic poverty and repression. Compared to this gigantic cover-up about the world, the cover-ups of Watergate and even Irangate were minimal.

In theological terms, what this shows is that in this world of ours there are idols. I am disappointed that so much of Western theology in the 20th century focuses only on the question of God's existence or nonexistence. You know the terms—faith and unbelief.

Idolatry goes beyond that. Idolatry means that there are historical realities which present themselves as divinities with the characteristics of true divinities. They are something ultimate. They don't need to justify themselves. They are untouchable. They offer salvation to their worshipers although in fact they dehumanize them. Worst of all, in order for these idols to survive, they need victims.

So I think we live in a world of idols. Idols are not trees or images which so-called primitive people worship. Idols are existing realities which every human being, no matter how well-developed or scientific he or she is, worships.

In El Salvador, as Archbishop Romero used to say, there are two main idols: the accumulation of wealth, and the doctrine of national security. Our national interest becomes ultimate, something untouchable. This has happened in El Salvador; national security now means that anybody who disagrees with the official policy, especially that of the army, will be persecuted and killed. When you touch an idol, you get burned, and you get killed.

Now these Jesuits—and so many others—simply told the truth about the country. They unmasked the lies—the efforts to cover up the scandal of the country—and they touched the idols. The same thing happened to them as to Jesus of Nazareth, to Martin Luther King, Jr., and to Archbishop Romero: They were killed. So El Salvador is not just a terrible anecdote in present history, it's one case among many that show the kind of world we live in.

The killings also show what we normally understand to be true: Sin is central to an understanding of Christian faith. Without sin, conversion makes no sense. And without conversion, there is certainly no Christianity.

In the First World, sin is dealt with usually more from an individual point of view, which raises many questions. I think that in the First World, many theologians don't know what to do with sin.

There are many reasons why people don't take the world's sin seriously, but I think we should. We see so many human beings around the world dying like Jesus Christ on the cross. We say that Jesus died for our sins; but if we instead rephrase it and say that Jesus dies *because* of our sins, because of the sin of the world, then it becomes obvious that there is indeed sin in the world. And if sin is what gave death to Jesus Christ, and so many people are still dying like Jesus Christ, sin is still very present.

But in spite of so much sin, so much death, so much suffering, there is something in our history which gives us hope. I ask myself so often, How is it possible that there is hope? Why haven't these people of El Salvador and Guatemala committed collective suicide? After so many centuries of being oppressed and repressed—new governments, new superpowers—why haven't they said, "History makes no sense"? Because they have hope.

Hope for what? Just to live. These people don't take life for granted. For those of us who take life for granted, life cannot be an object of hope. That's why so many Christians in the First World, when they think of hope they think, "Well, maybe there is another life." For the poor of El Salvador, living on this earth is a matter of hope.

I think, for me, this is one of the ways in which this ultimate mystery which we call God is revealed. In the presence of death, life itself makes sense. It is good to live. There is something positive in history. In order to have life, many people work for it.

These Jesuits, among others, reacted with compassion and mercy toward those who are deprived of life. Compassion and mercy are not just psychological responses; they are the reaction toward people who suffer, by the very fact that they suffer. El Salvador is a whole country in suffering; therefore, the appropriate name for compassion and mercy is justice. Justice is mercy—and compassion for the majority.

At times this mercy and compassion become heroic. They become love. They become the greatest love in people who die innocently—like the poor in El Salvador who are killed because of the very fact they are poor—or in others who give up their own lives in a very conscious way. They are ready to give everything. And there you have the greatest love.

Would you say that it has always been true that the role of the martyrs is to unmask the world's cover-up, to bring to light the idolatries that exist and by doing so, make conversion possible?

In Latin America in the last twenty years there have indeed been martyrs. But there have been martyrs since the first centuries of Christianity. I am convinced that the type of martyrdom we have now is the type of martyrdom Jesus went through. Christians today are killed, historically speaking, for the same reasons Jesus was killed. They want justice, they unmask lies, and in this way they show they believe in God—but a God of life, a God of the poor.

In other centuries it might have been different; the Archbishop of Canterbury was killed to defend the church's rights. But Romero was not killed, or these Jesuits, or the North American church women, defending the church's rights. They were killed for defending the rights of the poor. To find a parallel to this you have to go back to the beginning, to Jesus of Nazareth.

The scriptures often speak of the cross of Christ as a moral clash with the principalities and powers of this world, with the ruling idolatries. You speak of the cross so often in your writings. The centrality of the cross has been very much clarified these past months, it seems to me.

At times even my friends in Latin America have told me, "You stress the cross too much, you should speak more about the Resurrection." I think that for me the cross is central. Our risen Lord is not just a corpse who came back to life, but somebody who was assassinated.

Peter describes the Resurrection of Jesus in the first chapters of the

Acts of the Apostles as a drama in two parts. First he says, "You people of Israel, you know Jesus of Nazareth, and you know human beings killed him." That's the first act of the drama. In this Jesus was innocent; history is such that it produces innocent victims.

And then the second part of the drama: "This Jesus, this man whom you killed, God has raised from the dead." The Resurrection of Jesus of Nazareth is not primarily a promise of an afterlife. The Resurrection of Jesus is primarily a symbol of hope for the victims of this world. At least in one case, a crucified victim triumphed over his executioners. But if you don't have the cross, Resurrection makes no sense, Christian faith makes absolutely no sense.

Now what I want to add is that when I make the cross central in faith and theology, it's not because I am a masochist. It is because I don't see how you can show love in this world of sin without being in solidarity with the victims of this world. And if you are in solidarity with the victims of this world, I don't see how you can avoid the cross. The theology of the cross is the theology of love in our real world.

You are often described as a liberation theologian. What do you think is the essence of liberation theology now? Is it the same as it was two decades ago? What are the challenges and what is at stake now?

Although it has reacted, the strongest accusation against liberation theology has not come from the Vatican. The strongest accusation has come from the Rockefeller Report, the Santa Fe Document, the multinationals, those who really want to accumulate wealth.

Some well-trained theologians who read Gustavo Gutiérrez's books years ago say that while liberation theology is interesting and was inspiring at first, now it's out of fashion, passé. The notion that liberation theology, as such, is passé is absolutely false.

Let's remember the origin of liberation theology. If there is no oppression, the word "liberation" makes no sense. The reason liberation theology arose is because theologians and other Christians saw that there was oppression in Latin America and in other parts of the world. So the question is, Is there oppression today in the world? Unfortunately, the world is getting worse, from the point of view of the poor.

I recently read in *Time* magazine—ironically it was in a section called "Business"—that up to 60 to 80 percent of the Latin American population—that means perhaps 300 million people—is on the path to becoming another Bangladesh, which in today's world is the symbol of utter poverty. *Time* magazine is saying that poverty is going to get worse—much worse.

That article also said that the wealthy people in Latin America have invested $326 billion in the United States alone. The gap between the

very poor and the very rich is getting wider. This is just one way of saying that there is still oppression in the world. If this is so, I cannot conceive of any theology which is Christian, which believes in a God who
created human beings, which believes in Jesus of Nazareth, which
doesn't take this fact as central for its faith today.

I am very much aware that liberation theology has many limitations.
We don't have much time to think, we don't have libraries. Our own
library in El Salvador was partially destroyed. But we've seen one thing
very clearly: You cannot be a believer in God today in this world if you
do not take oppression seriously.

What is at stake here is not theology. It is not whether you go from
existentialist theology to liberation theology or to process theology.
What is at stake here is faith and humanity.

This problem is not only for Christians but for any human being. I
don't know how you can be a human being on this planet today if this
growing oppression and poverty is not your central issue. I don't know
how we can avoid being ashamed of our being human beings if we don't
take this as the central problem of our human family.

To be a Christian today in our world is to look a little bit like Jesus.
The task is not simply to imitate him; we can't do that for many reasons. It is to take seriously the reality of creation, to make this so-called
option for the poor, to be really compassionate and merciful and to
make something ultimate out of that mercy and compassion.

If the churches are not built around this central message of the life
and presence of Jesus of Nazareth, then they are simply religious institutions with doctrines and ideologies. Archbishop Romero changed
Salvadoran society not because he was an analyst, but because he was
convinced that there is a God and that we have to please God. He
believed that it is good that there is a God of love, of tenderness, of
mercy for the poor, and that this is good news for this world of ours. If
you have that conviction, then you act in a different way. The poor find
hope; they find meaning.

I also used to say that long before the church made an option for the
poor, the poor in Latin America made an option for the church. The
poor have so much against them: governments are against the poor;
armies are against the poor; the wealthy are by definition against the
poor; and many universities, churches, and cultures are against the
poor. Why do the poor make an option for the church? They have
found, perhaps subconsciously, that a church which keeps Jesus of
Nazareth alive will be for them. That is good news for them.

*Isn't what's happening in the church of the poor the only future the
church really has? Isn't our only future always to go back to Jesus?*

I am convinced of that. Throughout the centuries there have always been movements which could be called the church of the poor. All great saints, especially in crisis times—whether Francis of Assisi or Ignatius—have the same insight: Let's go back to Jesus, and to his poverty. Wealth, abundance, power, and privilege are not the places for Christian faith. That's what history shows.

The miracle is that twenty centuries after Jesus, in this case in Latin America, this has been rediscovered. That means that the gospel has a power of its own.

The powerful of this world, including the churches, so often have tried to suffocate the basic message of the gospel. But as long as there are groups—even small ones—who again preach the beatitudes and the parable of the final judgment, then there is hope.

In the world, authority comes from wealth or a position of power; but from the gospel point of view, authority comes from suffering in some way. There's a paradox in the fact that a tiny country that has suffered so much, named "the Savior," is somehow being offered almost sacramentally for the salvation of the world.

The sacramental aspect of El Salvador is clear. I have often compared the Salvadoran people to the Suffering Servant of Yahweh.

The most obvious connection is death on the cross. But second, El Salvador sacramentalizes the responsibility of the world because, as in the case of the servant, the poor people in El Salvador are innocent. Their basic sin is that they are poor.

The third connection is faith. It is said that the servant was put by God as a light for the nations. Is it possible that light can come into the world from El Salvador? I am absolutely convinced that it is. As these Jesuits so often said, we see more from below than from the top.

As it is said of the servant, the poor of El Salvador offer salvation. Within the text of Isaiah we have a theoretical model of how the Suffering Servant can be salvation and expiation. And when we have approached this servant of God—the Salvadoran people—when we have tried to be with them, salvation has come upon us.

What does salvation mean? That our lives and our faith make sense. Deep sense. The Salvadoran people convey grace to us. As in the case of sin, I don't know what theologians in the First World do with grace. Grace is something we receive unexpectedly and undeservedly. And in general, the anthropologies of the First World are based on the opposite: Salvation is what you achieve. And this notion of grace, at least historically speaking, is difficult to grasp.

But that's what you experience in El Salvador. These people are grace for us in a very specific way: They forgive us, not by absolving us of sin, but by accepting us.

I'll always remember something I read a long time ago: Only he or she who has experienced himself or herself as forgiven can understand himself or herself as a sinner. In El Salvador you really experience that you belong to this sinful world but are simultaneously forgiven. And that is the experience of grace and salvation.

My friend, you are very vulnerable. Your brothers were killed in the house where you were living while you were gone. What does your vulnerability mean for your future as a theologian, as a Christian, and as a human being?

When I heard the news of the killings, obviously it came to my mind how vulnerable I am. But that thought soon disappeared. For me, what is more important is the question of where to get the strength to go on.

I see the Salvadoran people striving for so many years and being crushed so often. And now it seems we must start all over again.

How to really go on? These days a quote from the book of Micah has often come to mind. In a very solemn moment, the prophet says, "It has been declared to you what is good and right, what God expects from you: that you do justice and love kindness and that you walk humbly with God."

The first part is absolutely clear. No matter what has happened to these Jesuits, no matter what could happen to us, it is absolutely clear we have to work for justice; otherwise we cease to be human.

The second part is more obscure. How do we interpret walking humbly with God in history? I remember the great love shown by these Jesuits and so many others, or I look at the faces of poor people, and then walking in history makes sense. Faith means trying to do justice in the world—which we do by walking with God in history, and walking towards God.

So my main question has not been my vulnerability, but rather how to go on. Where do I get the strength to go on working in a world which is so tragic and so absurd? There is an answer for that: Remember Jesus of Nazareth and remember these people. Look at the poor, and you feel carried by them.

Albertina Sisulu

"I'll Never Bow Down"

"I feel strange. I can't believe it." These were the words uttered by Albertina Sisulu on July 31, 1981, the day the South African government lifted her seventeen-year banning order. For this steadfastly courageous woman, government persecution had become the normal fare of life.

Albertina Sisulu has been banned, harassed, tried for treason, imprisoned, and placed under house arrest. In 1964 her husband, Walter Sisulu, a leader in the African National Congress, was sentenced to life imprisonment in the same trial that put Nelson Mandela behind bars. Her outspoken son Zwelakhe, editor of the opposition newspaper *The New Nation*, has also been jailed as well as an adopted son. Three of her other children are in exile.

Through decades of suffering, Albertina Sisulu has served her people as a nurse and midwife, raised five children of her own and three whom she adopted after the deaths of relatives, and offered her life in testimony to the goodness of God and the evil of apartheid.

She has been granted the high honor of being named one of the three presidents of the broad-based United Democratic Front. And she has been given an "honor" from the other side as well: So threatening is she to the defenders of apartheid, the South African government singled her out and gave her individual restrictions when it effectively banned seventeen organizations in late February 1988.

Albertina Sisulu is a marvelously gracious woman, whose home has an open door for everyone from Soweto's children fleeing the police to a sympathetic North American stranger in awe of her courage and humility. Those keeping a watch on that door will never understand what greatness is inside.

Albertina Sisulu has ushered countless new lives into the world, each one likely, in time, to join the struggle for freedom. Her own children have followed her dauntless example. She has been midwife and mother to a movement, with an impact that spans generations.

She has one prayer: "I pray to God that one day I will see my people free." Surely, by her faithfulness, it will be answered in time.

Albertina Sisulu was interviewed in her Soweto home in April 1988 by Joyce Hollyday.

Walter Sisulu was released from jail two years later with Nelson Mandela.

When were you first banned?

My first banning order came in 1964. It was a five-year banning order, followed by ten years of house arrest. After that I was given two years of banning, which expired in 1983 when there was a blanket lifting of the banning orders.

And you have also been in prison several times?

Quite a number of times. I was in prison in 1963 with my first-born, who was 17 years old then. We were arrested under the 90-day detention, which was the Suppression of Communism Act.

In 1982 I participated in the funeral of a member of our federation [Federation of South African Women] by giving her life story. I was arrested because in the church was a flag—which they said was an ANC flag because it was green, black, and yellow—flying over the coffin. And they said we were furthering the aims of the ANC.

I spent seven months in jail while on trial. And I was sentenced to four years of imprisonment, two years suspended. I appealed the case. They allowed me bail of 1,000 rand [about $500].

While that case was still pending, I was arrested again in 1985 for the treason trial. I was in prison again for seven or eight months. And in all those times, I was in solitary confinement.

What was happening with your children during all this time?
With the first arrest in 1963, it was pathetic, because they were very young then. The baby was 4 years old. And when my brother from Cape Town came to fetch the child, he was refused, because there was an order from the commissioner here that not one of the children could be moved out of the house. So the children were depending on relatives and friends, who really looked well after my children. Every woman was here to help.

Walter was sentenced to life imprisonment in 1964. Do you get to see him?
Yes, there are opportunities monthly. But because it is so far, we can't afford that. I see him three, four times a year. And in between, the children do the visits.

Recently your son Zwelakhe was also imprisoned. Why was he detained?
Well, actually nobody knows, because the government is dodging about his detention. We have a feeling that he's detained because the newspaper [*The New Nation*] wouldn't bow down to the government's order that they must not publish anything that would be against the government.

When the lawyers applied for his release, they said they can't release him because he is a member of the NECC, which is the National Education Crisis Committee. We just don't know why he is still there, because the paper now is banned—and so is the Education Crisis Committee.

Where are your other children?
Out of my eight children, three are in exile: my first-born, my fourth-born—a daughter—and my sister-in-law's son. My brother-in-law's son is serving five years of imprisonment on Robben Island for "furthering the aims of the ANC."

How does that make you feel as their mother?
Well, like all parents, I'd like to be with my children at all times. And especially when there is a young girl who is not sure of her future in exile. She phones at times but we never know what country she's phoning from. She was arrested in 1976 and released a year later; she had to leave the country because the police were still following her.

It was worst when they arrested her, the little one. We couldn't see her for almost a whole year. We didn't know where she was. And when she came out of jail, she was mentally affected because they were torturing her. She has long hair, and she told me, "Mama, they would pull

my hair and knock me against the wall. And I would pass out, Mama."
That makes you feel you must work harder to see the end of apartheid.

I am bitter. And that is why I'll never bow down to any order from
the government. That is why I'm prepared to go on with the struggle
until the last day of my life. And, I dare say, I'll do that.

The government knows that—that is why I've really been pulled
about, because I'm on the right track. And I will never deviate.

*Obviously the fact that your children have had both of their parents
in prison hasn't scared them away from being involved in the struggle.*

In fact it has made them stronger. They never had a comfortable
home, with both parents at home. And there they are now, in and out
of jail.

*The government's desire has been to deter you by putting you in
prison, placing you under house arrest, and banning you. But, like
everyone else we've talked to who has been imprisoned, you have come
out even more determined. It seems that the government's plan is back-
firing. Is that true?*

It's very true. If you are being punished for being innocent, you have
nothing to lose. By being so brutal to the black people of this country,
the government is not helping itself. Instead, the government is organizing the people to be together.

When the government started being brutal to the children in 1976,
children were just doomed like flies in the streets. Whatever street you
turned on, you saw corpses of children shot by the police, by the people
who are supposed to be the protectors.

If your child is missing, you must get to one of the police cells, where
you find a pile of corpses of children in [school] uniform. You must go
through them to see if your child is there underneath. And in most
cases, you find your child under some other corpse.

And what do you think parents are going to think now about a government they thought was kind? The people now are so united they are
saying: "Let the devil do what it feels it can do, but we are not turning
back. We are going forward."

*What do you think happens to these children who have survived the
brutality—those who have been detained and tortured and beaten and
shot at in the streets?*

They are no longer afraid of the police. They are no longer afraid of
being jailed because they have been there.

I'm going to show you a very good example of two young things who
have been detained more than once. [She calls in two young boys]. We
found them here one evening. They were naked, hungry. They had
nowhere to go. They were being chased around by the police just

because they—small boys, school boys—quarreled with their teacher in school. The bigger boys naturally reacted and went to the house of the teacher. Every child in that school now is being harassed by the police. They are being arrested left and right; these children are all over now. We just have to accommodate them.

Do you think that the confrontation is going to become much more violent because of the bitterness of the children? What do you see happening in the long term for South Africa?

It's difficult to say, but if the government keeps on provoking the people, anything can happen. Since 1976 the government has been killing the children. I mean, really, nobody can excuse killing.

Again, in 1985, it was worse. The SADF [South African Defense Forces] were running about the townships in their casspirs [armored personnel carriers], killing children playing in the playgrounds, getting into school premises, shooting and killing children in front of other children. And the government thinks that by so doing, it's frightening the other children not to go on with the struggle.

It's making the children worse, because they resent their classmates being killed in front of them. Nobody can stand that. And some have no home now. They are determined that the only alternative is revenge.

What about the parents of these children? Are they getting involved in the struggle because they're seeing their children being brutalized?

You'd be surprised. We have church women who used to say, "Oh, we don't want to be involved in politics." They are the ones who are waking us now during the night to say, "What is the next step?" You can imagine, if a mother doesn't know where her child is, she doesn't sleep. She must go around asking other women, "What do you think we should do?"

The churches are involved now. But this government does not care who is a church member and who is not. As long as you are black, you must be guilty. Whether you are innocent or you have done something, you must be killed.

Sometimes they kill just for fun, to see if they can aim well. Can you imagine practicing how to aim on a human being?

Three weeks ago, led by Leah Tutu, women came here after church and just filled my house. They were protesting the restrictions against me. They had formed a committee to join the women's organization and do one action at a time.

What's the nature of your current banning order?

I must not be with more than ten people at a time. I must not address meetings. I must not be involved in five organizations: UDF [United Democratic Front], FEDTRAW [Federation of Transvaal

Women], FEDSAW [Federation of South African Women], the Youth Congress, and the Soweto Civic Association—the residents' organization for complaints to the councilors. How can I not be involved? I've got complaints right now while I'm sitting here about what is happening in the township. I must be involved.

I must also be in the house from 6 P.M. until 5 A.M. the following morning. And during that time, nobody can enter this gate; I must be alone here. And they check on me at unholy hours of the morning—1 o'clock, 3 o'clock, 4 o'clock—as often as they feel like, just to harass me.

Do you think apartheid will end during your lifetime?

That's my hope, really. And I think it's not far. What makes me so optimistic is that the government of this country is aware that the whole world is against apartheid—and in such a way that they are losing friends from the outside world.

Now, even if they pretend as though they don't notice that, it's bad as far as they are concerned. They don't want any more journalists from outside the country. They are muzzling the media. Nothing can be said against the government in our papers. Nothing.

For many whites, their first question is, "What do you think will happen to us when the black people take over?" Even if we can take over, it does not mean we will not choose a white man if we feel that the white man is the right man to lead us. But white people are afraid because of the atrocities they have caused in this country. They think people will take revenge. That's not the way. This is going to be a democratic, non-racial, peaceful country after apartheid.

We don't say they must go to the sea or go back to Europe. Everybody who was born here has a right to be here. We say, "Let's be equal. There should be no division among us. Let's be friends and share our views and be sisters and brothers."

They are rich because they are exploiting the poor black people. Black people have no salaries in this country. And yet they are the people who bring the riches to this country. They have been exploited left and right. We say let's be equal.

For decades you have defied the South African government, and you've suffered so much personally. Where do you find the strength to continue with the struggle?

I wouldn't be alive if I weren't staying with God. I'll give you an example of how God is guarding me.

One morning I was coming back from town. At the train station before mine, there was a little boy, well dressed and with a parcel from town. The two guards on the train wanted tickets. This little boy didn't have his ticket; I'm sure he must have dropped it on the train. The guards gave him a good clip.

And I said, "Listen, what is the matter? He has no ticket. He is a child, a school boy. Must you assault him? How much from here to there?" The guard said, "Nine cents." Can you imagine? So I gave the little boy nine cents.

When I was getting off the train, someone met me and handed me two rand.

At home, the young boys staying with me had made a fire, the water was boiling, but there wasn't a cent in the house. No mealie meal [corn meal], no sugar, no tea. The boys were home from school, and they were hungry.

When I came they said, "Mama, we are hungry. There is nothing."

I said, "Wait. I'm going to give you something. I'm going to give you money to go buy food." Then I just looked up and thanked God, and the tears just rolled down.

I think that nothing will happen to me, since they didn't kill me during the time when they were killing the children. Next to here there's a school. I had a fence, and the children would jump the fence and just fill up this house. And the police would come running with guns pointed at me.

"Open the house," they would demand.

I would answer, "There's no child in this house. I am not going to open the house for you." And they'd just go on.

God is a wonderful man. And if you believe in him, you're never disappointed. I'm telling you—he's the only man who is guiding me and keeping me alive.

Your children must also be a source of strength and pride. You have given them a tremendous example, and they have followed.

That's what I have been praying for. You know, when my husband was taken away, I prayed that God must help me with the children. God was really with me in putting my children in the right light.

That you see Zwelakhe and the others today peacefully fighting for the freedom of everybody in this country pleases me more than anything else. God is the one who has made it possible for them to be what I have wished them to be.

You're a nurse, a midwife, a mother—in many ways a very ordinary woman, and yet a very extraordinary woman. And the government is so threatened by you that they ban you. Why are they so afraid?

They are afraid because they know that apartheid is the source of evil. And they will never part with apartheid. The fact that they are a minority ruling the majority should really always, at all times, make them feel that they are wrong. So when they get people like us who are trying to show the people the right thing, they are always threatened. They feel threatened, quite rightly, because they know very well that if the people really turn against them, they have nowhere to go.

You've suffered so much, but you're still full of hope.

My hope is based on the world's history; there's nothing without an end. We have read the history of the Roman Empire crumbling, the British Empire crumbling. We have seen what happened in Zimbabwe. My hope is that one day even our government will be down on its knees.

As much as I was born here, as much as my great-grandfather was born in this country, he was not a citizen. I am not a citizen. An immigrant from overseas coming here is given only three years to be cleared as a citizen. But that doesn't worry me because I know that there's nothing without an end.

They [the government] may be happy now because they are comfortable. And they may be happy now because they can do anything—because they have got arms, they have got everything. But the day God takes away those arms, those thousands and millions of days they have been enjoying will be just like one day, because God loves us all.

They call themselves Christians, but I fail to understand, because in the very Bible they are carrying it says, "Thou shalt not kill." But they are busy killing the children, busy killing the people in jail.

In the Bible there is no black and white. God calls us his children—all of us.

[Postscript: After the end of apartheid Albertina Sisulu was elected to the South African Parliament.]

Sister Dianna Ortiz

Death's Dance Broken

by Rose Marie Berger and Julie Polter

"In spite of the memories of humiliation, I stand with the people of Guatemala. I demand the right to heal and to know the truth. I demand the right to a resurrection."

On Thursday, November 2, 1989, at 8 A.M. in Antigua, Guatemala, Sister Dianna Ortiz was dragged into hell. The 28-year-old Ursuline nun, originally from New Mexico, was kidnapped by two men from the Guatemalan security forces and taken 45 kilometers to a secret prison at La Escuela Polytecnica (the old police and military training school) in Guatemala City.

Twenty-four hours later, when a man called Alejandro shouted for the men to stop mid-rape, he put his boot in a door which, for most abducted Guatemalans, is closed irrevocably by death. Alejandro led Ortiz to a gray Suzuki jeep, back into the autumn light of Avenida La Reforma, ten blocks from the U.S. Embassy. No longer "disappeared," she escaped from him toward the Old City, the cathedral, to become one of the "undead."

Every step Ortiz has taken since her escape has been toward learning the truth of what happened to her. Truth is the necessary ingredi-

This profile appeared in the July-August 1996 issue of *Sojourners*. Since then Sister Dianna Ortiz, with the help of Patricia Davis, has told her story in *The Blindfold's Eye: My Journey from Torture to Truth* (Orbis Books, 2002).

ent for healing her shattered life and reclaiming her violated body. Truth enables a survivor of abuse to overcome the isolation described by Salvadoran poet Claribel Alegria: "Don't come any closer/there's a stench of carrion/surrounding me."

Truth, however, is the first casualty of war. In Guatemala in 1954, the CIA sponsored and trained mercenary forces to overthrow Jacobo Arbenz's democratically elected government. The CIA-engineered coup put Col. Carlos Castillo Armas in power. Armas reversed the Arbenz land reform programs, abolished taxes for foreign investors, eliminated the secret ballot, and plunged Guatemala into a reign of terror.

For thirty years Guatemala suffered a revolving door of military dictators, including the notorious Brig. Gen. Efrain Rios Montt, who was an elder in the Guatemalan Church of the Word (El Verbo). Finally in 1986, Vinicio Cerezo's Christian Democratic Party replaced the juntas; but by 1989, kidnappings, death threats, bombings, and murders were again on the rise. Black handkerchiefs were again nailed to the doors of teachers and catechists. Rios Montt maneuvered to get his name back on the ballot.

In August 1989, human rights offices in Guatemala City were bombed. In September, four students from San Carlos University were murdered. Newspapers reported an increase in U.S. military presence in Guatemala—Green Berets training Guatemalan paratroopers and Black Hawk helicopters with mounted machine guns patrolling the highlands. The counterinsurgency campaigns left 150,000 Guatemalans dead and 45,000 missing.

The scars on Ortiz's wrist and back are reminders that all politics is personal. Almost seven years after requesting information on her case from the U.S. and Guatemalan governments, and receiving nothing in return but slander, excuses of "lost" files, and lukewarm sympathy, Ortiz took her case to the White House. While the Clinton administration kindly said they had no reason to disbelieve her story, they also had no reason to believe that U.S. intelligence agencies were connected to her torturers.

Ortiz's silent vigil for truth, begun on Palm Sunday, lit a small flame in Lafayette Park, across from the White House, then spread like wildfire across the United States and abroad. The Internet hopped with requests for information and ways to offer support. In San Salvador's plaza, thirty people kept a silent witness for Ortiz. In Owensboro, Kentucky, supporters held a candlelight service in front of the federal building. As news coverage increased, people from throughout the D.C. area came to sit, pray, hand out flyers to tourists, bring flowers and fruit, and spend the night with Ortiz.

She had a small, low-set hut, covered with a bright blue plastic tarp, to serve as a rain shelter and storage place. A blanket was spread in front, and Ortiz sat there on pillows 21 hours a day. She wrapped up in quilted coats and sleeping bags during the cold early days of the vigil and later blocked the sun's harsh rays with a large umbrella.

At least two people stayed with Ortiz at all times; sometimes as many as thirty ringed the area. At night supporters slept in shifts in sleeping bags around her. Several of the homeless men in the park became part of the vigil, including Elijah, whose first day of homelessness was Palm Sunday. He spread his tarp and sleeping bag behind Ortiz's shelter every night.

On April 29, with Ortiz's permission, the community surrounding her turned up the heat on the government. Every morning for a week, people gathered at 9 A.M. in front of the White House for civil disobedience. They included government workers, lobbyists, a flight attendant, a 70-year-old woman visiting her son in Baltimore who decided to join him in getting arrested, teachers, nurses, students, rabbis, priests, and especially Catholic sisters from at least six orders, coming in support of one of their own. For about half of all who participated, it was their first time being arrested.

The illegal liturgy began and ended in prayer. The morning community read responsively from Guatemalan poet Julia Esquivel's "Threatened With Resurrection": "Be with us in this vigil/and you will know what it means to dream . . . /how wonderful it is/to live threatened with resurrection." Ortiz draped a length of red Guatemalan cloth over a large wooden cross. While she remained in the park, a Franciscan priest bearing the cross led the rest of the group, singing and praying, across the street to the White House sidewalk, where it is against the law to demonstrate without official permission.

The U.S. Park Police cleared the area of tourists and issued warnings over a bullhorn that the group was in violation of federal regulations—a dissonant counterpoint to the comforting melodies of "Ubi Caritas" and "Peace Is Flowing Like a River." In the midst of the group's ongoing song and scripture reading, the police officer approached each person, handcuffed them, and led them to the police wagon to be searched and photographed. Ortiz stood silently, watching.

After five hours of processing, the arrestees returned to the vigil and Ortiz greeted each one with a sign of peace. When more than 100 people had been arrested, the State Department released several thousand pages of documents, and Dianna prepared to make another public statement.

Ortiz's simple prose style disarms the cynics and confounds the blusterers. She opened her May 6 press conference this way: "Over five weeks ago, I stood in Lafayette Park, along with other survivors of torture in Guatemala. The tulips were only slips of leaves; patches like open hands. During two of the past five weeks I have fasted, losing 25 pounds. In Guatemala, approximately 10 people have been tortured since the tulips budded and bloomed." Hardened cameramen wept.

The State Department documents revealed two things. First, the U.S. Embassy in Guatemala initiated a smear campaign against Ortiz immediately upon report of her abduction. Second, a March 19, 1990, document refers to needing to "close the loop on the issue of the North American named by Ortiz. . . . The EMBASSY IS VERY SENSITIVE ON THIS ISSUE." Two completely blacked-out pages follow.

While the documents are insufficient, Dianna's vigil clearly opened a portal for the Holy Spirit. In early April, while waiting to appear on NBC's Today Show, Ortiz met Jeanne Boylan, an expert forensic artist who had drawn the sketches of the Oklahoma City terrorists and the Unabomber.

After hearing Ortiz's story, Boylan, a Pentecostal Christian, offered her services. For four intense days, she worked with Ortiz to reconstruct her memories of the torturers and of Alejandro.

"At first it took Dianna an hour to look at Alejandro. She hyperventilated and then passed out," Boylan recounted. "I'm stunned at the credibility question. It's part of my job to look for falsity factors. With Dianna I found nothing to indicate deception of any kind. Her descriptors were phenomenal, highly identifiable."

The torturers' names are still secret, but at the May 6 press conference their faces were unveiled. "This is the one dressed as a policeman," she said in a strong, clear voice. "This is the neat one. This is the indigenous man they called José."

As her mother and sister convulsed in tears, Ortiz pointed to the Anglo man in curly black wig and sunglasses. "This is Alejandro. He is not a figment of my imagination. He is real. I have felt the evil of my torturers dance within me. I was afraid to get close to anyone because I would contaminate them with my evil. But today, with the release of these sketches, that evil is no longer within me. Today I can say, I am free."

With the revelation of the sketches to the press, and the receipt of a letter to President Clinton signed by 103 members of Congress asking for the declassification of all U.S. information on human rights cases in Guatemala since 1954, Ortiz's dramaturgy moved toward a close. She concluded the vigil on the feast of St. John at the Latin Gate with a beautiful service in the park. Her mother and sister looked on while Ortiz burned the sketches of her torturers in a clay pot with sage. While the community sang "Amazing Grace," she released brightly colored balloons into the warm spring sky.

On Palm Sunday, March 31, 1996, Sister Dianna Ortiz stood in Lafayette Park, across from the White House, and for the first time spoke in public of the most difficult parts of her torture.

Today, I begin my silent vigil for truth in front of the White House— not a silence of complicity, but a silence of commemoration for those who have been tortured, assassinated, or disappeared in Guatemala in the last 30 years. Our own United States government has been closely linked to the Guatemalan death squads, and has a great amount of detailed information about those of us who have survived as well as those who have perished. We need and demand this information so that we can heal our wounds, bury our dead, and carry on with our lives.

Many of you know my story. I was in San Miguel Acatán, teaching Mayan children to read and write and to understand the Bible in respect to their culture. For a long time I received death threats. Then on November 2, 1989, I was abducted from the back yard of the Posada de Belén retreat center in Antigua by members of the Guatemalan security forces. They took me to a clandestine prison where I was tortured and raped repeatedly. My back and chest were burned more than 111 times with cigarettes. I was lowered into an open pit packed with human bodies—bodies of children, women, and men, some decapitated, some lying face up and caked with blood, some dead, some alive—and all swarming with rats.

After hours of torture, I was returned to the room where the interrogation initially occurred. In this room I met Alejandro, a tall man of light complexion. As my torturers began to rape me again, they said to him, "Hey Alejandro, come and have some fun." They referred to him as their "boss." Alejandro cursed in unmistakable American English and ordered them to stop, since I was a North American nun and my disappearance had become public.

Like a knight in shining armor, Alejandro seemingly came to my rescue. He helped me on with my clothes, then escorted me to a gray Suzuki jeep. In poor, heavily accented Spanish, he told me that he was taking me to the U.S. Embassy to talk to a friend who would help me leave the country.

For the duration of the trip, I spoke to him in English, which he understood perfectly. Alejandro professed that he was concerned about the people of Guatemala and consequently was working to liberate them from communism. He kept telling me in his broken Spanish that he was sorry about what happened to me. He claimed it was an honest mistake. He spoke to me about forgiving my torturers. I asked him what would happen to the other people I saw tortured. At this point, he switched to distinct, American English. He told me not to concern myself with them and to forget what happened. He made it clear that he had been given the videotape and photographs that would incriminate me of crimes I had been forced to participate in. This was an obvious threat.

The memories of what I experienced that November day haunt me even now. I can smell the decomposing bodies, disposed of in an open pit. I can see the blood gushing out of the woman's body as I thrust a small machete into her. For you see, I was handed a machete. Thinking it would be used against me, and at that point in my torture wanting to die, I did not resist. But my torturers put their hands onto the handle, on top of mine. And I had no choice. I was forced to use it against another human being. What I remember is blood gushing—spurting like a water fountain—and my screams lost in the cries of the woman.

In spite of the memories of humiliation, I stand with the people of Guatemala. I demand the right to heal and to know the truth. I demand the right to a resurrection.

George Tinker

Survival and Self-Determination

George Tinker has a passion for the American Indian community. He is, as he describes it, of mixed blood: "Osage is my tribe of enrollment on my father's side; my mother was a Lutheran." These days both lines of his heritage interact to define just who he is.

In the mid-1970s, Tinker spent several years in Berkeley, California, first studying for ordination at Pacific Lutheran Seminary and then for a doctorate in biblical studies at Graduate Theological Union. While in the Bay area, which has the largest concentration of American Indians in the United States, Tinker organized a ministry to work as an agent of healing with Native American people in San Francisco, Oakland, and San Jose.

Tinker believes that the church, which has historically been part of the oppressive authority over the Indian community, must participate in healing—"self-healing" with Indian people. After years of organizing at the local level, Tinker made the difficult transition into the academic world by accepting a position at Iliff School of Theology in Denver teaching multicultural ministries. As associate pastor of Living Waters, a joint Episcopal-Lutheran parish, he brings together his faith

and heritage into a common tapestry, and at Iliff he shares that vision with a new generation of pastors-to-be.

George Tinker was interviewed in October 1990 by Bob Hulteen.

You are planning an alternative in October 1992 to the "celebration of Columbus's discovery of America" 500 years ago. You have said about the anniversary that white people should be thinking different-ly, that we misunderstand the event. How would you say it should be characterized?

I think the whole notion of celebrating Columbus Day is part of the American foundational mythology. It is an illusion that people on this continent live with. My argument would be that living that illusion is not healthy for white Americans, that it is in fact living a lie.

You have to understand that from an American Indian perspective, celebrating the Columbus quincentenary is in fact celebrating Indian genocide. Indian people like to remind white Americans that the only thing Columbus discovered was that he was lost. About half a world lost.

Actually Columbus didn't even discover that he was lost. He died thinking that he had found Asia.

The myth of Columbus begins with the notion that he was a scientific adventurer who was trying to prove that the Earth was round. But flat-Earth notions were only held at the uneducated popular level in Europe. The academicians all knew the world was round. In fact, notions of a round Earth go back to Greek philosophy in the West. Many American Indian tribes already knew that the world was round.

So for more than half a century before Columbus sailed, people had been playing with the notion of making that trip; they had plotted it and planned it. The only question was, How long before you landed? There was no notion of falling off the Earth.

Another aspect of the Columbus mythology that needs to be shattered is that he was an esoteric scientist trying to make a point. In fact, that voyage was engaged in for one purpose only—to become wealthy. Columbus expected to become wealthy. He had promised his bankers, and the King and Queen of Spain, Ferdinand and Isabel, that they would become more wealthy. And in the long run they did exactly that.

The other side of it for Indians is the result of Columbus' misadventures: ten years after Columbus' arrival on the island of San Salvador, the entire population, estimated to be 100,000 people, perished. Within thirty years, nearly the entire population on the island of Hispaniola perished. Bartolomé de Las Casas [sixteenth-century priest and historian] says there were three million people on Hispaniola alone.

Within 58 years—by mid-century in the 1500s—the population of Mexico was reduced by 80 percent, from 25 million to five million. That's the kind of genocide we are talking about.

For American Indian people, it's not a matter of being anti-Hispanic or anti-Italian. But Columbus becomes the symbol of the continuing genocide of Indian people, because of what happened in the Caribbean, and then in Mexico, and then in South America.

It happened under the aegis of the British in Virginia and the English Puritans in the Northeast. And it has simply continued, usually with some pretense of wanting to take care of the Indians, civilize them, Christianize them. That's especially true when people want to deprive Indians of their land.

Part of the problem today is that Indians are such a small minority of the population on this continent. What may have been 25, or 30, or even 40 million people in 1492 has been reduced in the United States to one-and-a-half million. Unlike black people, who are a political factor because they approach 20 percent of the population, Indians are not a political factor.

There's a clear line through history, both here in the United States and in countries around the world, of the ongoing genocide of indigenous people. Is there any multinational effort to bring together the peoples who are being killed, primarily at the hands of historically European people?

For centuries, Indians in the jungles of Peru, Brazil, and other Central and South American countries were left largely undisturbed, because the jungles were uninhabitable by the European immigrants and economically unfeasible. Now, as the population has grown and technologies have been developed to clear the jungle, Indians' lands are being taken away from them.

We in North America seem to have an ecological interest in saving the rain forests. But we are also complicitous in causing their demise, because we control the economic system that has generated such a horrendous Third World debt that the Third World countries can only satisfy the debt by using up the resources they have. One way of doing that is clearing rain forests and creating cattle ranges to provide Burger King and McDonald's with ground beef.

What happens to the people living in these areas when such change occurs? The reports we get, repeatedly, continually these days, especially from Brazil, state that Indians are simply being massacred in order to deprive them of their land. They are being massacred by private armies of entrepreneurs and big ranchers who are laying claim to the land, homesteading it.

A number of Indian organizations are struggling to make their voices heard. I suppose that's the hope for the future—some sort of coalition among "Fourth World" peoples around the globe, including aboriginal Australians and Pacific Islanders. The Maoris in the Pacific are particularly strong on some of these issues. Indigenous people include many Africans, many Asians, and many oppressed groups in India.

What would you say to the environmental movement that focuses its attention on the rain forests, with little concern for the people whose entire subsistence is being destroyed? Is there a difference between the ecological concern and the justice concern?

At one level you'll find Indian people in general support of the environmental movement for religious and theological reasons, not just for survival reasons. To treat the Earth with respect is an Indian way of existing.

On the other hand, the justice concerns of people, and not just Indian people but all people, have to exceed issues of peace and ecology. The World Council of Churches, since Nairobi in 1975, has consistently talked of justice and peace, not peace and justice. Justice must precede peace.

The WCC tried to get it right with "Justice, Peace and the Integrity of Creation." Some of us think they were just playing pin the tail on the donkey and that maybe there's a religious concern, a spiritual concern, for creation that needs to come first as the foundation for justice. But that is not solely an ecological concern.

There's been criticism from a lot of poor people—marginalized people—that the ecology movement has detracted from justice issues. I think that's a legitimate concern.

Could you say a little more about the importance of the land and the sense of creation preceding justice? It is very hard for most white Americans to comprehend an Indian's perspective on land and its ownership.

Indian people look at the land as generative. It is where we come from. It's not something we possess or own. Land ownership is a Western European philosophical notion that's become rooted in political and economic systems.

When the Europeans first came to this country, they created legal and theological fictions that allowed them to take over Indian land. They said the Indians didn't really occupy the land, because they just roamed the land. Doctrines of vacant domination developed. And if Indians died in a plague, the Puritans considered it an act of God to open it up to them because then there weren't enough Indians to occupy it.

There were consistent efforts in the 19th century to teach Indians private ownership of property because it was considered the civilized way of existing. Of course, what it did was destroy the structure of Indian society and culture and meant that Indians were reduced to levels of existence that forced codependent relationships upon the U.S. government.

As Indians were no longer able to take care of themselves, they had to rely on government subsidies and handouts. That codependency continues to this day—in the relationship of Indian people to the church as well as to U.S. government agencies such as the Bureau of Indian Affairs and the Indian Health Service.

Indians believe that the Creator put them in a specific place and that is their place. To move to another place is a very hard thing to do, and people die when they move. The Osages did not thrive when we were moved out of Missouri and into Kansas. And when we were moved out of Kansas and into Oklahoma it became even worse. That's the story of many, many tribes that were relocated in Indian territory, where they had to learn to live in relationship to a new land.

The relationship to a land is not only a spiritual relationship; it's one of physical economy as well. You know the land; you know the sacred sites; you know the medicines, the herbs, the foods that grow there and where they grow.

When you are moved to a new place, you suddenly don't have access to those things anymore, so that many of your patterns for religious ceremonies and observances are broken. How can you have a ceremony if you don't have access to the various things of the land that you need to conduct that ceremony?

And I guess I should say straight out that the gospel was not liberating for Indian people but was a form of bondage. It's not the gospel that's not liberating, though; it's the proclamation of the gospel that puts Indians in bondage. Consistently the missionaries of the European churches in all of our denominations confused gospel with European culture. The gospel they proclaimed was the gospel of "civilization," of a "superior culture." Steven R. Riggs, a nineteenth-century Presbyterian missionary in South Dakota, literally called it the "gospel of soap."

One wonders if we have to give up our Old Testament in order to leap into the New Testament—the new covenant in Jesus. Yet Indian people were forced to disassociate themselves from their old ways— from their religion and their culture.

In order to do that, they have to engage in an act of self-hatred and self-denial. They have to look at what they were and say, "All of that was evil." The Puritans said it straightforwardly: "The Indians are the legions of Satan."

Are they still doing that today?
Of course. I think there are white missionaries who are trying to be much more sensitive. And some are extremely good and extremely faithful. But we have two problems. One is that we have a lot of white missionaries in all of our denominations who buy into that colonial mentality and are about the business of whipping Indians into shape culturally. It happens.

The other problem is that the institutional structures of church, just like the institutional structures of government, continue to impose themselves on Indian people. It may be on a subconscious level, but they nevertheless forcefully, powerfully, require a cultural shift toward assimilation. I suspect that most people in our North American churches believe in their heart of hearts that the solution to the "Indian problem" is assimilation.

And they become so angry when efforts toward assimilation aren't welcomed. They condemn Indians' desire for self-sufficiency, and they do it in pious language.

That's right. It's, "How dare you Indians be that way when we offered you what we never offered black people, in order to make you white?" The oppression is different in those two cases.

You see, white America wants change to happen on its own terms. White people want reconciliation. They can't understand that their insistence on reconciliation is an insistence that it happen on their terms.

My colleague [at Iliff] Vincent Harding has an interesting analogy. He's a black historian of enormous repute. He says that for years white America was busy building this house, and then had people from different cultural groups living in the yards or the shanties around the house.

The liberal contribution since the civil rights activity of the 1960s has been to say, "We have to open our house and invite these people to come in and stay." But the problem, as Vincent says, is, "It's still their house. We're still guests." We need to think about building a new house where everybody gets equal say in its design and has equal ownership. Then we need to tear that old house down.

Liberation theology as it's been given to us by Central Americans, South Africans, and others has helped people who are oppressed to find their place in the gospel story. You are a New Testament scholar. Do American Indian people find themselves in the Bible story?

I think the gospel can speak forcefully to Indian people. There's no doubt about that. But I think Indian people have to be free finally to determine what the gospel is themselves instead of being told what the gospel is.

The problem is that too many missionaries seem to be under the impression that Indian people are incapable of having a spiritual thought without pastoral coaching. I think liberation theology can eventually have an impact on Indian people. It hasn't yet.

We haven't figured out liberation modes for interpreting the gospel. We are consumers of the denominational theologies of our churches, period. That's what has to change.

The problem with Latin American liberation theology, first of all, is that it is given over to Marxist thought. For American Indians that is wholly inadequate and inappropriate. It is replacing one Western philosophical economic system with another. Marxist thought does not pay attention to the realities of indigenous cultures. It can't. It is a social and political movement that lumps people together into some amorphous, cultural whole called "the people."

What's happened in Latin America is that Indian people have consistently been oppressed—and not only by Third World governments that are rightist, but by leftist governments as well. Sometimes in the debate that goes on, one is led to believe that there are only two options—capitalism and Marxism. Indian people by and large would stand opposed to both because of their cultural, economic, and social impact on Indian people.

Indian people would far quicker say, "We should simply be allowed to have our own way of doing things." And since 1492 that has not been the case. Things have been imposed upon us by an outside, military, superior force. And of course Europeans confuse military superiority with cultural superiority.

It seems to me that Indian people have much to evangelize white America about in terms of finding some of those things that white America has lost.

I'd go a step further and say that Indian people may have an understanding of the gospel of Jesus Christ that is more authentic than white Americans' understanding of the gospel.

It seems to me that much of the gospel has been interpreted throughout history by Europeans and Americans. Before long it is not the gospel that is being interpreted but an interpretation of the gospel. Some things become so commonplace that you can't think of understanding them differently. The kingdom of God has consistently been understood in temporal terms by Europeans, primarily Lutheran New Testament scholars, beginning a century ago. The kingdom of God was dealt with as a question of when it is going to happen. The question of where it is was consistently disallowed. That's not at stake.

It's a question of eschatology: When will it happen? And you get all these jargonized responses of realized eschatology, actualized eschatology, imminent eschatology.

I would argue that the European intellectual tradition is fundamentally temporal, with spatial aspects being subordinate to this primary category of time. But Indian people are just the opposite. We're spatial, rooted in the land. And when we read about the kingdom of God, the first and only thought to come naturally to Indian people is, "Well, we don't know much about kings and kingdoms, but it must be someplace. It must be somewhere."

As Indian people we wrestle with that, and I've wrestled with it out loud with numerous Indian groups and Indian people: The kingdom of

God has got to be right here. In other words, it becomes a metaphor for creation.

Jesus' call to repent, to return to the kingdom, is a call to come into a proper relationship with the rest of creation, and with the Creator. A proper relationship recognizes that I am simply a part of the creation, one of God's creatures along with the other two-leggeds, the four-leggeds, the wingeds, and the other living, moving things—including the trees, the grass, the rocks, the mountains.

All those things are relative. That's the universal Indian notion of the interrelationship of all things in creation. Human beings are a part of creation—not apart from it and somehow free to use it up or abuse it.

This is a whole different slant on the kingdom of God and, immediately and implicitly, on the gospel of Jesus Christ.

The New Age movement claims to have adopted what its leaders say is a native spirituality or outlook on creation. How do you feel about that?

I think it is misguided, for a number of reasons. One is that there is a great romanticizing of Indian people and Indian spirituality.

There is also a great dearth of spiritual rootedness in white America, so people are really searching. And that's real, that's legitimate. But they're searching in the wrong places. They are searching to appropriate somebody else's spirituality instead of working within their own culture to uncover what is there.

When people come to the Indian world and try to appropriate Indian spirituality in that New Age fashion, a number of things happen. New Age thinking quite often is economically motivated. A lot of New Age people out there are ripping off Indian things and making money at it.

For some people it is just a way of enhancing their own private spirituality. In fact, for most New Agers, Native American beliefs provide a way of enhancing private spirituality. That is as un-Indian as you can get.

White people come out to dance in order to accumulate some sense of spiritual self-worth, when in fact one doesn't dance the sun dance for that reason. We dance the sun dance so that the people in that place might live. Why would somebody drive all the way from Texas to South Dakota to dance the sun dance so that the people in Rosebud might live? Well, they don't. They drive that far to prove themselves.

And in the process those lies creep into Indian thinking. I find it horribly destructive of Indian people for whites to be involved in Indian things that are that intense, that private, that intimate.

I don't think that Indian people ought to try to make Indians out of white Americans. We can model our spirituality in ways that enable our white brothers and sisters to reclaim their own spirituality. That is part of evangelism because, you see, there is no doubt in the Indian mind that white Americans are brothers and sisters, relatives, just as much as the others of the four nations of the Earth—the black nation, the red nation, the yellow nation, and the white nation.

The white American church needs to hear this, especially since it has been a part of the problem, not the solution. In my opinion, part of the churches' own spiritual need is to engage in acts of confession and repentance, of reconciliation and healing.

But still I draw inspiration and energy from my church more than anything else, and from the people. I am the associate pastor of an Indian church in a very poor community. My church is a community of people who are really struggling to affirm both their commitment to the gospel of Jesus Christ and their Indianness at the level of culture, ideas, spirituality. We are struggling to understand the gospel from an Indian perspective.

It's very clear that we will no longer have an interpretation of the gospel imposed on us by anyone. We will even resist having the structure of the congregation imposed on us by judicatory authorities.

We've tried to say consistently, "No, we'll decide what we ought to be doing, and what will be healing to the Indian community." The vision is one of healing and wholeness for the Indian community, so that my congregation is extremely active in the urban Indian community, and many are active still in their connections back home on the reservation.

When we are together in prayer several things happen. First of all, we bring our Indian identity into the liturgy. Second, we show respect always to the traditional religion of our tribes, to the traditional spiritual leaders; and in conversation with them we have brought some of that with us into our liturgy. We might quite naturally have a medicine man in church on Sunday, and we would have that medicine man pray for us. Usually those people would also come to Communion.

Third, we affirm our Indian identity and we bring those things from the tradition into our service. We use a drum and we sing traditional ceremony songs, prayer songs, not Christian, as the proper preface to our Holy Communion.

When we celebrate Communion, our people are very, very clear that Christ is present on the altar. More clear I think than white Episcopal and Lutheran churches. The power of Christ is present in body and blood and spirit.

The fourth item is that our people speak for themselves. They don't need pastoral leadership to tell them what it is they are about. When we go to conferences, Indian ministry conferences, it is invariably the case that as we go around the room it is the pastor or ministry director who gets up to report. When it comes around to Living Waters, somebody will reach over and touch me on the shoulder and say, "It's all right, we'll take care of it."

Last summer we had eight people in the congregation who danced in four different sun dances. Of course the missionaries have said all along that those ceremonies are pagan and we can't do that. Our people insist that they are free in the gospel, free in Christ Jesus, to participate in Indian religious forms and ceremonies. We intend to live in that freedom.

III

BLESSED
ARE
THE MEEK

Jean Vanier

Welcoming the Little Ones

In August 1985 Jean Vanier, founder of the L'Arche Community in France, came to Washington, D.C. The L'Arche movement, which began in 1964 and now includes dozens of communities around the world, serves physically and mentally handicapped people. During his stay in Washington, Vanier and Sojourners Community had the following conversation.

We feel a kindred spirit with you and L'Arche, and you're often in our thoughts and prayers. Could you tell us what you feel is at the heart of L'Arche, and what are some of the struggles your community faces?

We have now seventy L'Arche communities. In all of our communities, the people with handicaps are really at the heart. They are a real gift. They evangelize us. They change us. They call us forth. They call us to humanity. They teach us how to celebrate.

But there are always struggles. One is the struggle to live our community life. I don't think we can live without Jesus. I don't think we can see the value of the wounded person unless we are in the dynamics of the gospels, the Beatitudes—blessed are the poor and so forth.

So how do we find the right spiritual support? That is a big question for a lot of our communities. Where do we find the spiritual nourishment? Sometimes we find the priests and pastors, but other times we don't.

We could get very caught up in the busyness of doing things, in the crises in the homes, in working with psychiatrists and psychologists. We could get caught up in all this and forget the real reason why we're there—which is to somehow create community with the person who is handicapped, to create a body. That's what community is—a body in which the handicapped person is the most important. So there's the question of spiritual nurturing, and the answer is not entirely clear.

Another big area of concern is handicapped people who are aging. That's no small reality. In my own community, the mean age is now 37. In 10 years it will be 47. And in 20 years it will be 57. You begin as a dynamic community with everybody working in pottery and that sort of thing. But what happens when you move into a situation where you almost become a nursing home? How are we going to make these transitions?

There is also the question of nurturing. How do we get the churches interested and to see what we're doing as valuable? We have meetings where we get together with all the priests, the pastors, and the ministers in a particular region. But it's still not a high priority for them to really see the wounded person as a value. To really believe in the words of Christ, "Whoever welcomes one of these little ones in my name welcomes me. And whoever welcomes me welcomes the One who sent me."

I think our culture remains deeply ingrained with an idea that some people are cultivated at the top, and the others at the bottom are more or less forgotten. Those at the bottom take a lot of time. They take a lot of money. Is it really worthwhile putting a lot of money and energy into them? So we're struggling with that, trying to bring interest into the churches. And it's coming a bit.

We can enter quite quickly into the situation of doubt, because the results are not great. After years of struggle, where are the results? There's a witness, there's a context, there's love, but where are the results? We can all be tortured at one moment with doubt.

What is the value? To believe. To believe that just living this life of community is what Jesus wants. It's a tiny witness.

Living without results. We can identify with that. On the other hand, you have to live with the danger of success. At the same time that L'Arche is accomplishing tiny things, you are widely admired. The success of recognition, admiration, and adulation is in some sense as spiritually dangerous as the lack of results.

I agree with what you're saying about the dangers of success. As I look to our communities, I just see people who are tired and struggling. I see much more pain in our communities than I see adulation. Where I see the danger is in fearing to take risks. Somewhere the fundamental motivation and trust in God wanes.

There is the danger of the ghetto mentality, in the sense that we're so busy that we only know what's happening in our own community. I sense a very great need—and I'm not sure we're attentive enough to it—for the crisscrossings of communities. Things that you say can awaken us; things that we say can awaken you. We have to see what's happening in the wider church, or the wider reality of humanity, and see the questions you are bringing up.

One of the tensions I feel very strongly is how to say no to so many demands and needs. It's the problem of being so busy that we begin to feel the lack in the life of our community with one another.

How do you deal with that issue? Do you say no to people? How do you not become so overwhelmed and caught in despair because there's so much need and there's so little we can really do?

I think the danger is not the fact that we don't say no but that sometimes we can become insensitive to needs. You have only so many beds in the house, and once you've got them filled up the demands are still immense. So in a way there is actually a danger of a hardening of the heart with respect to the immensity of the need. That's what I sometimes see in myself. You feel it when you've had the third phone call from a mother saying, "I just can't stand it. My seven-year-old son is going through a crisis, and every place says no."

One of the greatest ways of nurturing is a retreat or "interlude" for handicapped people. Normally it's on a one-to-one basis. An interlude is a sort of renewal program for people with handicaps.

We touch very fundamental questions, like, "Why am I handicapped?" "What is a handicap?"—you know, those questions that are almost taboo. "Was I loved by my parents?" "What is my relationship to them now?" "What happened in the institution?" "Why did I come to L'Arche?" These are some of the questions which are almost too explosive to be brought up in daily living, if they're not handled with care.

We just had a retreat a few weeks ago with maybe thirty people in all, fifteen with handicaps. There was one particular assistant, one of our house leaders, who had hit his limit. He was on the point of departure. But he came back so refreshed, and he said, "You can't believe the honesty, the truth, the beauty in what these people were saying—the pain, the acceptance."

One of our communities in the north of France took a weekend retreat not too long ago. One of the men who was up there had been in my community—he's a very simple man. They were talking about a text of the Apocalypse, where Jesus knocks on the door. And Jesus will dine with whoever opens the door. This man said, "I know what I'll eat when Jesus comes to dine with me. We'll have pancakes. We'll have muffins. We'll have cider." And then he said, "And Jesus will say something. He'll take me in his arms, and he'll say, 'You are my beloved child.'"

What seems to nourish the most is when there is a direct experience of the presence of God, the presence of light, a prophetic utterance from people who are so little and so broken. Although this doesn't happen on a daily basis—perhaps once a year—it nonetheless happens. It is a very marked and profound experience when people seem to experience that God is present in another person who in so many ways appears devalued and is driving us up the wall. Such moments bring deep conversions in people.

One of the difficulties we've always had is an inability to find disciplines that seem to work for us activists in our diverse ministries. Especially with children in our community, it just doesn't seem to work for us to, for example, get up in the morning at the same time and go to one place together to pray.

Are there things in the community life of L'Arche over the years that have proven essential to your sense of nourishment?

One of the things we sense really helps assistants is what we call "accompaniment." Young assistants will come to our community full of enthusiasm and a desire to serve. And then within some number of months, they touch their point of pain. They're fed up. They're angry. So there's a period of disillusionment, and it happens everywhere.

We see that if these new people are well-accompanied, if there is somebody walking with them and meeting with them every month, they will be able to say, "We all go through this. It's all right, and it's really important." And they can verbalize what they're going through. They can say they're fed up. This is the phenomenon of touching your pain.

Also almost every community or every home has evening prayer. And we find nourishment in the way we celebrate. In a community in Liverpool, there were a lot of wounded people. And they started washing each other's feet and developed a whole liturgy around it. Now on Maundy Thursday, in many of our communities, we talk about how God brought us together, and then we wash each other's feet. The whole month before Christmas we're preparing for its arrival. And we also celebrate birthdays. A lot of assistants will tell me that the feast was so great that they feel totally refreshed.

I think we're discovering something in L'Arche: the meaning of celebration. It's not just a prayer, but a celebration in which we laugh, we sing, we dance, we let out all the tension. We eat well, we have wine, it takes time. It's well-prepared, we're dressed up. And it will last. We really, really have fun, and we laugh from the guts. And there's a fantastic liberation in celebration which is a holy act, not a liturgy in a sense, but a holy act. We're celebrating that we are a body and giving thanks to God.

We give thanks in the way we dance. Each home has its own traditions, its way of celebration. One of the essential nourishments is the quality of celebration, which is a religious act and a very human act. We are also learning how to "live" meals well—just the ordinary meal—so that the meal becomes a little wedding feast, a celebration of unity.

There seems to be something about attentiveness that is at the heart of everything we've said about nourishment, whether we're talking about time on retreat, or time in prayer, or celebrating a birthday, or taking time just to hear from another and sense Jesus in that person. I've been working a lot in our own community with the quality of our life and what nurtures us.

What we're talking about is attentiveness, attentiveness to the moment of what is given. I think if there's too much success, we're no longer celebrating. We'll celebrate victory, which is something very different from celebrating bonding. Maybe the less success we have, the more we have to be attentive to the present and the celebration of bonding. Just as we are, in our brokenness, our pain, our land of success, we celebrate that we're united together. And that is our comfort, our joy, and our gift.

Clarence Jordan

Theologian in Overalls

by Joyce Hollyday

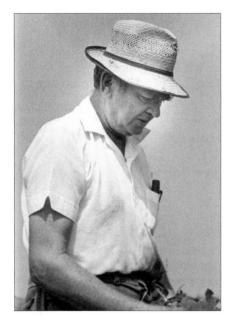

A minister was showing Clarence Jordan around his church. The minister pointed with pride to the church's imported pews and other fancy trappings.

As they stepped outside, the sun began to set. A spotlight came on and highlighted a huge cross on top of the steeple. The pastor boasted, "That cross alone cost us ten thousand dollars."

Clarence looked at him and said, "You got cheated. Times were when Christians could get them for free."

Such was the wit—and the direct way—of Clarence Jordan, a preacher and "theologian in overalls." Born in the deep South near the beginning of the century, Clarence founded the Koinonia community on a rundown 440-acre farm near Americus, Georgia, in 1942. Its name came from the Greek word that was used to identify the early church in Acts, which pooled its resources and shared the life of Jesus in an atmosphere of reconciliation.

The particular reconciliation that was so desperately needed at that time and place was between black and white. The Koinonians hired a

Joyce Hollyday has edited *Clarence Jordan: Essential Writings* (Maryknoll, NY: Orbis Books, 2003).

former sharecropper to help with the farm. They all ate their meals together, and this breach of Southern tradition brought on the first hostility toward the community.

In a story that has been told many times, Clarence again showed the courage and quick wit that became his trademark. A group of men came to the farm. Their spokesman said to Clarence, "We're from the Ku Klux Klan and we don't allow the sun to set on people who eat with niggers."

Clarence glanced over at the western sky and noticed that the sun was creeping low. He thought a bit, swallowed a few times, and suddenly reached out, grabbed the man's hand, and started pumping away, saying, "Why, I just graduated from Southern Baptist Seminary, and they told us there about folks who had power over the sun, but I never hoped to meet one here in Sumter County."

They all laughed, and nobody noticed that the sun had slipped down below the horizon.

Despite the hostility of white neighbors—including gunfire in the night—the farm soon became a success. Clarence invented a mobile peanut harvester and established a "cow library," through which poor neighbors could check out a cow for a period of time so that they could have milk. He built a deluxe chicken house that was the envy of some Koinonia members, whose own houses were austere by comparison. The luxurious chicken quarters were the target of many jokes from the neighbors, but when Clarence began getting more eggs than anybody else, those same neighbors were soon asking him for advice.

Meanwhile, Clarence's reputation as a powerful, uncompromising preacher was growing. As he travelled the country preaching pacifism, social justice, and community, he drew people to the experiment at Koinonia.

His wife, Florence, remembered that people who came to visit the farm were always surprised to meet Clarence. They always expected to see an "older, intellectual-type person," rather than this large man who had earned his doctorate when he was 26 years old.

A distinguished professor once came to the farm while Clarence was working on a tractor. The man said, "I wish to speak to Dr. Jordan."

Clarence wiped off a greasy hand, extended it, and said, "I am he."

The man responded, "No, I wish to speak to Dr. Clarence Jordan."

Clarence insisted that he was the one the man was looking for.

After repeating his request, the professor finally got in his car and left.

Perhaps Clarence's most widely known contribution is his unique "Cotton Patch" version of the New Testament Scriptures. Clarence brought the biblical characters home and set them in the towns, on the roads, and between the cotton and peanut rows of southern Georgia.

He stated in the introduction to his first Cotton Patch book, "We want to be participants in the faith, not merely spectators." And so he wrote a version of the New Testament that would bring its messages home to the people of his time.

Described as "a colloquial translation with a Southern accent," the Cotton Patch version states that Jesus was wrapped in a blanket and laid in an apple box at his birth; he was killed by lynching; and when he came out of the vault on Easter morning, he came to his disciples and said, "Howdy."

The humanity of Christ is central in this version. It is Christ who brings reconciliation between white and black, just as he brought reconciliation between Jew and Gentile in the traditional version.

The incarnational theme so important in the Cotton Patch versions was also a powerful concept in Clarence's preaching. He saw the resurrection not as an invitation to heaven when we die, but as a declaration from God that he has established permanent residence on the earth and comes home with us, bringing all his suffering sisters and brothers with him:

"And we say, 'Jesus, we'd be glad to have you, but all these motley brothers of yours, you had better send them home. You come in and we'll have some fried chicken. But you get your sick, naked, cold brothers out of here. We don't want them getting our rug all messed up.'"

Clarence Jordan lived in direct confrontation to such a way of thinking. He had a plan for the rich to share their resources and for the poor to find new hope and security in their lives. But he wasn't talking about charity or paternalism; he was talking about a partnership. His idea was for farmers to work together, providing for one another and returning any excess in resources back to a fund so that more land could be purchased for others.

Businessman Millard Fuller helped to launch the Fund for Humanity. Clarence called those around him to return to the Old Testament idea that the earth is the Lord's and to live out Jesus' proclamation that a new order had arrived—to live out in a permanent way the spirit of the Jubilee year when slaves were freed, debts forgiven, and land returned to its original owners. His vision was to have eventually one million acres of land for the poor.

By 1969 the farm covered 1,400 acres. Plots of land were sold to area residents at whatever price they could pay.

The community, now Koinonia Partners, carried the idea of partnership into their fast-growing pecan industry and into housing. Over the years dozens of houses were built from the Fund for Humanity.

Clarence lived to see the first house almost completed. On October 29, 1969, at the age of 57, he died in his writing shack.

In the last hour of a visit to Koinonia in 1979, I walked through the fields and past the pecan groves to the shack. It was a holy experience for me, this pilgrimage. I wished, like many who have come to the community since Clarence's death, that I had met and known this man.

As I approached the small building, I made my way through the patch of small trees that has grown up around it. I stepped inside.

The shack had been used little since Clarence's death. Marked original manuscripts of speeches and Cotton Patch writings were on the shelves. A copy of a 1959 *Encyclopedia of Candy and Ice Cream Making* sat next to Clarence's Greek New Testament. As rain fell softly on the roof, I was struck with the gentleness and strength that were part of the life of Clarence Jordan.

A blade of wheat, dried with age, lay on Clarence's desk. I picked it up, wondering how it came to be there and how long it had lain in its place. It seemed appropriate to find it there. I can think of no better symbol for Clarence's life.

"Unless a grain of wheat falls into the earth and dies, it remains alone; but if it dies, it bears much fruit."

Later, I went in search of a Cotton Patch version of John to find this verse from the twelfth chapter, hoping to draw some kernel of wisdom from Clarence's unique translation of it. I discovered that it was the manuscript of John that was on his desk when he died; he had completed only the first eight chapters of the book.

I felt cheated by the discovery. And I began to understand even more deeply what a loss it is to us all that Clarence died at the age of 57. But on the heels of that feeling of loss came a sense of gratitude that for those fifty-seven years he lived in such a way that his spirit is with us still.

In the introduction to his *Cotton Patch Version of Luke and Acts,* Clarence wrote:

> Jesus has been so zealously worshipped, his deity so vehemently affirmed, his halo so brightly illumined, and his cross so beautifully polished that in the minds of many he no longer exists as a man. He has become an exquisite celestial being who momentarily and mistakenly lapsed into a painful involvement in the human scene, and then quite properly returned to his heavenly habitat. By thus glorifying him we more effectively rid ourselves of him than did those who tried to do so by crudely crucifying him.

Clarence lived in contradiction to the tendency of those around him to make Christ less than a man by making him more than one. Bringing home the incarnation was the motivation for Clarence's writing, his preaching, and his living.

He believed that the incarnation was the only method of evangelization, that "We haven't gotten anywhere until we see the word become flesh." This was true in his own life. His words about justice were applauded by the local whites around him, until they discovered that he meant to live out what he preached from the pulpit.

Clarence learned that reconciliation at the lunch table, where black and white shared together, was as scandalous to his neighbors as reconciliation on a cross.

Yet he was a man who conquered the fear that paralyzed others of his time. He spoke about fear as "the polio of the soul which prevents our walking by faith." Its purpose is self-preservation. Only by living with the assurance of the victory over death can faithful witness shine forth.

Clarence had given up his life to God, and thus lived with the knowledge that no one could take his life from him. He understood deeply the connection between life and death, the impossibility of sharing resurrection without participating in crucifixion. And so he endured excommunication from his church and gunfire from nightriders, living as a man who knew that local hatred and the Ku Klux Klan had no more power over his life than Pilate did over Christ's.

He lived the incarnation in his fervent love for the poor. He saw that it was a suffering and disinherited Christ who shows us the way to love the same among us now.

And, believing that it is a spirit-filled community rather than the empty tomb that is proof of Christ's presence with us, Clarence pointed to Koinonia as evidence of the continuation of the incarnation.

Millard Fuller was unable to convince the coroner or county medical examiner to come to the farm to pronounce Clarence dead: "Even in death, Clarence Jordan was rejected by the high and mighty, by those in authority, in the area in which he lived. But this was not surprising to me, as it never had been to him, because the Bible promises that a prophet is never with honor in his home area."

The medical examiner insisted that Millard rent an ambulance and bring Clarence's body to the hospital. But Millard felt that Clarence would have objected strongly to having money spent on a dead body.

"So we loaded the body in the car.(I smiled as I went through town with Clarence sitting down. I knew he would have gotten a terrific charge out of that."

Clarence's body was lowered into the red Georgia clay in a simple pine box, a crate that was used to carry a fancier coffin. His grave remains unmarked. It is a fitting memorial for a man who, though thunderous in his preaching and exhortation, was gentle and humble in his living. He was a man who never made himself the center of the community that was his dream, and thus the dream has endured his death.

Just a few weeks before Clarence died, a reporter asked him, "When you get up to heaven and the Lord meets you and says, 'Clarence, I wonder if you could tell me in the next five minutes what you did down on earth?' What would you tell the Lord?"

Clarence's reply was simple: "I'd tell the Lord to come back when he had more time."

William Stringfellow

Keeper of the Word

by Jim Wallis

Karl Barth, the famous German theologian and author of the Confessing Church's Barmen Declaration in resistance to Nazism, made a trip to the United States, where he noticed a young attorney from New York's Harlem. "This is the man America should be listening to," said Barth. The man who most impressed Karl Barth on his U.S. visit was William Stringfellow. Karl Barth was certainly not the only one on whom Bill Stringfellow made a lasting impression.

I met Bill at a conference at Princeton Theological Seminary in 1971. The conference organizers had invited both of us to speak and wanted us to meet. Our little group of seminary students in Chicago had just begun publishing *The Post-American*, the forerunner of *Sojourners*. I'll never forget that first time I heard Bill speak.

He talked very quietly, and, at times, I had to strain to hear him. And yet there was a force and power in his words, an authority I had never encountered in anyone before. He always spoke from the Bible, and, from my first hearing of William Stringfellow, I felt that the Word of God was being opened up to me. The way he explicated the scriptures caused a deep excitement within me.

After an evening session, he invited me to go for a walk. A long, late stroll across the Princeton campus was the beginning of a friendship that lasted fourteen years, until William Stringfellow died on March 2, 1985.

William Stringfellow, a man who taught us the meaning of the Word of God and showed us the possibilities of living with the incarnation at the center of faith, was a theologian. In my opinion, he was the most significant U.S. theologian of the last three decades. His own modest definition of a theologian was anyone who reflected on the meaning of the Word of God for their lives and their history. Bill spent his whole life doing just that and doing it better than anyone else I know.

In response to government surveillance, he once said he humbly hoped that the official scrutiny of his life, or the life of any Christian, would just further expose the Word of God. On another occasion he told me that when he knew his phone conversations were being listened to by the FBI, he would make calls and read long passages from the Bible. "I think they need to hear it," he would say.

William Stringfellow was radically rooted in the Bible. That is what gave his social commentary and political dissent such insight and power. Bill never would have regarded himself as a pioneer. Yet, in so many things, he was the first to see something, to take action, to make a crucial connection, to provide the clarifying word.

Long before poverty law practice or Christian ministry to the inner city were much discussed, William Stringfellow was doing both in Harlem. His was one of the first voices to cry out the agony of the city, to speak truthfully about white racism, and to warn of the judgment to come.

Bill was an early critic of the war in Vietnam, exposing its criminality and hypocrisy. He had a unique capacity to go to the root of things and draw out their biblical significance. Behind the war he saw a growing tendency in the United States toward what he called lawless authority taking over the society's leading institutions while usurping both law and conscience. He attributed the nuclear threat to the ascendancy of technology over all of human life.

All of these developments Bill related to the biblical description of the principalities and powers, which had been all but forgotten and dismissed in the seminaries and churches. Not only did he renew our understanding of such doctrines as the powers and the Fall, but he gave us a more comprehensive biblical description of the United States than anyone else even attempted. While liberals ignored the Bible and evangelicals fought over the various theories of its inspiration, William Stringfellow applied the biblical Word to our lives and times like no other contemporary Christian.

Racism, poverty, civil rights, Vietnam, women's equality, nuclear weapons, abusive political and ecclesial authority, the exercise of conscience—all these issues and more William Stringfellow insisted be brought into the heart of the church's life and examined with biblical scrutiny.

At his memorial service, Bill's old and well-used New Testament was brought forward and placed on the altar with these words: "No one in our time was a more perspicacious student of the Word of God in scripture than Bill. This is his Bible, most unsanctimoniously weathered, rumpled, underlined, cryptically annotated. We offer it among the gifts of bread and wine, as truly a medium of grace and life to the world. But now who will open it for us as he did?"

Bill loved the church, but it was the kind of love that called the best out of the church while refusing to be silent in the face of its accommodations and cowardice. He cared enough about the church to call it to account by its own scriptures and traditions.

Time magazine once referred to Bill as "one of the most persuasive of Christianity's critics-from-within." When the church ignored its country's racism and its own, Bill brought it out into the light. When the church sanctified war, nationalism, and official deception, Bill was the first to say it was wrong. When his own church attacked women seeking ordination, Bill was the attorney for the defense.

I was at the Washington National Cathedral in Washington, D.C., in 1976 when Bill Stringfellow defended Rev. William Wendt in an ecclesiastical trial. Wendt had invited Allison Cheek, one of the first Episcopal women to be ordained to the priesthood, to celebrate the Eucharist at his church. The woman's ordination had been deemed "irregular" and had not yet been officially accepted by the Episcopal Church.

It was the first church trial and display of canonical law I had ever witnessed, and the drama was very high. I watched Bill as he rose to make his closing argument. He was a brilliant lawyer and a powerful speaker, and his command of the legal issues at stake was absolutely masterful. But after he made the compelling legal case on behalf of his defendant, he turned to the gospel. Bill looked at Bishop Creighton, the presiding officer of the court, and said:

> Perchance, there is another way altogether to act today, albeit more audacious, which would redeem this day, a way more suitable to your capacity as *pastor pastorem;* I would like to think more compatible with your spontaneous inclinations as a human being.
>
> In a moment good Father Wendt will stand before you to be sentenced. In the name of Christ, whom, even now, we await eagerly as the Judge of the living and dead, will you say *this* to him? "William Wendt, the ecclesiastical courts of this diocese have found that you have offended my authority as your bishop. If that be so, I forgive you."

The entire assembly was stunned and silent.

On another occasion Bill was invited to speak at Trinity Church Wall Street in New York. It is said to be the richest church in the United States, with an annual budget of more than $200 million. Bill was always one for noting the significance of the day, liturgically or otherwise. He kept, by his dining room table, little books with holy days, saints' birthdays, and other memorable events to help celebrate each day. The day William Stringfellow was invited to preach at the richest church in the United States was both auspicious and ironic, albeit unbeknownst to his church hosts; he preached his sermon that day on the occasion of Karl Marx's birthday.

To his own Episcopal Church and to all the churches of his day, William Stringfellow was both a prophet and a priest, though he always cherished his status as a layman. He was always the thorn in the side and the voice of conscience. The church hierarchies rarely received Bill very well in his life, but, a few months after his death, the Episcopal Church, gathered in national assembly, made the following resolution: "This 68th General Convention gives thanks to God for the life, witness, and ministry of William Stringfellow."

I had met Bill after he left New York for health reasons and moved to Block Island, off the coast of Rhode Island. The island became a place of refuge, retreat, and reflection for me—the only such place I have ever really known. I made the pilgrimage many times over the course of the last decade and a half, taking either the one-hour-and-fifteen-minute ferry ride or a short flight on a small, single-engine plane from the mainland.

I remember vividly my first visit. It was at the end of a long and busy speaking tour, and I was still running in high gear. The pace at the island house was so peaceful and contemplative that I had to consciously slow myself down in order to fit in. The house was like a monastery—but one with the radio news on most of the time.

The word "discernment" best fits what seemed to be going on all the time as the most natural activity in the home that was named Eschaton. While serious issues of faith, politics, life, and death seemed to pervade the place, the atmosphere was never heavy or overwhelming. Rather, the house literally abounded with humor, hospitality, and very human relationships.

I confess that I was in awe of the place and of William Stringfellow in particular at my first meal there. I expected an evening of very weighty conversation, in which I might find answers to most of my theological and political questions. Bill began to offer a prayer before the meal. As I waited to hear something quite profound, Bill prayed for healing for one of his dogs who was sick! From that moment on, I was always struck by how merely and marvelously human everything seemed to be at Block Island and how much more human I felt when I was there.

My favorite place was around Bill's big dining room table in front of the large window with a magnificent view of the Old Harbor. Countless hours were spent around that table in listening, talking, laughing, praying, and enjoying some of the best meals of my life (Bill was an exemplary cook and host). Bill's table was where all of us congregated who made regular pilgrimages to Block Island. It became a place of nourishment, companionship, and spiritual formation.

I've often said that I learned more good theology around Bill's table than around any seminary. On my last trip to the island, I loaded that old table into the back of my car and brought it back to Washington, where it now sits in my apartment and where I am writing this article.

The truth is that I learned more from listening to Bill Stringfellow, from watching him, and from just being around him than I have from anyone else. He was a man who genuinely knew how to live life, perhaps because he understood death so much better than the rest of us.

I'll always remember him waiting for me at the boat dock or the little Block Island airport in one of his many circus hats, or endlessly waving good-bye until my ferry or plane was completely out of sight. I can still picture Bill at the Block Island beach with his little body and littler bathing suit, all tanned and looking like Mahatma Gandhi, reading his *New York Times* or working on a book manuscript over the picnic table and eating hot dogs for lunch.

Bill lived with constant pain during most of his last years. He died at the young age of 56 and, even then, lived longer than many expected him to. But his mind was always razor sharp, his heart full of passion, and his spirit indomitable. He was always full of surprises.

A few days after Bill died, I was sitting in his study and spotted a magazine ad recently cut out and placed by the telephone. It read: "NEED ACROBATIC PEOPLE FOR RIDING ACT—For 1985 Season—Good Opportunity—Send Resumé and Photos to Circus Vargas, North Hollywood, California." It seems Bill was contemplating a second vocation.

William Stringfellow was a mentor and spiritual father to me. He treated me like an adopted son. For many of us, he was our most formative theological influence. Daniel Berrigan spoke for us all when he said at Bill's funeral, "For thousands of us, he became the honored keeper and guardian of the Word of God."

At that service I led the intercessory prayer for Bill. In part the prayer said,

O Lord, thank you for William Stringfellow, who was a Christian among us and in the world.

Of all the souls we have known, Bill Stringfellow was one of the most truly human. That was his great blessing to us, his friends, and his great threat to the rulers and powers of this age.

In his vocation and by his example, he opened up to us the Word of God.

We pray now, not only for Bill, but for ourselves in his absence from us.

May we always remember William Stringfellow, and may his memory make us strong and faithful.

May we know that he is and always will be with us. Amen.

Henri Nouwen

A Heart's Desire

by Brett Grainger

At the time of his sudden death in 1996 at the age of 64, Henri Nouwen, a Dutch priest and author, was one of the most popular spiritual writers in America. He was also a long-time friend and contributing editor to *Sojourners*. Several of his books—on compassion, desert spirituality, prayer, and ministry, first appeared in the magazine in multi-part series. For the past ten years he had served as pastor of the L'Arche Daybreak community in Richmond Hill, Ontario. It was there that he was buried. Brett Grainger, a former *Sojourners* editorial intern living in Montreal, attended Nouwen's funeral and wrote this story.

Passing the unofficial boundary marking Richmond Hill, Ontario, from the surrounding suburban sprawl, the first thing I noticed was a sign proudly declaring "Home to Elvis Stojko." Yes, the heart-throb of Canadian figure-skating might have grown up here, but my guess is that the majority of the 100,000 or so other souls who today call this town home did not.

The "golden horseshoe" of rich farmland that once stretched around Lake Ontario's northern shoreline is today more of a pale crescent, whose waning is the result of decades of overdevelopment. Whole towns and communities, some of which existed independently for centuries, have been absorbed into a fast-paced urban orbit around Toronto. Richmond Hill, like all towns close to large cities, suffers from a modern sense of homelessness.

I was going to Richmond Hill to visit the L'Arche community of Daybreak and spend some time speaking with community members about the recent death of their friend and pastor, Father Henri Nouwen. Nouwen was best known for his steady stream of spiritual writings, writings that influenced a generation of Christians from the seminary to the streets of Sarajevo and which will place him in the company of the most significant spiritual writers of this century.

I missed the driveway three times before finally picking out the modest sign identifying L'Arche Daybreak in the fading twilight. This says much about the humility of a group that is the oldest L'Arche community in North America. With about 120 members, consisting of "core members" (the permanent handicapped residents of L'Arche) and "assistants" (those who live with and assist the core members), it is also one of the largest. This is the place where Henri Nouwen, a foreigner, an academic, and a restless heart in the classic sense of St. Augustine, finally found a home for the last ten years of his life.

Perhaps "home" became such an anchor in Nouwen's writings because he spent so much time away from the land of his childhood. Born in 1932 in the town of Nijkirk in the Netherlands, Nouwen soon left behind the sunflowers of his father's immense gardens to pursue ordination in the Catholic Church. At the request of his bishop, Nouwen pursued further education in psychology and a post at Notre Dame soon followed. He knew, however, that his true interest lay in theology, and after returning to seminary for further theological training, he took a position at Yale.

Despite the accolades that Nouwen started to receive as a writer, his restless heart would not let him settle down to a life of quiet academic reflection and study. The explosive political convulsions that rocked Latin America in the late 1970s called him to resign from his post and go serve the poor however he could. Travels in Bolivia and Peru brought him into direct contact with the stark contrast of lifestyle in the First and Third Worlds, but he also learned the difficult lesson that his gifts and skills as a pastor and writer were of more use to the South back in the North.

So his unsettled spirit carried him back to North America, this time to a position at Harvard Divinity School, where Nouwen hoped to enlist his experiences in a "reverse mission" that would awaken the wealthy and advantaged to the plight of the poor. But he soon found himself enfolded in the cycle of ambition and competition that he had sought to escape at Yale.

Much of Nouwen's life was the story of his deep unhappiness with these ambitions, and his inmost hunger for connection, for a taste of peace and rootedness in a place that he had described so often in his books, but which seemed to elude his grasp in the very grasping. As Carl MacMillan, director of development at L'Arche Daybreak, told me, "Henri had talked about home, he had written about home, but he was always flitting off places."

The road that brought Nouwen to Daybreak went through Trosly, France, where the first L'Arche community (French for "ark") was established by Jean Vanier. Jean Vanier, himself a restless heart and expatriate who abandoned a promising academic career in Canada, founded the original Trosly community when he invited two mentally handicapped men to live with him in a modest little cabin in the French village. Nouwen visited the Daybreak community in Richmond Hill and, after a brief courtship, was invited to become their pastor. He accepted.

The shift from life as a Harvard academic to life in community with the mentally handicapped was not an easy one. Stories abound at Daybreak concerning the adjustments Nouwen had to make when he first arrived. As one legend goes, in his first week, the formerly coddled ex-professor appeared before a community member, laden down with dirty shirts and underwear. "Who do I give my laundry to?" he asked. Nouwen soon received a sobering initiation into the mysteries of modern laundering technology.

While it is true that Nouwen did not bring many practical skills with him, it is also true that Henri's role at L'Arche was never one of charismatic leader or figurehead. As Henri wrote, "My sense of being called to L'Arche was based more on what I had to receive than on what I had to give. Jean Vanier said, 'Maybe we can offer you a home here.' That, more than anything else, was what my heart desired."

In fact, each member of L'Arche, regardless of apparent ability or intelligence, is held up in a network of relations that many call a "mutuality of care." It is in part this emphasis that distinguishes these communities from traditional social work agencies.

L'Arche assistants truly believe that they are fed by living in the presence of those whose bodies are physically broken but whose spirits reveal a humanity often obscured and warped by the complications of "normality." In attending to the brokenness of these bodies and minds, assistants often find healing for their own inner experiences of fragmentation and brokenness. In a way, the practical, daily dependence upon others that the handicapped experience becomes a symbol for the universal brokenness that places all in a relationship of radical neeu ₁ᵤₗ God and for one another.

If Nouwen received much from Daybreak, he certainly returned as much. Besides his friendship, perhaps his most enduring gift to the community was his ability to evoke spiritual gifts. Despite the presence of many ordained clergy, Nouwen developed a pastoral team of lay people that empowered them to use their gifts in spiritual direction. In some ways, this gift also prepared the community for the death of their senior pastor.

A telling example of this came from a core member a few days after Henri's death. In his halting speech, Michael Arnett said, "I'm going to miss that guy." Then, pointing at Nouwen's clerical robes, he said, "I . . . want . . . those . . . robes. I . . . want . . . that . . . job!" As Carl told me, "Mike saw that he could wear the robes, and in fact he was an altar server." Daybreak member Geoff Whitney-Brown added, "Henri really gave us each a sense of our priesthood."

As I drove home from Nouwen's wake with a friend late on Friday night, we listened in the darkness to a documentary on the process of grieving. The speaker expressed his sense that grieving a great loss carries with it the potential to deepen the soul of any who go through it. This is not to say that suffering is good, but only to admit that as finite creatures we are deeply defined by our limits and the pain associated with a changing world.

Through grieving, the speaker continued, we come into contact with our own finitude. It is this temporary encounter with clarity and the tenderness it engenders that eventually allows us to transcend the loss and incorporate it into our larger lives. Deep grieving, as painful as it is, offers an opportunity to be strengthened in our sense of what it is to be a creature with a weight inaccessible to us otherwise. It is the final gift from the dead to the living.

I began to think of how Nouwen himself had given much thought in his later years to the subject of death, in particular his own. It might seem odd that Nouwen considered his death—all deaths—to constitute not the end of our giving to others, but rather its fullest consummation. In imitation of Christ, our death can be a gift that eclipses anything we can give in our lifetime.

Henri developed this idea most recently in *Our Greatest Gift*, but it had been percolating through his thoughts for years. After a near-fatal accident in 1990, Nouwen wrote in *Beyond the Mirror*, "In this perspective, life is a long journey of preparation—of preparing oneself to truly die for others. It is a series of little deaths in which we are asked to release many forms of clinging and to move increasingly from needing others to living for them."

Saturday morning took me back to Richmond Hill for Henri's funeral, this time to the cavernous Cathedral of the Transfiguration. The cathedral sits alone in a wide open field, a curious stone ark through whose doors poured a steady two-by-two stream of people from every race, class, and creed.

Outside the weather was poor, and a light rain drizzled continually as we joined the thousand or so people seating themselves there. I was surprised to find the mood not one of somber seriousness but of celebration. During the Mass, songs from the French community of Taize, accompanied by guitars, flutes, and violins, replaced the usual stoic selections from hymnals; actors and actresses breathed life into the gospel reading (the story of the Prodigal Son, one of Henri's favorite passages) through a dramatic rendering of the parable; dancers, from wheelchair and from tip-toe, lifted praise to God through the joyful movement of their bodies. Sunflowers and irises were carried in by a flood of children until they surrounded the altar, transforming the barren Communion table into a garden of delight bursting out in yellows, greens, and browns. The flowers, evocative of his father's own gardens, anchored the table in the rich soil of Holland, home also to Van Gogh, whose work Nouwen had loved so deeply.

Henri's body rested at the center of the gathering in a modest pine casket. At his request, it had been handcrafted by members of his own community at The Woodery, Daybreak's carpentry shop. Core members also created colorful drawings that were then transferred to the lid of the casket by an artist from the community.

The effect was not unlike walking into an elementary school classroom in springtime. Dazzling colors and joyful figures crowded around houses, flowers, and a rainbow to announce a deep thankfulness. Through their combined efforts that day, the service announced a covenant of mutuality between brother and sister, between the dead and the living, between the broken and the breaking. It announced a "cold and broken hallelujah," the only kind permitted to restless hearts like Nouwen's, who found a home between rest and restlessness, a restlessness which keeps us hungering after its source, the "first love" of which Henri spoke so much.

The carnival atmosphere of the day reminded me of something else: Carl had told me about Henri's relationship with "The Flying Rodleighs," a troupe of trapeze artists who toured Europe and with whom Nouwen had gradually developed a relationship. His father, I was told, also loved the circus. I imagined the scene: A 60-year-old writer of spirituality and his 90-some-year-old father going to the circus every year, hanging around the popcorn and high-wire usually associated with small children. It reveals a certain playfulness and capacity for wonder which Nouwen possessed and which fed his writings and community life.

One year, Nouwen traveled with The Flying Rodleighs for ten days across Europe. His experiences became the basis of an unfinished book in which he sought to reflect on the parallels between the trapeze artist and the life of faith—a far cry in spirit from Calvin's solitary soul before God or the angst-ridden cliff-jumper of Kierkegaard.

Under the big top or outside in the world, Nouwen understood that there are two types of people: "flyers" and "catchers." The catcher's role is the most difficult and important role, because he or she is responsible for performing the catch. The flyer cannot try to catch the catcher, but must remain totally loose and rely on the ability of the catcher to be caught.

This became a crucially important image for Nouwen. He always glimpsed the playfulness and joys of the life of faith, but without dangerous sentimentality or illusion. He knew personally that each member of The Flying Rodleighs had experienced the serious injuries that come with the acceptance of a life of risk.

But rather than allowing risks to keep us earthbound, Nouwen also understood that life is only truly lived out on a flying trapeze bar, where the lights are bright, the grip is sweaty and unsure, and the script, though rehearsed over and over again, can always go differently for the first or the last time.

Before I left Daybreak for the final time, Carl spoke to me about how Henri had himself struggled to be a flyer: "He ended his life at a time when he had the confidence to be a flyer. He had been a wonderful catcher for so many people. But to be a flyer and to have that kind of faith, he would illustrate this with his whole being, just reaching out. He had a way of using his body on stage. He was reaching for the sky and shaking like a leaf.

"He had that kind of grace and confidence at the end of his life, and he didn't have a great deal to prove anymore. He did have friends, he did have a home. He was peaceful with his own family. So he died at a time when he was peaceful, which was saying a lot for Henri, because he lived most of his life restless."

IV

BLESSED ARE THOSE WHO HUNGER AND THIRST FOR RIGHTEOUSNESS

Martin Luther King, Jr.

Dangerous Prophet

by Vincent Harding

In 1968, just a few months after our friend Martin King was assassinated, my wife, Rosemarie Harding, was visiting in the home of two poor, older black women in Atlanta. In their two-room apartment, up on the wall in the place of honor next to the picture of Jesus, was a picture of Martin Luther King, Jr. One of the women told Rosemarie that King had come to her a number of times since his death. That seemed right, and totally at one with the meaning of Martin Luther King, Jr., in our lives.

As I have reflected on that, what is also clear, especially in light of the establishment of the King holiday, is that there is a tremendous danger of our doing with Martin King precisely what we have so often done to Jesus. That is, put him up on the wall and leave him there, or use his birthday as a holiday and an excuse for going wild over buying things, or domesticate him—taking him according to what

Vincent Harding, a colleague of Martin King, served as a consultant on the documentary of the black freedom struggle *Eyes on the Prize*. Harding is professor of religion and social transformation at Iliff School of Religion in Denver and the author of several books, including *Martin Luther King: The Inconvenient Hero*. This article, from the October 1984 *Sojourners*, was based on a speech delivered in Atlanta.

we want, rather than what he is demanding of us. The temptation is to smooth him off at the edges and forget what the assistant director of the FBI said about him in 1963: "We must mark King now, if we have not done so before, as the most dangerous Negro of the future in this nation." A dangerous Negro, now a national hero. How shall we work with that?

What we have tried to do and are being tempted to do is forget that King was a dangerous Negro, a dangerous black man. He was dangerous in the midst of a society that had chosen to live in a way that was filled with inhumanity to itself and to the rest of humankind. He was dangerous to all of the keepers of the status quo and to all the lovers of a pleasant Christianity. He was indeed, I think, the most dangerous Negro in the future of this nation, partly because, unlike Malcolm X, lots of people didn't realize how dangerous he was, and still don't.

I would like us to think about the Martin King of 1968 and ourselves now, and to ask the question, "Where are we now related to where King was in 1968?" Then we can try to understand the challenge of Martin Luther King, Jr.

The last place we see King is in Memphis, Tennessee, not at a conference, convention, or theological consultation, not even on a vacation, but at a place he felt he had to be because garbagemen needed him to stand with them. And standing with them, he was shot down. That represents one of the first issues we have to deal with as we think about the King of 1968.

One of the reasons he was in Memphis was because he was struggling with the question of poverty in American society. He had been driven by the realities of life in America and elsewhere by his continued relationship to Jesus, who knew what life among the poor was, to grapple with the question of what to do about poverty and unemployment in America. He had not come to any absolutely clear conclusion. But there was no question in King's mind by 1967–68 that poverty in American society—whether for black people or Native Americans or whites or anybody else—would never be adequately addressed without fundamental transformation of the political and economic structures of this society.

What about us? Is King challenging us to realize that this society has structured unemployment into its very well-being? It attains the "highest standard of living in the world" for some of us by making sure that others of us will never have a job. King says, I cannot live at peace with that as a child of God, as a minister of Jesus Christ. I must find a way to see how this society can be restructured much more in the image of the righteousness of the kingdom of God.

How goes it with those of us who talk about the kingdom of God? How goes it with those of us who talk about loving Jesus and loving

God and do not in any way deal with the need for a radical analysis of how the children of God are doing in America, and why? Why is America, supposedly the most wealthy nation in the world, filled with millions of people who cannot get work? I think King would challenge us to think about that.

Toward the end of his life, King said this: "The dispossessed of this nation—the poor, both white and Negro—live in a cruelly unjust society"; therefore, "they must organize a revolution against that injustice, not against the lives of their fellow citizens, but against the structures through which the society is refusing . . . to lift the load of poverty."

Martin King was saying many things that challenge us. He was saying for one thing that there are adequate resources, human and natural, for the load of poverty to be lifted. He said this society *refuses* to lift the load of poverty; it insists on structures that will keep the load of poverty. Then society tells us that this is consistent with Christianity and all Christians ought to be capitalists. And we believe it.

Martin King challenges us here. He says this society is unjust because it *chooses* to be unjust, and we must find a way to organize (that dangerous Negro word) a revolution, meaning a radical change in the values of our lives in the structures of this society that cause injustice. Are we preaching about that yet? Is that in the Sunday School lesson yet? If not, how shall our people be prepared for that which must come?

This is connected to another challenge that King left. One of the last times I saw him was here in Atlanta, in what was then Ralph Abernathy's church, at a gathering that King and others had called together. It was one of the most exciting, stimulating, and scary things I have ever seen. For the first time, Native Americans, blacks, Hispanics, and poor whites were all beginning to talk about the ways in which we might, together, find a way to speak to the poverty that cuts across all racial lines. This was fascinating, for it was moving toward what was to be the Poor People's Campaign.

King was trying to deal with two things there. He was trying to find a way of organizing folks to deal with poverty through some form of revolutionary nonviolence. But more importantly for us at this particular moment, this was also King's way of dealing with racism in American society.

King said that the way to deal with racism is to find a common vision that will join you together. Find a common task on which those of all races can work together, hold hands, and move forward together. That is the best way to deal with racism in American society. A thousand conferences will not do what a gathering of people can do when they are convinced that across their racial lines they have a common goal that they must work for, sacrifice for, and die for.

That was the way King was moving toward dealing with racism. Being equal in a society like this was beside the point. He was seeking to organize across racial lines to transform the society, not to be equal in it. As my friend Howard Dodson likes to say, a fundamental difference exists between, on the one hand, seeking equality of opportunity to be exploiters and on the other hand, participating in struggle across racial lines to create a new non-exploitative society. King was about the latter.

This was hard, and King had to deal with some issues of how his leadership would fit into this kind of multiracial situation. It was clear to him that the heritage of our struggle made it absolutely necessary that black people take the lead in moving toward the transformation of this society.

It could not be left to anyone else—neither professional liberals nor professional revolutionaries. Black people, who had come so far, would have to have the courage to keep going and to take leadership for a new day. In other words, to be dangerous Negroes.

By 1967–68 King was calling for a new political and economic order. Is that a Christian agenda? Some Christians doubt it, saying that it is not our concern, it is not our business what this economic order is doing to the lives of other people here and abroad. Yet there is no Christian here who is not quite ready to sit and take the benefits of the present economic order.

If it is not our business, then we need to leave it and not take its benefits. But if it is our business, then we have got to put our lives in it and decide what shall be done to bring this society some inches closer to the vision of the kingdom of God.

King also said that the black movement was forcing America to face all its interrelated flaws. This is the beautiful thing about what came up from us. It started out as a black movement, and all of a sudden you look around and everything is going on—women, Native Americans, Chicanos, and Gray and Black Panthers were organizing. Everything was rising up because we had begun to tell what we saw from the underside of American society.

The black movement opened up our eyes, and even the mainstream churches began talking about change. King said the black freedom struggle was exposing the evils that are deeply rooted in the whole structure of our society. It was revealing systemic flaws and suggesting that radical reconstruction of society itself is the real issue to be faced, no longer simply black or women's equality.

King, by 1967–68, had seen that what we are faced with is the need for radical transformation of the major institutions of the society, reshaping them with the needs of the poor, rather than the well-to-do, as our primary guide. How do we put that together with the people who are telling us now that what black people really have to do is learn how to use the political process—meaning the Democratic and Republican parties?

How do we preach, teach, and pray about this? What message do we get from the living Word about this? We will get no message unless we go seeking, hungering, and thirsting after a message. And we will not go hungering and thirsting if we think that this has nothing to do with being "saved and sanctified and meeting the Lord in glory."

But if being saved means being saved from the blindness of going along with the conformity of this age, if being sanctified means really finding a new righteousness and a new holiness that can be shared with all people, if meeting the Lord in glory means meeting Jesus wherever he is to be found among poor people, then it has everything to do with being saved, sanctified, and meeting the Lord in glory. King challenges us to deal with that.

King was pressed into looking at the rest of the non-white world by the war in Vietnam. That war opened up a whole new arena to Martin King, and he came forth from his congregation in Ebenezer Church to Riverside Church in New York City and said that this country, the country that he loved, had managed to get on the wrong side of a world revolution, and it seemed to insist upon staying there. King began talking about Vietnam, about the murderous policies of our nation there. He began lifting that up wherever he went.

Lots of people said to him, "Martin King, you're crazy, because that's not Christian stuff, that's not civil rights stuff, and besides Lyndon Johnson is going to have your behind if you keep doing that." And King said, "I have been fighting against segregation all my life, and I refuse to segregate my conscience."

Some people can be very excited about black and women's rights in America, but are absolutely silent about what this country is doing to the people of Nicaragua today. King said he could not participate in that kind of moral segregation. In other words, he told us that we who have known what it is to be black in America have a particular responsibility to listen to the cries of those who are non-white and under the American heel all over the world.

Lots of people now in the so-called Third World are asking, "Where do black people in America stand? Have y'all gotten it so good in your middle-class newness that you no longer see, feel, or hear anything about what it costs us in Nicaragua and South Africa, Peru, and the Philippines for you to be well-off in New York and Atlanta?"

I remember well how happy we were in the 1950s and '60s when voices from all over the non-white world came in telegrams, speeches, and lectures, saying, "We are for the black freedom movement in the United States." Now it's our turn to stand with them—often against our government's anti-revolutionary policies. As the old folks used to say, "God don't like ugly."

But the question is not simply what we are going to say about what our country is doing to the rest of the world. As King saw it, the question is what are we going to do about our own participation in a world of the middle-class, materialistically oriented values that create that kind of exploitation? Is there any way that we who have known oppression in America can hook up with those who have known oppression from America?

In the last year of his life, King proposed that all of those who believe in revolutionary nonviolence in America should try to find the brothers and sisters in Latin America who believe in revolutionary nonviolence and somehow hook up with them. He said that this country has caused so much of the misery in Latin America that we here in this country ought to take special responsibility to connect with the revolutionaries there.

People asked King why he was concerned about all of these people all over the world who have nothing to do with Negroes in America. He replied, among other things, that it was because he was a minister of Jesus Christ, who loved his enemies so much that he was willing to die for them, and so he had a different way of dealing with enemies than the State Department does. We need to think about that, those of us who want equal access to the State Department.

King went on to say, "I must be true to my conviction that I share with all men [and of course now he would say all people] the calling to be a son [child] of the living God, beyond the calling of race, or nation, or creed. Beyond the calling of race or nation, or creed is this vocation of sonship [and daughterhood] under God, and because I believe that the Father is deeply concerned especially for the suffering and helpless and outcast children, I come tonight to speak for them." King was suggesting that there may be something that goes even deeper than our Christianity, that our fundamental identity is to be found in our evolving life as children of the living God, who has children everywhere, of every kind, of every religion, of every color.

King moved forward from that theological position because he understood that it is not enough to say that you are going to be a child of God and act as if it doesn't affect your life, your commitment, and the way you see the world. As a child of God, as a minister of Jesus Christ, King recognized that, by and large, America is using its military power to keep the oppressors in place—largely because they support our anti-communist myopia and provide opportunities for our economic and military forces. Therefore, he said, I cannot encourage black young men to go into the military service to support such repressive governments. How about that for a dangerous Negro?

We have to face the personal and collective implications of the fact that King was talking in February and March 1968 about going around to black churches as well as white ones and trying to organize all the young people he could reach as conscientious objectors. What he said in other words, was equality of opportunity in the U.S. military is not what the black freedom struggle is about. What are we saying about that in our churches? Yes, I know. For so many hundreds of thousands of young people, that is the only place they can get a job, any sense of dignity and responsibility.

I know the military provides one of the most impressive outward appearances of successful integration in our society. But that itself is one of the most terrible things in the world; that a country can give so many of its young people no real work except the work of killing, that a society can provide for significant camaraderie only in the camps of war. And we are silent, or we say go and make a man of yourself. Spare us from such a definition of manhood, for that is part of what has brought us to this nuclear precipice.

But much to our discomfort in the churches, King didn't stop with calling rank and file young people to be COs. He didn't think that black (or white) ministers ought to escape these issues through ministerial exemptions or think that they have it made, morally or financially, by going into the chaplaincy. He was raising the question of how the 17th- or 18th-century Africans or the Indians felt when chaplains came along with the armies of destruction and colonization. He is asking us the same question: are we going to send chaplains with the armies of oppression in order to help our black young men be better fighters?

We can tell ourselves a lot of other things, but chaplains are there, according to the military definition, to increase the morale of the fighting forces. Is that what the church of Jesus Christ is meant to be about? I think King would not let us off easily on that one.

Moreover, what King would say to us now, I think, is that there cannot be an authentic, liberating, and visionary peace movement in this country unless black people are going to be part of its leadership. For even the peace movement folks can forget a lot of things about race that they ought not to be allowed to forget, so we had better be right in the middle of the leadership to make clear that peace and justice must be tied together. So King went into the leadership of the peace movement.

We must also recognize some of the things that King wasn't as clear on and be challenged not only by his strengths, but also by his weaknesses. King left us with the provocative question of how to put together revolution and nonviolence. How do we create a loving, tough, persistent, righteous, justice seeking revolution? King was struggling with that.

But he was very clear that revolution does not have to be synonymous with people going around shooting each other. So please lay that one aside. The deeper question that we must work on is how shall we prepare ourselves and our people for a struggle that will so transform our way of thinking and being that we will never be comfortable, quiet, or at peace until we have given ourselves to the task of overturning the injustice of this society?

As James Cone says, we must never assume that because we believe in love and nonviolence we cannot believe in revolution. King was grappling with how to put those together. I am quite grateful that he was unclear, because now it opens up to us not a law, not a set of guidelines, but simply a set of questions.

What shall we do? I think that whatever we do, we shall be unfaithful to Martin and to Jesus, to Malcolm and to Fannie Lou Hamer, to all of the great men and women of our time if we do not move forward, pick up these questions, and live out the marvelous tradition of the dangerous Negroes. And I would add all of the friends who want to move with dangerous Negroes, for we invite all of our friends and loved ones to be there and to enter into danger, knowing that "nothing can separate us from the love of God in Christ." (You don't have to quote that kind of verse if you ain't up against anything.)

I think finding a way of nonviolent revolution may be one of our greatest challenges. I want to remind you that if you told Gandhi, "But that has never happened before," he would say, "So what? Think of all the things that never happened before they happened."

None of us ever happened before we happened. And yet here we are, happening, right? Lots of things are going to happen that never happened. The question is, shall we be participating in the creation—with our creator God—of that which has not yet been but must be? Or will we be standing rigidly as frightened agents of the past?

It is in the search for the transformation of the people of God that the people of God will be able to participate in the transformation of God's world. We cannot stay as we are and expect to be soldiers in the struggle. King understood that and went on knowing that this was the case.

Four weeks before he died, King talked to the congregation of Ebenezer Church about his unfinished journeys, about his failings, and about his weaknesses. He was speaking for us as well as to us. He was speaking in this case of his life and his own disappointments and failures, and he said we are constantly trying to finish that which is unfinishable. We are commanded to do that, and so we find ourselves in many instances having to face the fact that our dreams are not fulfilled. Life, he said, is a continued story of shattered dreams, but one must strive always to hold that dream in one's heart.

He said there are times that all of us know somehow that there is a Mr. Hyde and a Dr. Jekyll in us. But he said even that truth should not cause us to lose faith in our dreams and our best possibilities. For God does not judge us by the separate mistakes that we make, but by the total events of our life.

So he said, "You don't need to go out this morning saying that Martin Luther King is a saint. Oh no, I want you to know this morning that I am a sinner like all of God's children. I want to be a good man. And I want to hear a voice saying to me one day, 'I take you in and I bless you.'" Then you understand that being a good man, to King, meant being a dangerous Negro.

I began with a dream, and that's the way I want to end. I had a dream a couple of years ago. In the dream, I was in my home church where I had grown up, on 138th Street in Harlem. I had been away from the church for a while, and I was back in my usual manner rehearsing with the junior choir. While I was singing I became conscious of the fact that, in that empty sanctuary, toward the back pews, someone was sitting. I looked over, and there was Martin, sitting in the pew all by himself. I had never seen King looking so much at peace with himself. Peace, fulfilled as if the journey had finally brought him to a new and magnificent place in his own evolving life.

I took that as a marvelous sign. I offer it as a sign and a challenge to you as well. A challenge to all of us not to worry about where we aren't yet, but to encourage us to move forward beyond where King left off in 1968.

Through some amazing grace that we do not understand, each of us clearly has been granted more time, more grace, more life than King was. Let us use it in the pursuit of the new dream, of the new peace, of the new justice, of the new person, of the new community that the world has not yet seen, but that must be if the world is to continue.

Myles Horton

Leaving the Best Heritage

In 1932 theologian Reinhold Niebuhr wrote an initial fund-raising letter for something called the Southern Mountain School, a project initiated by his former student Myles Horton. After a few years of study at Union Theological Seminary and the University of Chicago, Horton, a native Tennessean, had become inspired to return to Tennessee and begin an experimental school specializing in education for fundamental social change. That idea developed into the Highlander Folk School, now called the Highlander Research and Education Center.

In the ensuing decades, Highlander has served as a meeting place, training center, and catalyst for the movements of poor people, workers, and minorities throughout the South. In the 1930s and '40s, Highlander was an integral part of efforts—especially by the newly founded Congress of Industrial Organizations (CIO)—to organize Southern workers.

In the 1950s Highlander became a center for the then-embryonic civil rights movement. Rosa Parks, who helped spark the civil rights explosion by refusing to yield her seat on a segregated Montgomery, Alabama, bus, was one of the hundreds of black Southerners who were inspired and prepared to act by their experiences at Highlander.

In the 1970s and early '80s, Highlander became identified with the struggles of Appalachian people around issues such as land rights, toxic wastes, and strip-mining. Since then, while the engagement with Appalachian struggles has continued, Highlander has turned its attention back to the rest of the South as well.

Myles Horton served as Highlander's director from its founding until 1973. Since stepping down from the post, Horton continued to travel, speak, and teach throughout the world until his death in January 1990. He was interviewed at the Highlander Center in 1986 by *Sojourners* contributing editor Danny Duncan Collum.

In 1932 you started what was then called the Highlander Folk School. What was the dream for it?

We were interested in building a democratic society and were going to use education as one of the means to changing society. We were openly out to change society and have what we called a second American revolution that would be an economic democracy as well as a political democracy. The purpose of Highlander has always been the same: to try to contribute toward a genuine democratic society through radical social, economic, political, and cultural change in this country.

When I'm talking about democracy, I mean it in the full philosophical sense of people governing themselves and working out the systems that make that kind of relationship possible. Capitalism certainly isn't democratic. If you put things before people, there's nothing democratic about that.

One of the things that we felt was very important was to have a new type of labor movement, because at that time the American labor movement was at a very low ebb. We advocated that there should be a democratic, industrial-type union, and we hoped to get people in the mountains interested in unions and cooperatives and things of that kind as one of the means of building a democratic society. So that was a specific statement of purpose that more or less outlined the program of the school.

What do you mean when you talk about education? I'm not sure it's what people usually associate with that word.

Several years ago I was speaking at an alternative school conference. One of the people explained that Highlander was not a school in the sense of a college or any other kind of school because we didn't have classes, we didn't have credits, we didn't have this, that, and the other thing, and that we built on people's experiences instead of teaching them things they needed to know. And that's true. Highlander is not a school. But it is educational in the traditional meaning of the word "educate," which is to draw out instead of to pour in.

We think people become educated by analyzing their experience and learning from other people's experience, rather than saying there's a certain body of knowledge that we need to give them.

How did you see the religious impulse that was present when you started on this project being tied in with the kind of work that has happened at Highlander?

Well, we were not considered religious by most people because we decided early on that we were going to stay away from all kinds of sectarianism—religious, political, or otherwise. So we didn't have any church or religious affiliation of any kind, which was their way of deciding whether people are religious or not.

But we tried to work with the local community church and did, up until the time that we started getting a number of black students. The church people refused to let them come to the church, and we couldn't very well go without them. We couldn't tell the students that we had to go and worship the Lord but they weren't allowed to go along. We said we wouldn't go without them, so we dropped out of that. We still said that we'd be delighted to take part in any church service or religious service that would allow us to bring our students, but we got no offers.

If you think of religion as having something to do with morals, or ethics, or, as Paul Tillich said, the search for truth as a religion, then we never said we weren't religious. We just said we weren't church-related.

The philosophy of Highlander fits in well with the notion of a gospel that is good news to the poor and gives liberty to the captives.

You're absolutely right. We decided not to try to deal with all of society. We tried to carve out a segment of society to deal with what we thought was the most important—the poor, the working people, and the minorities.

If you say religion is to be judged by the way it treats the poor, then Highlander would qualify as religious. But we do that primarily out of an analysis of society. We want to bring about a fundamental change in society, and we think it has to come from the bottom up—it can't come from the top down. Anything that's given to people can be taken away. So we try to help people struggle to gain their own freedom.

That doesn't mean that we think it's our job, or could be the job of any institution, to make overall programs and analysis for minority people. What we do say is, "You decide what you want to do." As we said before civil rights times, back in the '50s, we think that blacks are going to have to liberate themselves, and however they go about it we'll offer to help.

One of the things that people always say about Highlander is that back in the '30s, '40s, '50s and even into the '60s, it was one of the few places in the South where black and white people could get together as equals and get to know each other in a new way.

Well, there was a Catholic school down in Mobile, Alabama, that quietly, off the record so to speak, had some black and white people. They tried to keep it kind of quiet, for good reasons. They would have been run out of town if they hadn't. Then there were other places where people would quietly get together. But Highlander was the place where people knew you could openly have social equality, and they knew it because Highlander brought down the wrath of the opposition. And since we were the only place that was attacked at that time for doing it, we were practically the only place that was known. That opened up the opportunity for us to work with black people and was well worth all the harassment and trouble.

Besides, it was a matter of principle with us. If we had denied that, then we would have had no reason for existence. If you don't practice the things you advocate, you're losing your greatest opportunity to educate people. It's the experience, the action, that educates much more than words or pronouncements. We were living out what we believed in, and that was the message. By the way we lived and the kind of policies we had, we thought of Highlander as a place to give people a glimpse of the kind of society you could have.

It's interesting that with all the supposedly radical labor activities and all the alleged notorious communists who came through here, or didn't, what ended up getting you in trouble with the law had as much to do with how you sat down to eat supper.

Yes, it had more to do with that. The worst thing that could happen in the South at that time, as you know, was intermarriage between blacks and whites. The next-worst thing was eating together, because that was a social ritual. So we defied the social ritual, which scared people more than anything else we could have done except get married.

How did this work out back in those days when the focus was on the labor movement? I assume that the white workers were white Southerners who had been socialized with all the racist mythology that white people were taught then. How did you bring black and white people together?

At first we had great difficulty getting blacks. We could occasionally find whites who would live with black people, but we couldn't find many blacks who would take the chance of getting lynched. So we used to have to bring people here for short periods. But gradually we got to the place where we could have a minority of blacks, and then we would try to get the students who had that experience at Highlander to go back and translate that immediately into their local unions. And to a very surprising degree that worked.

By actually living on the basis of equality together, the whites were easily persuaded that their union would be stronger and more democratic and they would become better leaders and have more influence in the union if they made that alliance with blacks. So a lot of our students went back and started working with blacks. Then they started sending whites and blacks together from those local unions. And so it spread.

Now all this was taking place before the civil rights movement. It wasn't framed as a civil rights issue because we put it all together on the basis of having a strong union, a democratic union, a union that could stand up and fight the bosses and get some benefits. And we said, "It doesn't matter whether you like it or not. You've got to take the women in. You've got to get old and young together. You've got to get everybody working together in a democratic set-up, or you won't have any strength." That was the angle we used. So the groundwork was laid, and although we weren't dealing with civil rights on a daily basis, a lot of black people and white people whom we worked with later became leaders of the civil rights movement.

How did what started as an economic struggle during the Depression evolve into a civil rights movement?

We finally came to the conclusion that we couldn't go any further in terms of economic, political, or cultural changes until we dealt head-on with this business of racism. We'd get so far, and then racism would be used against us. So in the early 1950s, around 1952 or '53—before the Supreme Court decision on Brown *vs.* Board of Education—we decided that we were going to have to consciously concentrate on dealing with the public aspects of segregation.

That's when we came to the policy of saying to black people: "OK, we'll work with you. You decide what to do, and we'll be supportive. We think that's the most important single thing we can do now, because we can't move on peace, we can't move on economic issues, we can't move on social life or anything else, until we crack that." Then we started trying to pull together people who would talk about racism, both white and black, and the basis for this was our old trade union people.

You see, to the labor people we added black people who, for economic reasons, were freed of influence from whites—preachers from black churches, beauticians, morticians, and other business people who only worked with other black people. A few people in education were involved, along with private people, black and white, who were more independent. But the basis for this was the labor people.

I understand that one of the first things to come from that work was the citizenship schools. How did that come about?

I guess that's what you'd call one of the Highlander success stories. Our policy has always been not to go out and do anything anywhere unless we have students who start something and then ask us to come and help. The citizenship school program is a typical example of that.

A fellow named Esau Jenkins had come to a workshop at Highlander, and he was trying to get people registered to vote in Johns Island, South Carolina, when he asked if we could help. After doing some real analyzing and thinking about the situation, we came up with a very simple idea that the black people there called the citizenship school. It was what most people would call a literacy school.

The law required blacks to read a part of the U.S. Constitution before they could register, and so it ruled out illiterates. If you had a certain amount of property or wealth, and you were white, you didn't have to be able to read to vote. But if you were black, you did. So our program was really a way to help people get to be citizens. That's why they called it citizenship school.

Out of that program grew a lot of leadership for the civil rights movement. Some people credit the citizenship school program for being one of the bases of the civil rights movement. It was simply black people teaching black people in a system of adult education based on what's called popular education now, especially in Latin America. It was based on the fact that if you know just a little bit more than the people you're teaching, you are closer to them and you can help them. You don't need to have expertise to do it, but you have to respect the people you're dealing with.

That program spread, and later on Martin Luther King, Jr., asked me if I would work out an educational program for SCLC [Southern Christian Leadership Conference], which didn't have an educational program. After spending a month or so thinking about it and visiting some of their programs, I came to the conclusion that the citizenship school program was ideal for them. They accepted the program, and that became the official program of SCLC. It became a big program, but it started out in the back of a little co-op which we'd helped set up.

You mentioned Highlander's relationship to SCLC and Dr. King. What is the story about Highlander's role in the explosion that began in 1956 in Montgomery, Alabama?

Well, we were bringing people together to discuss the problem of segregation. Rosa Parks had been active in the NAACP [National Association for the Advancement of Colored People] as a secretary, and a fellow named E.D. Nixon, who was a Pullman Porters Union organizer, was head of the NAACP in Montgomery. Nixon and two white

Alabama civil rights movement sympathizers, Cliff and Virginia Durr, decided that if Highlander could get Rosa a scholarship, they'd provide bus fare to send her up, because they thought it would be nice for her to come to Highlander.

When Rosa got here, she sat very quietly through the session, and she didn't take much part in the discussion. When it came to the end of the session where we'd ask people to make a commitment of what they were going to do about segregation when they got back to their home communities, Rosa said, "I really can't say that I'll do anything because I just don't see anything that can be done." Well, everyone knows what she, in fact, did do just a short time after she got back to Montgomery.

Was it during the period of involvement with the civil rights movement that Highlander really faced enormous persecution?

If you're not facing some kind of resistance from the people in power, then you must be a traitor to your cause. So you can be sure that if you're accepted by people who are struggling, then you're going to be harassed by people who want to keep the status quo. So in a way it's a measure of your involvement.

What form did that harassment take for you?

Well, I've had ribs broken and my skull fractured. I've still got a crack in it. I had teeth knocked out, collarbone broken, arms slashed, but all of it short of death. Now, I had to go to jail like everybody else, but that was no problem—you got a little rest. So on a personal level you had to take punishment.

One thing a lot of white people don't understand is that we have a certain advantage in the fact that we are white. They'd beat me senseless. But they'd kill a black person. They didn't quite dare kill me. That would have been embarrassing. In fact there were instructions in writing by the FBI to the officers in Mississippi when I was there not to kill me. There weren't any such instructions not to kill black people.

As far as Highlander itself was concerned, they tried every way in the world to harass us. They tried to have vigilantes come and run us off and try to burn the place, but our neighbors protected us. Then they had a state investigation to try to put us out of business, and that didn't work. Senator James Eastland's Internal Security Subcommittee came, but that didn't work. Finally they raided the school and set up a case over a two-year period during which they bribed local people to testify; but even after all that, most of them got mixed up and said the wrong things. They finally found a technical way of getting us by charging us with selling liquor without a license for having a cooler of beer with a collection cup beside it.

The one thing we pleaded guilty to was the one thing they were concerned about—running an integrated place. We very proudly said we'd been doing that for years and were going to continue to do it. And it was that issue that got us in trouble.

And you were raising a family during the worst of those times?

Yeah, I was raising two kids. My wife died when my kids were 10 and 12. All their childhood lives, they lived in this period of harassment during which I had to send them to a neighbor's house when we'd be attacked. And they used to hear all this hate stuff on television and radio and from the preachers and read about it in the paper. So they grew up knowing all about that, and they'd just kind of bear with it.

My daughter was going to a local school, and the teacher would say, "Comrade Charis, will you read?" And then the teachers would say, "Well, you better get back out there with those little nigger kids you live with." So the kids didn't have an easy time, but it was more than made up for by their growing up knowing wonderful people. They knew Rosa Parks just like family.

That's important because, as you said, when you take certain stands about how you're going to live your life, you can expect the things you experienced at Highlander. People may not fear that for themselves, but they fear that for their families.

I was asked at one of the state investigations of Highlander if I felt like I had some obligations to live a more normal life and assume my responsibility as a parent for my children. I was also asked what kind of heritage did I think I was leaving them. I said I thought I was leaving them the best heritage that I could. I thought it was important to leave them a heritage that they wouldn't be ashamed of. I thought that was much more important than playing Little League baseball with them or doing some of the things that the investigators thought were part of a parent's duty.

So I don't feel that you neglect your kids when you do something that they can be proud of. I'm happier now that my kids are not ashamed of Highlander, not ashamed of me, and not sorry about their own lives, than I would be if I'd left them conventional sorts of memories and money and things of that sort. And they're better off.

One thing that is pretty unique about Highlander over the whole span of the last fifty-four years is the role of culture, especially music, in the education and agitation work that's been done here.

Even before Highlander started, I was making notes on some ideas that I'd like to see incorporated into it. One of them was the use of culture, music, and drama as a way of saying things that you can't say otherwise. You can say things in music and in dance and drama and poetry that are not exactly the rational step-by-step sort of things. I always conceived of that being important.

"We Shall Overcome" was just one of the many songs that were brought to Highlander. It came from Charleston, South Carolina, where the American Tobacco workers were on strike. Like a lot of people, they made up songs based on their hymns. And they brought to Highlander a pretty rough-hewn song they'd made up. With my wife Zilphia's encouragement, that song grew. It had something to it that people just kept singing it. When Martin Luther King, Jr., heard it, he said, "This has got to be the hymn of the civil rights movement." Zilphia collected such songs and put out music books that spread all over the South and were used during the civil rights movement and the labor period.

There's a story that one of the verses for "We Shall Overcome" came into being much later at Highlander.

There was a black Baptist church youth choir from Montgomery, Alabama, and Septima Clark, a black woman on our staff, had made arrangements for them to come up. While they were eating and looking at a film, there was a raid.

People came in with guns and demanded that they put on the lights. But nobody would put on the lights. The people had flashlights and showed their guns and kept demanding that they turn the movie off and put on the lights. No one knew whether they were vigilantes or the law. It turned out that they were deputies and people who'd been deputized for this raid. Soon the kids started singing "We Shall Overcome," and they added that verse "We are not afraid." And Septima said it just infuriated those people, the whites, to have these black kids sing, "We are not afraid."

After decades of social struggle, what perspective can you offer to people who are involved now but haven't been at it for so long?

One of the ways it seems to me that people can keep going is to have a moral conviction about what they're doing, not just a rational analysis of society. However, you do need your rational analysis to size up the situation, because you've got to start where the people are. So you've got to be very firm about your convictions and very analytical about the situation.

If you're going to get ready for the long haul, you've got to be able to look down the road a ways and decide where you're going. You've got to make up your mind about the way, or the path, or the process you're going to use in getting there so you aren't always trying to rethink everything every Monday morning. If you're going to think in terms of staying with something until you get it done, you've got to have a vision that's worth spending a lifetime on.

You said that at Highlander fundamental social change is the objective and that at different times Highlander may work on toxic wastes or union rights or civil rights. How does your work on the specific issues, some of which you may win and others you may lose, relate to the larger objective?

I think there are two things involved. One is that what results in a revolution is a culmination of a lot of things that have their fruition at a certain time. But the revolution is being built all along.

What you do is build little cells of decency, little cells of democracy, little experiences of people making decisions for themselves, little philosophical discussions about civil rights and human rights. All of those get built into what's going to happen later on.

So you're really building for the revolution when you do something to develop local leadership. You get some satisfaction out of seeing steps as you go along, even though you don't get all the way.

Then, if you're around long enough, you see things like the industrial union movement, the civil rights movement, the anti-war movement, and other movements that seem to get something done. So you know people can do things. A lot of people today have never seen anything succeed.

I've seen things succeed. I know people can do things. I've seen the complete labor movement restructured; I've seen the civil rights movement. I know people can make changes. They're not making them now, but they're building things. The time is not being wasted. But it's not being fully occupied either.

The purpose of Highlander is not to solve problems but to use problems and crises as the basis for educating people about a democratic society. To make them want more, and make them understand they can do more.

A lot of people in the movement these days are starting to suffer from a kind of crisis-to-crisis, issue-to-issue burnout.

Don't tell me. I don't understand this kind of thinking, you know. I get the impression that the organizers have reduced the people they're working with to their own level of expectation. But these people are used to tough problems; they're used to defeat.

I think you need to challenge people. I think you stretch them as far as you can. I think you have expectations that you share with them and you give them hope.

If you believe in certain principles, you practice them. If you believe that people can learn, then you learn. If you stop learning, you'd have no way to help other people learn. You have to go through life sharing your own enthusiasm for your beliefs and trusting people and having a love for people so it can be understood by others. You help them understand that within them is the possibility of accomplishing things. You do nothing to limit people.

I feel very strongly that people have the capacity to go further.

You've got to deal with people's self-interest, some say. Well, I agree with that, but their interests are much broader than most people think. Their personal interest includes a willingness to struggle, a love for their country, a love for humanity. Those are personal interests too. It isn't just feeding your belly and getting some clothes on and getting a little security. Those are personal interests, they're valid and they're important. But these other things are personal interests too. And you can challenge people, you can build with people on those things. And if you don't, it seems to me you're minimizing the humanity of people.

Fannie Lou Hamer

Stepping Out into Freedom

by Danny Duncan Collum

In the late 1950s, something happened among black people in the South for which there is no simple explanation. Suddenly all the faith, courage, and endurance accumulated during 400 years of slavery and exploitation welled up into a massive nonviolent movement for human rights that, for a time, shook the country to its foundations.

The explosion was touched off by several circumstances. First, the long and tedious courtroom battles fought by the National Association for the Advancement of Colored People (NAACP) had begun to eat away at the legal basis for segregation and culminated finally in the 1954 Supreme Court school desegregation decision. Second, the struggles for self-determination of former colonies in Africa provided new pride and inspiration for many, especially younger blacks. Third, since 1947 small cadres of committed nonviolent activists had been experimenting with Gandhian tactics against segregation in the North and South. And, of course, the emergence of Dr. Martin Luther King, Jr., as a leader who could move a broad cross section of the black community helped galva-

Danny Duncan Collum, a *Sojourners* contributing editor, teaches writing at Rust College in Holly Springs, Mississippi.

nize the movement. But even these factors fail to explain the depth and magnitude of what began to happen.

Recently I asked a long-time activist in Mississippi how she had become involved in the movement. She replied, "I don't really know how I or any of us got involved. I just know that in Shelby, Mississippi, when we heard that the Freedom Riders were coming, we walked around for days asking each other, 'Are they here yet?' We were like soldiers waiting for somebody's army to join us." This grassroots, almost spontaneous character of the freedom movement was significant and mystifying.

Certainly the movement would never have had coherence and direction without the work and strategy of its organizers, lawyers, educators, and preachers. But the movement's primary impetus came from unlikely and ordinary sources, such as a seamstress in Montgomery who one day decided she was too tired to yield her seat on the bus; or a few young people at North Carolina Agricultural and Technical College who read a Fellowship of Reconciliation booklet about nonviolence and decided to eat lunch at the Woolworth's in Greensboro; or a young man named James Meredith who decided he should complete his education at the University of Mississippi; or a plantation worker named Fannie Lou Hamer who one day walked into the Sunflower County courthouse to register to vote.

Those most intense years of the civil rights movement perhaps can only be sufficiently explained as one of those times when the spirit of God blew like a mighty wind, and those who had faith in the most unexpected circumstances answered the call to step out into freedom. Fannie Lou Hamer of Ruleville, Mississippi, was one who answered the call without hesitation. When she did, the world saw powers of leadership, courage, and inspiration that it had thought were far beyond the reach of a poorly educated female farmworker. In the fifteen years after she stepped out to register, Hamer became a nationally recognized leader of the civil rights movement, a tireless servant to the poor people of Mississippi, and a beacon of hope to people struggling for justice all over the world.

Until 1962 Hamer's life was like that of most rural, poor, black women. She grew up the youngest of twenty children in the Mississippi Delta, then the poorest section of the poorest state in the union. The Delta, a triangle of rich flatland between the Yazoo and the Mississippi Rivers, has always had cotton grown mostly on large plantations as its economic base.

Since slavery days the majority population in the Delta has been black, and when Hamer was born in 1917 the white minority controlled all the political power and virtually all the wealth. The detailed Jim Crow segregation code daily reminded blacks of their place. All public facilities, including cafes, bus stations, and movie theaters were either segregated or reserved for whites only. Public buildings had "White" and "Colored" water fountains. Gas stations often had three restrooms marked "Men," and "Women," and "Colored." Public schools were segregated by law; black schools, woefully underfunded, were closed in the fall and spring so that the children would be available for field work. Blacks were kept from voting by an outlandishly complex literacy test, which only they were required to take, and a poll tax.

Like most Delta blacks, the members of Hamer's family were sharecroppers. The sharecropping system was the economic strand of the iron net that surrounded southern blacks. Devised to replace slavery as a source of cheap labor, sharecropping was a system under which poor tenant farmers were each assigned a piece of plantation land to work. The tenant was provided with a house and food, seed, fertilizer, and farm equipment on credit from the plantation owner's company store. At harvest time the landowner supposedly was due half the crop and the sharecropper half, though the sharecropper was required to pay for his supplies out of his earnings.

Somehow the bill at the company store always seemed to exceed what the sharecropper could get for his half of the crop. As a result, sharecroppers were kept in grinding poverty, enslaved by debt. The sharecropping system was not only cheap for the landowners, it provided a means to control the work force. Sharecroppers who rebelled or tried to move to another farm had their personal property confiscated as payment for their debt.

Hamer's family, through the hard work both of her parents and the whole brood of children, became one of the very few to work their way out of this cycle. Her father was able eventually to rent some land outright, buy his own animals, equipment, and even a car as well as fix up their house.

But the family's efforts and dreams were destroyed when a white man poisoned the feed and killed their stock, forcing the family back to sharecropping.

The sharecropper's daughter grew up and married Perry "Pap" Hamer, a tractor driver on a neighboring plantation. The couple was unable to have children of their own, and adopted two daughters. The first, Dorothy, was given to them at birth by a single mother, and the second, Virgie, they took in when she was five months old. She had been badly burned, and her natural parents were unable to give her medical care. For twenty years the Hamers worked on various plantations around Sunflower County.

Looking back on her years of farm work, Hamer said, "Sometimes I be working in the fields and I get so tired, I say to the people picking cotton with us, 'Hard as we have to work for nothing, there must be some way we can change this.'"

No way came into view until August, 1962, when at the urging of a friend, Hamer attended a rally sponsored by the Southern Christian Leadership Conference (SCLC) and the Student Nonviolent Coordinating Committee (SNCC). She later recalled that at the rally, "Rev. James Bevel [of SCLC] preached a sermon from the 16th chapter of Matthew, the third verse, 'discerning the signs of the times,' tying it to the voter registration. Then Jim Forman [of SNCC] talked about how it was our constitutional right . . . to register and to vote in Mississippi." At the end of the rally the call went out for blacks to go to the county seat the next week and register. Hamer answered the call, and at age 45 began a new life neither she nor anyone else could ever have imagined.

When she went to register, Hamer was confronted with the infamous Mississippi literacy test, in which she and other blacks were required to copy and interpret an arcane section of the Mississippi state constitution to the satisfaction of the county examiner. Not surprisingly, Hamer failed the test the first time. But she returned to try again, telling the clerk he would see her every thirty days for the rest of her life until she passed. She was finally registered to vote in January of 1963.

By that time Hamer had already been evicted from her plantation home as a result of her attempts to register, and had plunged full time into the movement as a SNCC field secretary. When her husband and daughters moved off the plantation to join Hamer in town, the owner confiscated all the family property, claiming that they owed him money.

The persecution that attended Hamer's first attempt to register set a pattern for the rest of her life. She received death threats by phone and mail, was wiretapped and kept under surveillance. The harassment came first from the Mississippi authorities and their allies in the Klan and the White Citizens' Council. Later these groups were joined by the FBI. The agency had set out to investigate the Klan but turned its attention to people like Hamer after the federal establishment came to consider the civil rights movement radical and uncontainable.

In her work for SNCC, Hamer traveled the cotton fields by day and spoke at churches by night, recruiting others to register to vote. In addition, she soon became one of SNCC's most effective communicators to northern white audiences, describing the desperation of blacks' situation in Mississippi and their determination to change it.

Less than nine months after she became a full-time SNCC worker, Hamer experienced her worst confrontation with white law and order. She and a group of SNCC and SCLC activists were returning by bus from a voter education workshop in Charleston, South Carolina. When they arrived at the Trailways station in Winona, they entered the white side of the terminal and were arrested. They were held for three days and brutally beaten. Hamer suffered kidney damage and developed a blood clot in her left eye that permanently impaired her vision.

The group was released only after intervention by movement representatives and the Justice Department. Hamer later reported that as she had sat bleeding in her cell she heard the officers "plotting to kill us, maybe to throw our bodies in the Big Black River, where nobody would ever find us."

"They offered to let us go one night, but I knew it was just so they could kill us and say we was trying to escape. I told 'em they'd have to kill me in my cell." Despite the beatings, Hamer refused to give in to hatred or revenge: "It wouldn't solve any problem for me to hate whites just because they hate me. Oh, there's so much hate, only God has kept the Negro sane."

Hamer was back in the thick of movement activity as soon as her wounds began to heal. The campaign for black voting rights picked up after the passage of the 1964 Public Accommodations desegregation law, and the right to vote became the symbol of black aspirations in Mississippi. Few in the movement, especially among the SNCC activists, had any illusions about the efficacy of the vote in the U.S. system. But the right to vote was a tangible goal. And since many of Mississippi's towns and counties had majority black populations, the black vote could make some cracks in the system and whet the people's appetite for bigger changes.

The civil rights forces planned to use the upcoming 1964 national election and its accompanying media attention to force home the demand for the vote. In the summer of 1964, Mississippi was flooded with thousands of mostly white student volunteers from all over the country. The volunteers were set to work helping black people in their attempts to register. When in early August two of these northern volunteers and a young black Mississippian were killed in Neshoba County, the nation was made grimly aware of the severity of the situation in Mississippi.

Shortly after the Neshoba County murders, the Mississippi Freedom Democratic Party (MFDP) presented its challenge to the Democratic national convention in Atlantic City. Republicans in Mississippi were remembered as the party of Reconstruction, so whites voted solidly Democratic, making the Democratic primary the only election worth noting; the general elections were so sparsely attended they were considered a joke.

But the Democratic Party was a "Whites Only" club. Blacks who had been able to run the gauntlet of the literacy test, the poll tax, and white harassment to become registered voters found they were still locked out of the Mississippi Democratic Party and thus effectively locked out of the political process. Ironically, liberal Democrats like the Kennedys and later Lyndon Johnson were getting great political mileage in the North out of their apparent support for black rights in the South. The freedom forces in Mississippi intended to exploit that irony to the hilt at Atlantic City.

In 1964 Lyndon Johnson was unopposed for the Democratic nomination and assured of victory over Barry Goldwater in November, so he had devoted much personal attention to carefully arranging every detail of the convention to make it his own week-long nationally televised coronation ceremony. But one factor Johnson didn't allow for was a grassroots uprising from the cotton fields and piney woods of Mississippi. Specifically, he neglected to allow for Hamer and the MFDP.

The MFDP had been formed in the spring of 1964 after blacks were excluded from Democratic precinct meetings. When Hamer had tried to attend a precinct meeting in Ruleville, her husband was fired from his job the next day. The MFDP constituted itself as a counter-party and set up its own delegate selection process, culminating in a state convention in which Hamer was elected vice-chair of the delegation. The MFDP delegates then went to Atlantic City and presented their documented evidence that the white delegation had been chosen in a fraudulent process. They asked the convention credentials committee to refuse to seat the "regular" Democrats and instead recognize the biracial MFDP delegation as Mississippi's representatives.

The MFDP was represented by the nationally famous civil rights lawyer Joseph Rauh, and presented the committee with a string of distinguished witnesses, including Martin Luther King, Jr., who testified regarding the undemocratic character of Mississippi politics. But Hamer grabbed the attention and conscience of the nation as she powerfully and dramatically told her story: the harshness she faced after trying to register, and how she had been shot at and beaten almost to death, all for attempting to exercise fundamental legal rights.

We are told in Matthew's Gospel that when Jesus finished the Sermon on the Mount, "the crowds were astonished . . . for he taught them as one who had authority, and not as their scribes." When Hamer finished her testimony at Atlantic City, the whole country recognized that she spoke with authority, in marked contrast to the many "scribes" assembled there. And like Jesus, the source of her authority was the potent combination of suffering and faith.

The attention of the nation was now fixed on the decision of the credentials committee; the liberal pronouncements of the Democrats were clearly on trial. The liberals failed the test miserably, and the MFDP challenge was rejected.

After Atlantic City, Hamer and the rest of the MFDP did not give up their battle for black voting rights. They went back to work preparing to take their case to the U.S. Congress. Since blacks in Mississippi had been prevented from nominating and voting for their own candidates, the MFDP ran a counter-election for Congress with a ballot listing the white incumbent and the MFDP challenger. Hamer was on the freedom ballot for the second district and received 33,000 votes against 49 for the incumbent, Jamie Whitten. Statewide, 70,000 blacks voted in the freedom election, and when the new Congress convened in January, 1965, the MFDP's elected representatives went to Washington, intending to claim that Mississippi's five congressmen had been chosen in a rigged election and should not be seated in the House.

Not until September did the subcommittee on election hear this case. Fifteen thousand pages of evidence were presented, proving legally what was obvious to the naked eye: 40 percent of Mississippi's people were being denied their constitutional right to vote. But again liberal Northern politicians declined to rock the boat. Hamer wrote later:

> Racial progress? Almost a hundred years ago [during Reconstruction] John R. Lynch placed this same kind of challenge before the House of Representatives. He was a black man from Mississippi, and he succeeded with Yankee white help. But we failed a hundred years later with native white Mississippi help and Yankee opposition. . . . So you see this is not Mississippi's problem, it is America's problem.

Though the MFDP challenges failed, they played a major role in generating the pressure that finally forced Congress to pass the 1965 Voting Rights Act, which opened the way for blacks to gain their right to vote. By the 1968 Chicago Democratic convention, a somewhat more moderate biracial delegation, called the Mississippi Loyalist Democrats, again challenged the old guard and succeeded in replacing them. Hamer was a member of that delegation and served three years as committeewoman for Mississippi's Democratic National Committee.

The defeat of the MFDP challenges marked a turning point in the development of the freedom movement. Until then the movement had been at the same time working in an uneasy partnership with the federal establishment and working against it. A choice had to be made between partnership and opposition, a choice made even more stark by the 1965 escalation of the Vietnam War. Hamer was foremost of those who considered the federal government part of the problem. While she remained willing to work with anyone through any channels, she was never willing to compromise the just demands of her people.

As Hamer gained political experience, she grew aware of the broader dimensions of the illness that infected the American system. She became an early opponent of the Vietnam War, attending and speaking at numerous antiwar demonstrations. She saw the movement's struggle as not solely for black legal rights but as a fight for human rights in conflict with a system whose leaders were "more interested in more profits and power for the rich and powerful people . . . and have no interest in helping the poor people." She helped to organize for Martin Luther King's last dream, the Poor People's Campaign, which sought to mobilize a multiracial coalition of the dispossessed to demand basic economic reforms.

While Hamer's political understanding grew, it remained firmly rooted in biblical faith. In 1968 she wrote:

> We have to realize just how grave the problem is in the United States today, and I think the sixth chapter of Ephesians, the eleventh and twelfth verses helps us to know . . . what it is we are up against. It says: "Put on the whole armor of God, that ye may be able to stand against the wiles of the devil. For we wrestle not against flesh and blood but against principalities, against powers, against the rulers of the darkness of this world, against spiritual wickedness in high places." This is what I think about when I think of my own work in the fight for freedom.

She was unceasing in her service to the poor people of Ruleville and surrounding Sunflower County. She helped lead the battle to get the Head Start program into Mississippi. Head Start was finally brought in under the auspices of Mary Holmes College, an independent black school, in order to avoid the governor's veto of poverty programs and to keep their control away from white politicians. The Head Start effort was one of the few success stories of the War on Poverty, and the low-income children of Mississippi still reap its benefits.

Deeply suspicious of the way politicians were using the poverty programs as a way to make blacks dependent, the bulk of her efforts in Ruleville were oriented toward helping the people become self-reliant. Hamer organized the Freedom Farm Cooperative to obtain land for plantation workers who were left unemployed by farm mechanization. Freedom Farm eventually grew to 680 acres. She raised money for the construction of 200 units of low-income housing in Ruleville and helped start a low-cost day care center that today bears her name. She worked to bring a garment factory to Ruleville to provide jobs for the unemployed.

A lifetime of hard physical work capped by more than a decade of pouring herself out in the freedom struggle took its toll on her health. In addition to the effects of childhood polio and the lingering consequences of the Winona beating, Hamer had long suffered from diabetes and heart trouble. In the mid-1970s she developed breast cancer. Although she underwent a mastectomy in 1976 and resumed her activities, the cancer continued to spread, and on March 14, 1977, she died in the Mound Bayou Community Hospital.

While she had given herself in the struggle to redistribute power and wealth, Hamer had remained poor. In earlier years, movement friends had raised money to build a house for her family, and when she died, again friends and coworkers raised money for her funeral. The service was held in the Ruleville Junior High auditorium, which overflowed with mourners from all over the country. After her death the Mississippi state legislature passed a resolution in her honor. The resolution was sponsored by four black state representatives who knew they wouldn't have been in the capitol had it not been for Fannie Lou Hamer.

It is twenty years since Hamer walked into the Sunflower County courthouse. In some ways Mississippi is a very different place. Young people nearing adulthood have never seen the "Whites Only" signs, and in many parts of the state the public schools are among the most racially integrated in the nation. Seventy percent of Mississippi's black voting age population is registered and is a political force that politicians can't afford to ignore. Mississippi is among the nation's states with the largest number of black elected officials.

But in other ways very little has changed in Mississippi, or in the United States. On the whole, people are as poor now as they were then, and they are getting poorer. And black votes in Mississippi and elsewhere still haven't been allowed to translate into a real shift in power.

Hamer is buried at the edge of Ruleville on land purchased by the Freedom Farm Cooperative. Her grave is marked by a simple marble headstone that carries the words which were her motto and rallying cry as she spoke and organized for justice: "*I am sick and tired of being sick and tired.*" Planted by the grave is a lone flowering cactus plant, seemingly misplaced in the damp, rich soil of the Mississippi Delta.

But the cactus is an appropriate symbol of Hamer's life. The social and cultural terrain in which she lived and worked was as harsh and inhospitable as any desert. But she managed to rise up to it, to become tough enough to survive the worst it had to offer and still blossom into a flower that offered hope to millions of struggling and sometimes hopeless people.

Once during a time of unusually frequent threats and harassment Hamer said, "I'm never sure any more when I leave home whether I'll get back or not. Sometimes it seems like to tell the truth today is to run the risk of being killed. But if I fall, I'll fall five feet four inches forward in the fight for freedom. I'm not backing off that and no one will have to cover the ground I walk as far as freedom is concerned." She never backed off. And she certainly left us a great deal more than five feet four inches further along the way to freedom.

Miguel D'Escoto

Priest of the People

On July 19, 1979, the Nicaraguan people, led by the Sandinista Front, overthrew dictator Anastasio Somoza, ending a brutal U.S.-backed dynasty that had lasted more than forty years. Augusto Cesar Sandino, from whom the revolutionary opposition took its name, had led the fight against the occupation of Nicaragua by U.S. Marines four decades before. In the first years after the overthrow, the revolution made dramatic improvements in literacy and health care for the people of Nicaragua, and made strides in redistributing land and resources, all in the face of a $1.5 billion debt inherited from Somoza.

In November 1982, the U.S. press exposed the presence of U.S.-backed forces, known as contras, on Nicaragua's Honduran border, formed largely from former members of Somoza's savage national guard. In February 1990, in the face of a brutal and intransigent contra war, the stranglehold of a U.S. economic embargo, and their own mistakes, the Sandinistas were voted out of power.

Miguel D'Escoto, a Maryknoll priest, served as Nicaragua's foreign minister for the decade that the Sandinistas were in

power. Below are excerpts from an interview conducted by Joyce Hollyday and Jim Wallis in Managua, Nicaragua, in December 1982, just after the presence of the contras came to light.

Humanity has been created in the image and likeness of God, created to be a co-creator with God in the unfinished task of making this a world after God's own design. I am reminded of a marvelous painting of the baptism of Christ in a gallery in London. It was painted by Leonardo da Vinci's teacher, Verrocchio. In it you see John the Baptist pouring water over our Lord in the river. An angel stands by the side holding the garments of our Lord.

Verrocchio had great love and admiration for Leonardo, his young disciple, and he wanted him to participate in this masterpiece. So he asked Leonardo to paint the angel. Of course, the disciple was better than the teacher, and what is most interesting in that picture is the angel, although the whole work is very good.

And so our Lord also makes us co-creators, wanting us to participate and share in the canvas. God initiated a process, and in his great love for humankind, decided not to do it all. Having been given that orientation, we cannot accept being reduced to the level of simple spectatorship in a game in which only a few play. We have a built-in need to actively participate with our God-given lights in the common task of searching for a more human and just society.

In Latin America the church had been for so long identified with the powers that be, with an established order that was not a Christian established order. We had been preaching resignation and helping the rich to continue exploiting, telling the people that later they would be rewarded if they accepted this exploitation. We were preaching a kind of idolatry toward the system just because it was.

To preach resignation indiscriminately is very dangerous. Resignation in the face of the inevitable is oftentimes a virtue, but some types of resignation are sinful. To resign yourself to the point that you become an accomplice with crime, with exploitation, is a total refusal to do the will of God and become a leavening and transforming agent in society.

A process of renewal in the Catholic church began after Vatican II permeated our reality through the historic meeting of Latin American bishops in 1968 in Medellín, Colombia. It filtered down and reached Catholic schools, where they began to have qualms of conscience that they were educating only the elite and helping them to live in a bubble separate from the rest of their brothers and sisters.

The schools began to foment the idea that young students should voluntarily help out in the poor barrios, in the poor neighborhoods, with parish priests who were working among the poor. That's how the students discovered the plight of their brothers and sisters and began to search for what to do. From there they went to the mountains and joined the Sandinista Front. The great growth in the Sandinista Front occurred when the church began this process of renewal in Nicaragua and consciences began to open.

Do you know the apostle Thomas? Most people are like Thomas. They can't simply accept that the Lord was resurrected, and so the Lord says to them, "Come and put your finger in my wounds." Christ wanted to show Thomas his credentials, because Thomas demanded to inspect them.

We preach the message of our Lord. But the people want credentials. Where are our wounds, what are we suffering? In every Gospel you will see what our Lord is promising you: persecution. The inevitable consequence of doing the Father's will is the cross. And the Father's will is that we proclaim the brotherhood and sisterhood of all of us under God and therefore necessarily denounce whatever stands in the way of achieving this brotherhood and sisterhood. Do that, and our Lord says that we will be persecuted as he was persecuted; the disciple is no greater than the Master.

Eight years before the insurrection, after the earthquake, I talked to the archbishop. And I said, "Archbishop, don't you see how this is going to explode?" To me it seemed inevitable that sooner or later in spite of the great patience of our people—everything human is limited—that patience would run out. I said, "Bishop, it is going to be terrible, there will be so many dead people, so much destruction and death. Why don't we go into the streets? You lead us, armed with the rosary in our hands and prayers on our lips and chants and songs in repudiation for what has been done to our people. The worst that can happen to us is the best, to share with Christ the cross if they shoot us.

"If they do shoot us, there will be a consciousness aroused internationally. And maybe the people in the United States will be alerted and will pressure their government so that it won't support Somoza, and then maybe we can be freed without the destruction that I see ahead."

And the archbishop said, "No, Miguel, you tend to be a little bit idealistic, and this destruction is not going to happen." And then when it did happen, the church insisted on nonviolence.

To be very frank with you, I don't think that violence is Christian. Some may say that this is a reactionary position. But I think that the very essence of Christianity is the cross. It is through the cross that we will change.

I have come to believe that creative nonviolence has to be a constitutive element of evangelization and of the proclamation of the gospel. But in Nicaragua nonviolence was never included in the process of evangelization.

The cancer of oppression and injustice and crime and exploitation was allowed to grow, and finally the people had to fight with the means available to them, the only means that people have found from of old: armed struggle. Then the church arrogantly said violence was bad, nonviolence was the correct way.

I don't believe that nonviolence is something you can arrive at rationally. We can develop it as a spirituality and can obtain the grace necessary to practice it, but not as a result of reason. Not that it is anti-reason, but that it is not natural. The natural thing to do when some-body hits you is to hit them back.

We are called upon to be supernatural. We reach that way of being, not as a result of nature, but of prayer. But that spirituality and prayer and work with people's consciences has never been done. We have no right to hope to harvest what we have not sown.

Our Lord never said that we should take our cross and walk. He said, "Take your cross and follow me." Our Lord was the first to be nailed, spat upon, and crowned with thorns. He led as Martin Luther King led. That is why I always look upon King as the Christian who most exem-plifies what it means to follow our Lord today.

No one has influenced my own life more than Martin Luther King. For years and years it was his book *The Strength to Love* that I used in chapel for meditation. I gave a copy to many priests. And it was Martin Luther King's picture that hung in my office when I was in New York. But I used to look upon the picture with a certain amount of guilt or shame, because I admired him so much and wanted to follow what he had done, but I was afraid.

And then it came to me one day as we were preparing for Lent and I was alone in my office thinking. "Well, another Lent, and the same old mediocre me. What am I to do? You may say you are not going to eat hot dogs or do a particular thing; well, that doesn't help anyone. So what am I going to do for this Lent?"

I stayed there for a long time oblivious to everything, and then a prayer formulated: "Lord, help me to understand the mystery of your cross. Help me to love the cross and give me the guts to embrace it in whatever shape or form it comes."

And everything was different all of a sudden because the cross became to me a symbol of life, the beginning of life. I began to see it inseparable and indistinguishable from resurrection. Why? Because we come to understand in John that life is love, and greater love has no one than to give his or her life. The cross is the greatest act of love, and therefore the greatest manifestation of life.

During the revolution I was greatly uplifted by the experience of praying and offering the sacrifice of the Mass, celebrating the Eucharist with people who were in the struggle. It was a wonderful experience because for the first time I realized that we were not only repeating the words of Christ, "This is my blood, this is my body, which is shared, which is offered for all." Our Lord didn't want us only to repeat those words, he wanted us to repeat them after we had made them our own. The people who were participating in those prayers were making them real, because we didn't know if at that celebration or immediately afterwards, we would share our own blood and give our life—and many people did.

I remember that one day, late in the evening, I came to a camp where some combatants for the revolution were sitting in the grass under a tree having a conversation. They saw me coming and asked me to celebrate the Eucharist. I had no bread or wine, but I was able to respond to their request to "give us some uplifting words from the gospel of our Lord."

As I talked I noticed that one young man was fidgeting and seemed very uneasy. Finally I said, "Hernand, it looks to me as if you want to say something."

"You are always talking about the Lord," he replied. "Who is this Lord? The Lord People?"

"No, not the Lord People," I answered, "although he is identified with the people and is the Lord of many."

At this point an older man broke in, "Father, don't be upset with this young compañero. He is a good boy, he's just very revolutionary and has gotten himself confused by reading a book written by the Spaniard."

"What Spaniard?" I asked.

"Karl Marx."

No one laughed, and the man continued, "I don't know how to read. But I can tell this little fellow who the Lord is, because my grandfather used to tell us about him."

At that everyone hushed, because they knew that the older man's grandfather had been a lieutenant with Sandino. The man continued, "I don't want to brag, but I remember what my grandfather said. He said it was all in the book—the Bible. There it says that God is the Father of all of us and that Christ is his Son and is both God and man. We are all brothers and sisters, and we must be willing to give our lives for one another.

"So that's why when I was at home in my little town near Honduras and we heard on the radio that we must go to free our people, all of us Christians knew that we were supposed to be willing to risk our lives. And so we went in obedience to the Lord."

My father died three months before the triumph. He knew he was dying, because his heart was getting bigger and bigger and this was making it difficult for him to breathe.

I was living clandestinely at the time and couldn't visit him. But I heard that a bomb had been placed in his house, and it exploded where he usually sat. Somoza's people were looking for me, and after the bomb exploded, thirty-six armed men came and threw my father to the floor and demanded to know where I was.

After the men left, my father called me because he was afraid that news of this event would weaken me, make me worried. And he said, "I want you to know that your mother and I wanted to call and tell you not to worry about us because no one can really kill us." This is a new understanding of death: they can shoot our bodies but they cannot kill us.

And he said, "Don't be afraid yourself to die. I am praying with your mother one more rosary." (By now they were up to about six, because for everything that I got involved in he was praying another rosary.) "I am praying with your mother that you have the Christian guts to accept Calvary, if that is what the Lord wants."

But our struggle didn't end with the overthrow of Somoza, because we are still working for *Patria Libre o Morir*, a free country or death— free from internal tyranny, from external oppression, domination, and control; free to do what we believe is in the best interest of our people and will result in a social situation that will be certainly compatible with our Christian faith and belief. And in that commitment we continue.

In fact, that freedom began when the inner shackles of fear were broken, by the grace of God. All liberation must be first spiritual and internal. A free people can then proceed to free a nation, with freedom to do what it feels is the right and the just thing to do, regardless of the consequences.

What we are striving to do is to create a new Nicaragua, a Nicaragua that is really a Nicaragua of all of us, not just of a certain class. One doesn't choose the cradle; one chooses only the alliances that one makes.

I happened to be born into a class that enjoyed everything, which the majority of my brothers and sisters in Nicaragua did not. We could not continue to pray the Our Father because the hypocrisy of saying it became very repugnant. I can only say Our Father if I am concerned for the lot of every individual as if he or she really were my brother or sister. I could not honestly pray or go to communion. Then I realized that "I" was "we," we Nicaraguans, because this is a collective experience that led us to assume this position that took us to where we are now and for which we are being penalized. Pray that we can embrace the cross and endure being penalized for doing the Father's will, for proclaiming in word and deed the universal brotherhood and sisterhood of all of us.

Nicaragua has embarked on a project destined to secure for the first time real autonomy, sovereignty, and independence for our nation so that we can create a social, political, and economic situation that would allow us to live as brothers and sisters and respect the God-given dignity of each individual. Now we are confronted with this very aggressive attitude from people and governments that prior to this time were able to get along so well with the system that oppressed our people and condemned us to a most inhuman existence.

The triumph over Somoza has come, and we can begin, as patriots and Christians, to build this new country. It is only natural for the church to participate by developing the inner spiritual disposition among the people, so that their disposition would be up to par with what the revolution demands. The revolution demands that we abandon ideas of only ourselves becoming better off. It demands a great amount of brotherhood and sisterhood and sharing and thinking not only of myself but of *us*.

But soon after the revolution I saw that unfortunately there were some members of our church in very high and prominent places who opted to side with the small minority, who could not be satisfied by a popular revolution because they could not retain the privileges and prerogatives that they had enjoyed of old. And we had some inner church conflicts, which not only involved us as priests sympathetic with the revolutionary process, but at this point in time, as those exercising positions of responsibility within our government. It was alleged that we were doing something not in keeping with our responsibility as priests. It was even pretended that our actions were somehow against our Christian and priestly commitment.

But thank God we have the Gospels and the parables and the many ways in which our Lord tried through different means to clarify his message. When these conflicts arose I began to think more and more about the good Samaritan, because, like him, and the priest who went ahead and the other religious man who followed him, I was on the way to Jericho. My life had a very specific agenda. I had my work cut out for me, but all of a sudden the unexpected happened. There was my fellow countryman bleeding by the roadside, and I had to get off the beast and forget, for the time being, going to Jericho.

We go and we do, not what the priest did or the second man, but the one whom the Jews said could not be saved—the Samaritan. And so, we must be obedient to the Lord who calls us in many ways, and sometimes through events in which you, all of a sudden, find yourself immersed.

I am a man, a Nicaraguan, a Christian, and a priest, all of which demand of me certain things, but not contradictory demands. Being a Christian and being a priest means that I have to fulfill even more abundantly and completely the demands made upon a man and a citizen of a country. And I would never, by the grace of God, for fear of any reprisals, betray the people, who must be always the most important thing—the people for whom our Lord became incarnate, lived, died, and was resurrected.

And if, in trying to be faithful to what I believe is what our Lord demands of us in unusual circumstances, I suffer consequences, I will accept them. I have been told that I cannot celebrate the Holy Eucharist in public or private because somehow I'm supposed to be a scandal. It was the very center of my life. Well, I accept that. But when I was told that, I cried the whole night.

So, we go back to prayer: only to understand it, to love it, and to embrace it. You must join me in prayer that I will never betray the people, that I will accept the consequences of solidarity with the people who hunger for justice and for peace and for brotherhood and sisterhood.

Sojourner Truth

A Pillar of Fire

by Joyce Hollyday

The blaze of a fire threw shadows across the walls of the damp cellar. The pine logs crackled and sputtered, and from time to time Baumfree, tall and gaunt, rose and poked at them.

The night was filled with stories, as Baumfree and his wife, Mau Mau Bett, recounted to their two young children the events they had witnessed. Mau Mau, a mother who had seen ten of her children sold from her, wept as she told how Michel and Nancy had been taken away.

One snowy winter morning, five-year-old Michel had heard bells outside and ran excitedly to see the horse and sleigh that had stopped by the door. His delight turned to horror as he saw a man take his little sister Nancy and shut her in the sleigh. He ran screaming into the cellar and tried to hide, but the slave traders soon had him as well.

Such stories must have convulsed young Isabella with a sense of dread as she listened and watched eerie shadows dance on the walls. She would one day rise to the stature of her father, whose well-chosen Dutch name meant "straight as a tree," but as a child she was small and thin. And she had learned at an early age that there is no security for the children of slaves.

The world that her owner, Charles Hardenbergh of New York, gave to her was limited to this dank cellar beneath his tavern. Loose boards thrown over oozing mud served as the floor of the slave quarters. Here men, women, and children slept crowded on pallets of straw and tried to fight off rheumatism, fever sores, and palsy.

But Mau Mau Bett expanded the world of her young daughter and Peter, her only remaining son. On clear nights she took them outside to sit beneath a canopy of stars. "My children," she told them, "there is a God who hears and sees everything you think and do." Isabella was overtaken with this great mystery.

"When you are beaten or cruelly treated, or you fall into any kind of trouble," her mother continued, "you must ask his help. He will always hear you and help you." Then they knelt together as she led the children in the Lord's Prayer, spoken in a Dutch dialect.

As surely as the fireside stories blazed fear in the soul of Isabella, these starlight lessons kindled in her the warmth of comfort and the mystery of faith. It was these lessons that she carried with her as she traveled from slavery on a path that led her to embrace the name Sojourner Truth and a vocation as God's pilgrim.

Isabella's acceptance of God's mercy and comfort was put to its first severe test in 1806, when she turned nine. In that year Charles Hardenbergh died, leaving his relatives to decide the fate of his slaves. Baumfree, now a bent, old tree, was losing his sight and beginning to suffer the crippling effects of rheumatism. No one wanted the liability of Baumfree, so he and Mau Mau Bett were given their freedom and permission to live out their years in the cellar. Such "generosity" was in fact a way for the Hardenberghs to shirk responsibility for a failing couple that had given them the best years of their lives.

Mau Mau Bett's greatest fear came true on the auction block at the Hardenbergh estate: Both Isabella and Peter were sold away. Isabella was sold to John Nealy of Ulster County, New York, for a paltry $100. It has been conjectured that her "thin and bony" frame, or her "lack of feminine charm," were the reasons for the low price. One report has it that a few sheep were thrown in with her to make the deal more palatable to her new owner.

Isabella spoke no English, and her Dutch jargon was incomprehensible to her new owners. Their instructions left her confused, and if ordered to bring a teaspoon, she would as likely return with a bucket or dishpan. She was cruelly treated, forced to walk in winter without shoes and made victim of various abuses and indignities.

One Sunday morning Isabella was instructed to go to the barn. There Nealy was waiting for her. He tied her hands together and whipped her with a bundle of rods until deep gashes were cut into her flesh and blood streamed from her wounds.

The scars from her beating stayed with her forever, burned into her flesh by the hatred of a white man toward a ten-year-old girl. These, too, she carried on every step along her journey.

While she was Nealy's slave, remembering her mother's comforting words under the stars, Isabella began to talk in earnest with God. She asked God to protect her from her persecutors. As the abuse grew worse, she pleaded with God to tell her what she was doing against God's will to bring such tragedy upon herself.

Before long, she knew that her only true prayer could be one for deliverance from the Nealys. She begged God to send to her her father, whom she believed could be the vehicle of her deliverance. A short while later, Baumfree limped through deep snow to her door and heard his daughter's plea.

Not long after, Martin Scriver from Kingston, New York, came to the Nealy estate and bought Isabella for $105. Scriver was a fisherman and tavern owner. He and his family were simple and honest people. Isabella thrived and grew strong in the midst of their boisterous life, unloading boats at the wharf, hauling herbs and roots for the tavern's liquors. While with the Scrivers, she acquired the habit of smoking a pipe and speaking a brand of English that immediately identified her with a boat crew.

At 13 years old, Isabella had been transformed from a shy and frightened young girl into a tall and proud young woman. John Dumont, a nearby plantation owner, felt there was something striking about her and bargained with Scriver to buy her for $300.

Dumont was a kind man, and Isabella, known in the Dumont household as "Bell," soon became his favorite slave. He considered her "better than a man" because she could do as much as half a dozen others in the fields and still do the laundry at night. She soon incurred the envy and ire of the other slaves, Mrs. Dumont, and a white house servant named Kate, who took to throwing ashes in the potatoes Isabella washed every morning and then hurling vicious rebukes about the "dingy potatoes" her way.

While Isabella was with the Dumonts, Mau Mau Bett became very ill with palsy and a fever sore in one of her limbs. Baumfree returned from some chores one day and found her dead in the damp cellar—dead from sickness, toil, and unending grief over the loss of her last children.

Baumfree never stopped weeping. The last time Isabella saw him, he was sitting alone on a rock by the side of a road, disoriented, almost blind. Isabella tried to encourage him, informing him that the state of New York had agreed that in ten years all slaves would be freed, and then she could come and care for him.

"But my child, I cannot live that long," he answered to her young enthusiasm.

A few years later, Isabella, carrying her infant daughter, walked the twelve miles from the Dumont estate to the old cellar to give Baumfree the opportunity to hold—if not see—his grandchild. But the Hardenberghs had moved him out, and Isabella could not find him. Baumfree was discovered frozen to death in a miserable shack a short while later.

As a young woman, Isabella never questioned the master-slave relationship, believing it to be God-ordained and trying her best, as her mother had taught her, to be an honest and obedient slave. She in fact related to God and John Dumont in much the same way—as powerful men who recorded every move she made and meted out punishments and rewards.

Isabella made herself a "sanctuary" among some willow trees and daily continued the conversation she had begun with God years earlier. She always began with the Lord's Prayer, chanted in the Dutch her mother had taught her. Then she went on to recount her sins and sufferings to God, begging for forgiveness at times, commanding God to set things straight at others. She questioned and cajoled and bargained with her Lord.

She grew to love a slave named Robert on the neighboring Catlin estate, and the two desired to be married. Recognizing that if they would marry, all offspring would be added to Dumont's estate, Catlin tried to force them apart. Undaunted, Robert came to visit Isabella clandestinely. He was discovered one afternoon at the Dumont estate by Catlin and his son, who beat Robert with sticks until his head and face were pulpy, then dragged him bleeding home. Robert was later forced to marry a woman on the Catlin estate. The tragic series of events, in which Isabella felt completely powerless, struck a deep blow to her faith in the slavery system.

Isabella was given in marriage to a slave named Thomas. She gave birth to five children.

Since the day that she had informed Baumfree that all slaves in New York state would be freed, Isabella longed for July 4, 1827 to arrive. As the years crept by, Dumont even promised to free her a year earlier, since she had been such a faithful slave. But then Isabella contracted a disease in her hand that hampered her work, and Dumont withdrew his promise. Dumont's subterfuge dealt a further blow to Isabella's trust in this system that gave all power to white masters.

Isabella went to the highest tribunal and laid down the law. "Oh, God," she called out in the English dialect that would be her language from then on, "I been a-askin' you, an' askin' you, an' askin' you for all this long time to make my massa and missis better, an' you don't do it; an' what *can* be the reason? . . . Well, now, I tell you, I'll make a bargain with you. Ef you help me to git away from my massa an' missis, I'll agree to be good; but ef you don't help me, I really don't think I can be."

She knew she couldn't see well enough to escape safely in the dark, but she feared getting caught if she left in the daylight. She handed this dilemma over to God and waited for a response. She got her answer: "Get up two or three hours before daylight and start off."

"Thank you, Lord," she replied. "That's a good idea."

One fall morning at about three o'clock, Isabella arose, put a few articles of clothing and food into a cotton handkerchief, gathered up her infant daughter, Sophia, and set off. By the time the bright autumn sun crested the horizon, she had reached the summit of a hill a considerable distance from the Dumont estate. She looked down on the valley below her, brilliant with golden hues in the early-morning light, and felt both joy and alarm grip her. She was free.

She sat down for a moment to nurse her child, then knelt on the ground. "Well, Lord," she called out to the vast sky, "you started me out; now please show me where to go."

Isabella walked until late at night and came upon the home of a Quaker couple named Van Wagener, a house she later said had been shown to her in a dream. They ushered her into a spotless room with a tall, white bed. Never having slept in a bed before, she spent the night underneath it.

Dumont soon caught up to her. When she refused to go back with him, he threatened to take her child. The matter was resolved when Isaac Van Wagener, staunchly opposed to buying human beings, agreed to "buy the services" of Isabella and Sophia for the balance of the year.

The Van Wageners were staid Quaker folk. Their life held no excesses of either pain or pleasure. Isabella's roving spirit found life there too placid, and after several months another visit by John Dumont tempted her to return with him.

As Isabella started to climb into his carriage, she had an experience she described later in her *Narrative:*

> Well, jest as I was goin' out to get into the wagon, I *met God!* an' says I, "O God, I didn't know as you was so great!" An' I turned right round an' come into the house. . . .
>
> I could feel [God] burnin', burnin', burnin' all around me, an' goin' through me; an' I saw I was so wicked, it seemed as if it would burn me up. An' I said, "O somebody, somebody, stand between God an' me! for it burns me!"
>
> Then . . . I felt as it were somethin' like an umbrella that came between me an' the light, an' I felt it was somebody. . . . I begun to feel 'twas somebody that loved me. . . . And finally somethin' spoke out in me an' said, *"This is Jesus!"* . . . An' then the whole world grew bright. . . . An' I begun to feel sech a love in my soul as I never felt before. . . .
>
> An' then, all of a sudden, it stopped, an' I said, "Dar's de white folks that have abused you, an' beat you, an' abused your people—

think o' them!" But then there came another rush of love through my soul, an' I cried out loud—"Lord, Lord, I can love even de white folks!"

Truly Isabella's first encounter with Jesus was dramatic, showering her with the forgiveness that only Jesus can offer and inviting her to a love so profound that she was able to forgive even her white persecutors. As the years unfolded, she was challenged to return to that forgiveness again and again.

Her immediate desire was to get back her children. She discovered that Peter, age 5, had been illegally sold to a wealthy Alabama planter named Fowler. She determined to take on a whole class of society and an entire state, if necessary, to get her son back.

Isabella became the butt of scorn and contempt as she tried to find help among whites. Mrs. Dumont told her to stop making such a fuss over a "paltry nigger."

But the Quakers sent Isabella to the New York grand jury in Kingston to register her complaint. This former slave woman, barefoot and dressed in a plain cotton dress, with a large colored kerchief on her head, marched into the courthouse. Walking right up to a man she described later as "the grandest lookin' one I could see," she asked, "Sir, be you a grand jury?"

In the end, Isabella triumphed. Not only did she succeed in getting a white slaveowner arrested, he was made to post $600 for his court appearance. In 1828 a black woman taking a white man to court and winning was unheard of.

And she got her son back. At first young Peter, still in the custody of his owner, denied ever knowing his mother and begged the court officials not to take him from his master, blaming the scars and bruises on his face on Fowler's horse. But once out of his owner's brutal grasp, he tearfully told his mother about the kicks and beatings that left bruises and welts all over his small body. When she moaned for his pain, Peter said, "Oh, this is nothing, mammy, you should see Phillis. . . . She had a little baby, too, but Fowler cut her till the milk and blood ran down her body. You would certainly scare to see Phillis, mammy."

In her anguish Isabella cried out, "O Lord, render unto them double for all this!"

In 1829 Isabella moved to New York City. There she joined the Zion African Church. During a service she knelt in prayer and extended her hand to the woman who prayed beside her. There was something familiar in the woman's bony hand, and yet Isabella could not explain the strange sense of intimacy she felt with her.

A short while later, Isabella's sister Sophia came to New York and announced that their brother Michel was also in the city. Isabella remembered Mau Mau Bett's numerous recountings of Michel and the sleigh and could not believe that they would be reunited.

The reunion was a joyful one, though tinged with a note of sorrow. "If only you had come a little sooner," Michel said to Isabella. "Nancy, who was shut up with me in the sleigh, died a few months ago." As Michel described her dress and appearance, he added that she attended Zion African Church.

Recognition dawned on Isabella's face. "I have seen my sister Nancy; and now I see that she looked so like Mau Mau." The brother and two sisters quietly wept together for all that had been lost. "Oh, Lord," cried Isabella, "what is this slavery, that it can do such dreadful things? What evil can it not do?"

Isabella soon acquired employment with a wealthy New York family, the Whitings. But she grew increasingly uncomfortable with New York's corruption and vice, saying of the city, "Truly, here the rich rob the poor, and the poor rob one another."

She felt a call to take her message about Jesus to other parts of the land. On a summer morning in 1843, Isabella placed a few articles of clothing in a pillowcase and announced to the Whitings that the Lord was going to give her a new home. "Farewell, friends," she said as she left. "I must be about my Father's business." God's pilgrim was on the move again.

With only the sun to guide her and a quarter for the ferry to Brooklyn, she headed east. This pilgrimage felt to her like a break from all that had been before, and she wanted to leave everything behind, including her name. Every time she had been sold, her last name was changed to that of her master, and now she wanted a permanent name fitting of her calling.

As she was walking, the name Sojourner came to her, because she planned to "travel up and down the land" and be "a sign to the people." She prayed to God for a last name, and then exclaimed, "Thou art my last master, and thy name is Truth; and Truth shall be my abiding name till I die!"

The God who had once come upon her like a burning tempest now led her like the pillar of fire that went before the Israelites. She received hospitality from rich and poor alike and soon became recognized across the land as the tall, thin woman dressed in gray with mist-filled eyes and the love of Jesus in her heart.

She had a low voice that rang out when she sang and shook the gates of heaven when she preached. She could not read the Bible, and she often said that she preached from only one text: "When I found Jesus." Though she never learned to read or mastered English beyond a crude dialect, people of the highest intellect and education were swayed by her powerful message. Harriet Beecher Stowe, the author of *Uncle*

Tom's Cabin, said of her, "I do not recollect . . . anyone who had more of that silent and subtle power which we call personal presence than this woman."

Her wanderings took her through Connecticut and into Massachusetts, where she settled for a time in the town of Northampton. There she encountered several noted abolitionists, including William Lloyd Garrison, Frederick Douglass, and Wendell Phillips, who counted her among their company and affectionately called her "Aunty Sojourner."

It was in Northampton that Sojourner received her baptism by fire when a camp meeting was disrupted by a gang of ruffians. Mustering all her courage, she talked and sang the violent crowd into tranquility.

In this decade before the Civil War, the country was seething with unrest. Slavery was being hotly debated in all quarters. Women's rights were being pushed onto center stage, as the abolitionists and suffragists combined forces to set a social agenda for the nation.

Freedom burned in the soul of Sojourner Truth, and she added her voice to those of the advocates of equality for blacks and women. She was a black woman made steel by the searing, white heat of slavery, made compassionate by the tempering fire of Christ's love. She was possessor of both a warm heart and a tongue of fire.

Victim of the slaveowner's lash in her early years, she now became the target of lashes of the tongue from her many opponents. At an 1852 women's rights convention in Akron, Ohio, her presence brought scorn from the men-many of them clergy—who had come to argue vigorously against the issue, and from the women, who feared that their cause might be undermined if it were perceived to be sympathetic to the abolitionist struggle. Amid hisses and jeers, Sojourner rose proudly and delivered her now famous "Ain't I a Woman?" speech.

The scene was recorded in *Sojourner Truth: God's Faithful Pilgrim*, by Arthur Huff Fauset:

> The second day of the convention arrived. . . . Various ministers called on all their powers of persuasion to pour contempt on the movement which in a later day would result in the Nineteenth Amendment.
>
> "Why should not men have superior rights and privileges?" disdainfully asked one of these men. "Just look at their superior intellects."
>
> Still another pointed to Jesus Christ.
>
> "If God had desired the equality of woman," he opined, "he would have given some token of his will through the birth, life, and death of the Saviour."
>
> "Look at what happened on account of Eve," pointed out a third preacher.

The timid women folk were no match for the more experienced men. . . . A complete rout was in prospect.

All this time Sojourner Truth had scarcely lifted her head. But this was mere pose. Never had her mind been more gently agitated, her rage more vehemently stirred. . . . As Sojourner made her way to the platform, a hissing sound of disapproval rushed through the room. . . . Unmindful and unafraid, the old black woman moved on, with slowness and solemnity, to the front. . . .

"Well, chillun," she began with that familiarity which came to her so readily, whether she was addressing God or man, "whar dar is so much racket, dar must be something out o' kilter. I t'ink dat 'twixt de niggers of de Souf an' de women at de Norf' all a-talkin' bout rights, de white men will be in a fix pretty soon.

"But what's all dis here talkin' about?"

She wheeled round in the direction of one of the previous speakers. . . .

"Dat man ober dar say dat women needs to be helped into carriages, and lifted ober ditches, and to have de best place everywhere. Nobody eber helped *me* into carriages, or ober mud puddles, or give *me* any best place!"

She raised herself to her full height and in a voice as rumbling as thunder roared, "And ain't *I* a woman?"

A low murmur advanced through the crowd.

"Look at me," she continued. "Look at my arm."

She bared her right arm to the shoulder and dramatically demonstrated its great muscular power.

"I have plowed and planted and gathered into barns"—her voice was singing into the ether—"and no man could head me—and ain't *I* a woman?"

The murmur became more vocal.

"I have born'd five children and seen 'em mos' all sold off into slavery, and when I cried out with mother's grief, none but Jesus heard—and ain't *I* a woman?" . . .

"Den dey talks 'bout dis t'ing in de head—what dis dey call it?"

"Intellect," whispers someone nearby.

"Dat's it, honey—intellect. Now, what's dat got to do wit women's rights or niggers' rights? If my cup won't hold but a pint, and yourn holds a quart, wouldn't ye be mean not to let me have my little half-measure full?"

Now the crowd . . . rocks the church with applause and cheers, and echoes its approval of her words by pointing scornful fingers at the minister whom a few minutes ago it had applauded for sentiments in exactly the opposite key.

"Den dat little man in black dar," she continued, referring to another minister, "he say women can't have as much rights as man, 'cause Christ warn't a woman. Whar did your Christ come from?" she thundered at him, her arms outstretched, her eyes shooting fire. This was a lightning thrust. The throng sat perfectly quiet.

Then, raising her voice as high as it was possible for her to do, she repeated the query.

"Whar did your Christ come from?"

She hesitated a moment, poised over the audience like a bird hovering just before a final swoop down upon its prey, then thundered, "From God and a woman! Man had nothing to do with him!"

The audience was overwhelmed. It could not endure so much logic and oratory at one time. Pandemonium broke loose.

But Sojourner was not quite through. She turned finally to the man who had made a deprecating gesture at Eve, and rebuked him.

"If de fust woman God ever made was strong enough to turn the world upside down, all alone—dese togedder ought to be able to turn it back and get it rightside up again; and now dey is asking to do it, de men better let 'em."

Amidst deafening cheering and stamping, Sojourner Truth, who had arisen to catcalls and hisses, could hardly make herself heard as she shouted in conclusion, "Bleeged to ye for hearin' on me; and now ole Sojourner hain't got nothing more to say."

Sojourner was always ready with a quick retort for any detractor. A meeting in Indiana in which the noted abolitionist Parker Pillsbury was the featured speaker was overtaken by a violent thunderstorm. A proslavery Methodist in the crowd used the interruption as an occasion to state to the gathering, "I am alarmed. I feel as if God's judgment is about to fall upon me for daring to sit and hear such blasphemy." And then the low voice of a woman shouted over the noise of the thunder and rain, "Chile, don't be skeered; you are not going to be harmed. I don't 'spec God's ever heard tell of ye!"

The Fugitive Slave Law of 1860 criminalized escape from slavery and opened the way for more violence against blacks. In response, militancy increased among the abolitionists. Despairing that their speeches and petitions would ever bring emancipation of the slaves, many began to see armed resistance as the only recourse.

Frederick Douglass began to espouse this point of view. Sojourner Truth was present in the audience one day when he recounted the terrible wrongs done to his people and asserted, "Slavery can only end in blood." Waves of despair swept over the large crowd until Sojourner's voice rang out and charged the throng with hope. She admonished Douglass with one simple question: "Frederick, is God dead?"

Divisions began to plague the abolition and suffrage movement. A major split occurred between those who felt that universal suffrage was the only just goal and those who believed that it was important to first secure the enfranchisement of blacks (meaning black men) and later of women. Sojourner grieved the prevailing decision to take the latter course, only too aware that black women performed the same arduous work under slavery as men and suffered the same cruelties, along with the additional horror of sexual abuse.

At an 1867 equal rights convention in New York, Sojourner said about the fight for women's suffrage, "I am for keeping the thing going while things are stirring; because if we wait till it is still, it will take a great while to get it going again." Her words turned out to be prophetic: Once the issue of women's suffrage was set aside in the nineteenth century, several decades passed before the question was forced again into public consciousness.

During the Civil War, Sojourner settled for a time in Battle Creek, Michigan, attracted there by a spiritual community and the town's antislavery sentiment. Sojourner was now in her sixties. She was well-respected by the town's citizens and particularly loved by its children. They often gathered on her front porch and begged her to tell them stories, which she did between puffs on her white clay pipe.

She still had not learned to read. When a friend offered to teach her in her later years, she responded that her "brains [was] too stiff" to learn. In return for the stories she told them, the children read to her from the Bible. She preferred them as readers over adults, who seemed unable to resist interpreting the scriptures to her while reading.

She was rarely seen without her pipe. Some of her friends apparently criticized her habit. One reminded her that "the Bible tells us that 'no unclean thing can enter the kingdom of heaven'" and that nothing was filthier than the breath of a smoker. Her quick retort: "Yes, chile, but when I goes to heaven I 'spects to leave my breff behind me."

With so much brewing in the nation, Sojourner soon found it impossible to remain in Michigan. One morning in the spring of 1864, she announced to a friend that she was leaving for Washington that afternoon. She was now close to 70 years old and recovering from an illness. In response to her friend's "Whatever for?" Sojourner replied, "I'm going down there to advise the president."

Her friends protested that he was too busy and she was too old. But in words that could stand as a summation of her life, she retorted, "I never determined to do anything and failed."

The meeting of the two tall, gaunt fighters for black emancipation was historic. President Abraham Lincoln confessed that he had heard of Sojourner long before she had heard of him. At the end of their visit, Sojourner brought out the book she carried with her at all times, her *Book of Life*, whose pages bore the signatures and good wishes of all the interesting people she met on her journey. To such names as Susan B. Anthony, Elizabeth Cady Stanton, William Lloyd Garrison, and Harriet Beecher Stowe was added the inscription of a president: "For Aunty Sojourner Truth, Oct. 29, 1864, A. Lincoln."

She had come to visit a president, but the misery Sojourner witnessed in Washington compelled her to stay. An area by the city's Grand Canal teemed with thousands of former slaves, who had rushed across the Mason-Dixon line and into the city after the Emancipation Proclamation, with no possessions except the freedom given them by a dash of Lincoln's pen. Known in the North as "contrabands," they crowded into dark hovels and shanties, living in a squalor that bred disease and crime.

Upon seeing the poverty, this woman who had spent much of her life among white people preaching and agitating felt God call her to remain with her own for a while. Like a whirlwind, Sojourner attacked the problems that she saw, offering counsel, teaching hygiene, nursing the sick, finding work for her people. Raiders from Maryland frequently crossed into the Washington slum and kidnapped children, and Sojourner became a leader in the resistance to such activity.

In other parts of the city, marble edifices that radiated power and wealth were taking shape. Sojourner passed by these buildings in her journeys around Washington. She often paused at the Capitol, she explained in her *Narrative*, to thank God that the stars and stripes flying over the dome no longer symbolized the "scars and stripes" on the backs of her people.

But one day, with the picture of the children from the slums in her mind, anguish and anger overtook her as she gazed at the white, resplendent dome built at the nation's expense. She cried out, *"We helped* to pay this cost!" Her mind recalled all the back-breaking and unrewarded work that had been endured by her people. She later paraphrased the thoughts that came to her that day:

> Beneath a burning southern sun have we toiled, in the canebrake and the rice swamp, urged on by the merciless driver's lash, earning [for him] millions of money; and so highly were we valued, that should one poor wretch venture to escape from this hell of slavery, no exertion of man or trained bloodhound was spared to seize and return him to his field of unrequited labor. . . . Our nerves and sinews, our tears and blood, have been sacrificed on the altar of this nation's avarice. . . . Some of its dividends must surely be ours.

Justice burned in Sojourner's soul now as passionately as freedom once had. She put her energy toward what she hoped would be the crowning achievement of her life—a land grant for blacks in the U.S. West. She understood fully that land ownership was the crux of the issue: Those who had plowed and planted the soil for generations would never be truly free until they could do so to their own benefit. Huge tracts of land were being given over to the development of a railway system, and Sojourner reasoned that surely people were as deserving as the railroads.

With her body now slightly bent and her voice a bit huskier, Sojourner earnestly poured out her last bit of fire as she resumed her travels across the country. She preached and beseeched her audiences to sign petitions on behalf of the land grant. But she misjudged the intransigence of white racism. With slavery no longer an issue, many whites had lost their interest in the black cause, and she faced large opposition to her plan.

Sojourner continued the arduous work of serving her people, while still journeying far and wide in an effort to secure their civil and political rights. She took up the cause of temperance and child labor, having seen firsthand the ravages of alcohol in the slums and the exploitation of children. She spoke against capital punishment and on behalf of equal pay for equal work, long before the concept became a platform in the women's movement.

She delivered a petition about the land grant to the U.S. Congress and received a standing ovation from the Senate for her relentless efforts for freedom.

Sojourner continued criss-crossing the country, gaining more names for her petition from her supporters and insults from her tormentors. The wear of age and a lifetime of traveling now began to show. "Everybody tells me to 'stir 'em up,'" she confided to a friend. "But I ask you, 'Why don't *they* stir 'em up?'—as though an old body like myself could do all the stirring." Yet she persisted in the belief that if only she could acquire enough signatures, her dream of a place in the West for her people would be realized. She continued to pour her waning energy into a dream that would never be fulfilled.

In her last years, when exhaustion and despair could easily have become temptations, Sojourner found instead a new vision. Too perceptive to ignore the facts, but too faithful to yield to cynicism, she found hope in a truth far greater than her plan for settling her people in the West. She had a grander vision than others even dared to dream. Listen to the words of a proud, old black woman with fire in her eyes, words that stand as prophecy:

> These colored people will bring the whites out of Egyptian darkness into marvelous light. The white people cannot do it, but these will. They will teach the slaveholders the truth that they never had and never knew of. . . . These colored people are going

to be a people. Do you think God has had them robbed and scourged all the days of their life for nothing!

She found the faith to take the most difficult step of all on her long journey—the step of forgiving her white persecutors and envisioning their salvation. For Sojourner, this forgiveness became very personal in regard to John Dumont. A twist of fate brought an ironic conclusion to their relationship.

Sojourner had returned to visit her former owner and found him advanced in age and deprived of his wealth. He had changed his mind about slavery, now calling it the "greatest curse the earth had ever felt." Sojourner fervently praised God that she had lived to hear him utter those words.

She received a letter from her daughter a short time later, informing her that Dumont had moved West, taking along—probably by mistake—the few pieces of furniture she had left with him. "Never mind," said Sojourner. "What we give the poor, we lend to the Lord."

Sojourner's health continued to fail, and her ulcerous limbs left her in great pain. As the end came close and the suffering grew almost unbearable, she sang—often the same hymn, her favorite, that had quieted the Northampton mob:

> It was early in the morning
> . . . Just at the break of day
> When he rose
> . . . And went to heaven in a cloud.

Friends who were with her near the end talked about a remarkable serenity that enveloped her.

Sojourner Truth died at three o'clock in the morning on November 26, 1883. A few days earlier, a sorrowful friend had come to comfort her. "I'm not going to die, honey," Sojourner reassured her. "I'm going home like a shooting star." No doubt she shot straight to heaven and resumed her conversation with God where they left off.

A long line of carriages and a huge throng followed the hearse with its somber black plumes to Oak Hill Cemetery in Battle Creek. A stone was later placed on her grave, bearing her faithful proclamation and celebrated admonition to Frederick Douglass, "Is God Dead?" A witness reported that as her body was lowered into the ground, the sun appeared like a blaze of fire on the western horizon.

Sojourner Truth has been laid to rest, but the ground cannot contain this faithful wanderer. She moves like God's fiery pillar before us. She has blazed a trail for freedom and justice. And she beckons us, in courage and in faith, to follow.

V

BLESSED
ARE
THE MERCIFUL

Sanctuary

A Conspiracy of Compassion

On January 23, 1985, while the Inter-American Symposium on Sanctuary was taking place in the same city, John Fife, Jim Corbett, and Phil Willis-Conger were arraigned in Tucson, Arizona. They and thirteen other sanctuary workers had been charged with 71 counts, including conspiracy and harboring and transporting "illegal aliens." Evidence against them included tapes surreptitiously recorded by informants planted by the Immigration and Naturalization Service (INS).

Stacey Lynn Merkt was convicted of transporting refugees in May 1984 and given two years' probation. She went to trial again in February 1985 on similar charges.

As participants in the sanctuary symposium, Jim Wallis and Joyce Hollyday had the privilege of meeting and conducting the following interview with the four indicted church workers the day after the arraignment in Tucson.

At the time of the interview, John Fife was serving as pastor of Southside United Presbyterian Church in Tucson, Phil Willis-Conger was project director for the Tucson Ecumenical Council Task Force for Central America, and Stacey Lynn Merkt worked at Casa Romero, a hospitality house for Central American refugees in San Benito, Texas. Jim Corbett was a retired rancher.

Fife and Willis-Conger were later convicted and sentenced to five years' probation; Corbett was acquitted. Merkt served 78 days of a 179-day jail sentence, and was released to house arrest three months before she gave birth to her first child.

Could you talk about how your faith relates to the work you're doing, and particularly to your determination to continue doing the work in light of the threats you have received from the government?

Stacey Lynn Merkt: I think that I would start by saying that my faith is my work, and my work is my faith. I believe in the sanctity of life, and that has carried me through the last ten years or so.

It started out when I lived at Koinonia [in Americus, Georgia]. That's when I learned about living in community and about the social issues that we need to look at as Christians and as responsible persons today. More than that, I learned about the nitty gritty of seeing Jesus reflected in the face of my brother and sister. That is the essence of what faith is to me.

For me to start responding to the cry of the people in Central America meant that I had to start living and working and touching these people. When I went to work at Casa Romero, these people became more than names and numbers and faces and events. They became María, and José, and I put living flesh onto statistics.

I just seek to be a person who lives what I believe and who lives what God has asked me to live. It's clear to me that God asks me to love. The greatest commandment is to love the Lord your God with all your heart, soul, and mind, and to love your neighbor as yourself. And my neighbor is a world community of persons. That means I have to offer food to the person who's hungry, clothes to the person who has no clothes; I have to welcome the stranger in my midst, and I have to work for the day when those needs, when those deprivations, those injustices won't be. It's an outpouring of myself more than anything else. I believe that I am to love and in so doing, here I am.

Phil Willis-Conger: I grew up in a church that was real concerned about the social gospel and talked about social justice. My parents had been missionaries in Latin America. In growing up I gained some consciousness about some of the major social justice issues, such as racism and U.S. imperialism.

I have a definite sense of what is right and wrong, and I believe that comes out of the very core of me, which is God-centered. If there are people out there suffering, I can't ignore them. My upbringing won't allow me to just close my eyes to that.

I'm inspired by the words of people around me and the faith I see in the refugees, the hope that comes out of the incredible suffering and incredible hardship that these refugees are experiencing. They are Christ crucified, and yet the hope is still alive and still there. That keeps me going; that is an important part of my faith.

Jim, could you tell us how the sanctuary movement got started and how you got involved in it?

Jim Corbett: How it got started? You'll have to consult Exodus on that. It's very important to realize that the sanctuary movement is not something that someone, somewhere, suddenly invented. It has been around better than 3,000 years.

Those of us who are involved in the sanctuary movement have never, I think, really accurately anticipated what sanctuary would become when it was declared. It has been a process of discovery that doesn't seem to be over yet.

On May 4, 1981, a friend of mine was returning from Sonora [Mexico]. He had borrowed a van from me, and he picked up a hitchhiker in Nogales, Arizona, who was a Salvadoran, a refugee. At the road block just a little north of Nogales, this refugee was taken from him by the border patrol.

He returned the van that evening. Another friend was there, and we discussed what might happen to the Salvadoran refugee. I think the other friend may have been the one who had read an account of a planeload of Salvadoran deportees—deported from the United States—having been shot down right at the airport outside of San Salvador on arrival in December of 1980.

I'd been working prior to that with some semi-nomadic goat ranchers. I wasn't a Central America activist—I probably at that time could not have given the name of the bishop who had been murdered in El Salvador—but I had seen enough news that I knew that things were pretty bad, people were getting murdered. And that's where we left it that night.

But I woke up the next morning convinced that I really ought to find out where this guy was, what could be done for him. I was naive enough that the first thing I did was call the border patrol and then the INS and said, "You picked up a Salvadoran yesterday at a roadblock, and I want to find out whether there's anything I can do to help him." They said, "No, there's not, and you cannot even see him unless you have his name and are an authorized legal representative."

Well, my name is the same as the name of a former mayor of Tucson, now a judge, a person who is politically prominent here. So I found the name of the top people in the INS and called and said, "This is Jim Corbett here in Tucson. You picked up a Salvadoran at the Madera Canyon roadblock yesterday. I need to know his name and where you have him." The guy looked it up and told me.

He was in the Santa Cruz County Jail. Father Ricardo Alfred was suggested as someone to contact. I asked him if something could be done, and he got me a G-28 form, which establishes legal representation.

I took the G-28 and went down to the Santa Cruz County Jail and managed to talk my way in to see the refugee. I discovered there were more refugees there, and they in turn told me about other refugees who had been picked up at the same time or that they knew about—relatives, and women who were being held in another place. One woman they had heard about was being held more or less in isolation to try to break her, in the women's part of the Santa Cruz County Jail. About 50 in all had been caught in the previous few days.

The first step I took was to get that one G-28 signed and get out and get some more G-28s for these folks, these other refugees I'd run into. I went back to the Santa Cruz County Jail, and they had me wait and wait and wait, and it was getting close to the time I needed to rush to get back to file these things in Tucson. And so I said, "Look, when can I see those guys that I asked you about 30 minutes ago?"

"Oh, the border patrol came and got them 30 or 40 minutes ago," they told me. "There's no way of telling where they've gone."

So then I had to start searching. I found one in south Tucson and the other one up in El Centro [refugee detention center in California]. I was starting to get an education about the border patrol and INS.

There was a Salvadoran with me [on a visit to El Centro] who had a little recorder, which I took from him. The recording would have indicated that they [INS] had systematically denied these people their legal rights. So they locked me in El Centro and said they wouldn't let me out if I didn't give up the tape. Eventually they called their supervisor, who apparently said, "You've got an American citizen in there. You better let him out."

By early June my wife and I had set up an apartment in our house where refugees could stay while they were doing their I-589s, their asylum applications. I got a call from one of the refugees, who by that time was in Phoenix, who said that she had some relatives who had turned up on the other side of the border who were in trouble and didn't know what to do, and could I do something? I didn't know what I could do, but I went down on the other side at midnight and found them hiding under a house. I didn't know how to smuggle, but I got them through the fence.

I went over to visit the priest in Nogales, who is now indicted. He said, "There are refugees being held in the Nogales-Sonora Penitentiary. I give the Mass every Thursday, but they're held in a holding tank separately, and they have an urgent need regularly to contact relatives in the United States, relatives back in El Salvador, and so forth. If there was someone who could go in with me while I give the Mass and talk to these folks. . . ."

So I was "Father Jaime" each Thursday. I'd go in and get letters to Central America and telephone numbers of relatives in Los Angeles. We distributed a sheet with my name and number on it, names of organizations giving legal services, and what their legal rights were if they got across the border in the United States. This evolved into an ongoing program. Phil inherited that.

Willis-Conger: The difference perhaps between some of our actions and those of other Americans is maybe only that we've been more persistent about it. It's all about responding to your neighbor, Christ in each one of us.

Corbett: The personal contact makes the difference. The first week after I learned about the refugee problem, I learned that there was a Salvadoran woman with a bullet in her, who was hiding out and who needed a doctor but was afraid to get help. She'd been shot in El Salvador a couple of weeks before, and the bullet was still in her. I just started calling doctors to see who was willing to risk license, prison, and so forth in order to let us know what to do about this woman.

That's how it was all along. We didn't ever organize by running around and asking, "Will you become an active member of this secret organization?" When someone is in need, a lot of people respond.

How and why did you get involved in the sanctuary movement, John?
John Fife: I think that what Jim has suggested has been common

to all our experience. Our encounter with refugees has been the point at which we had to make some decision about whether we would turn our back on this overwhelming need or whether we were going to meet that need. As soon as you begin that with one refugee, you begin to hear about others. As we started off, we didn't realize we were standing on the edge of a whirlpool that just drew us in as we began to see the life-and-death plight of the people of El Salvador and Guatemala.

That started for me when a professional *coyote* [smuggler] abandoned 25 or 26 Salvadorans in the desert west of here in the middle of the summer [of 1980]. Half of them died of dehydration in the desert, and the other half were picked up by the border patrol and brought to Tucson to be hospitalized. INS put a hold on them, so that as soon as they were released from the hospital, INS would put them in a detention center and start the deportation process.

Some immigration lawyers came to the churches and said, "We've been talking to these people, and they're terrified of being sent back to El Salvador. The churches need to help us."

At that point I couldn't have put El Salvador on a map. That encounter meant that I had to hear about death squads, and about churches being machine-gunned, and about priests being murdered. The real driver for me was the persecution of the church.

The only thing we could think to do was what I assume people of faith have always thought of first, and that is, "Let's pray." We said we'd start a prayer vigil for the people and the church of Central America, and we'd do it every week, and we'd invite our congregations and others to come and join us. That's been going on for four years now; every week we meet to pray for the people of Central America. That became a gathering place where people who had bumped into refugees, or immigration lawyers who encountered them in the detention centers, would come, and we'd talk about the latest need and how the churches could start helping.

That went on until somewhere around April or May of 1981. Then the government's policy in terms of treatment of refugees changed. As we encountered that hardening of policy, it became clear that we couldn't do the work as individual congregations any longer.

We pulled together a meeting of people who were at that prayer vigil from different churches. We formed a task force under the Tucson Ecumenical Council—65 Protestant and Roman Catholic churches—and said we're going to try to meet those needs. We entered into an agreement with a paralegal organization. The churches would raise money for bonds, try to meet the expenses of the paralegals, and they would do the work in the detention centers, filling out political asylum applications and filing I-589s.

The next step was to go to the regional detention center. We made an absolutely crazy decision at that point. I don't understand how rational people can sit down at a first meeting and say, "Okay, we're going to raise $35,000 in the next month, and $120,000 in collateral, and we're going to take a bunch of volunteers from Tucson and go over to California and bond out all the Salvadorans that need to be bonded out in one group a month from now." And we did it!

We raised that much money. Some people put up their homes as collateral. On one day we brought 140 Salvadorans and Guatemalans out of that detention center, and then said, "Now what do we do?"

We had this enormous social service responsibility to relocate people and get them in touch with families if they had any, and bring them to Tucson and Los Angeles and put them in the churches. It took about a month before everybody was settled.

The paralegals went back to the detention center, and the government had another 200 refugees. We obviously couldn't sustain that kind of effort or that kind of fund raising, so we put together a long-range plan. We set a policy in place that we'd try to raise enough money in collateral to bond out 10 people a week, those who had been in the detention center the longest. What we needed to do was give refugees who were under threat of deportation or in the detention center some sense of hope that if they held out, we'd get to them eventually. Hanging on in there was really tough, with the conditions in the detention centers and the harassment and coercion.

That effort continued for two years. And we've got somewhere around three-quarters of a million dollars—just the churches in Tucson—in collateral, in bonds. We've been expending somewhere between $60,000 and $100,000 in legal defense efforts. And that effort goes on. So if you hear from INS that what those church people ought to do is try to work within the law first, we did it. And we did it with as much energy and imagination and creativity as we could.

At that point everything I was doing was very Presbyterian. Presbyterians understand legalities. We live and die by a book of order and legal procedures in our institutional life. I was doing everything possible within the bounds that had been set by government and culture to serve refugees.

Then Corbett started talking to me about theology and ethics. He said, "If you're really serious and you really think God is calling you to serve the needs of refugees, then you're working at their needs on the wrong end. After they're captured and in detention centers, the process of deportation is inevitable. All you can do is buy time." And he was right.

"If you really think that God is calling you to serve the needs of refugees," he said, "then you must meet their most critical and apparent need, which is to avoid capture and inevitable deportation and death." He was already doing it, helping people cross the border safely, bringing them to his home. When I first went to Corbett's house, he had 21 people living in one room.

At any rate, Corbett says to me, "We've filled up our house. I've got other Quakers' houses filled up in town. Can I bring people to your church? You're already keeping Salvadorans that you've bonded out of detention centers in your church." And I said, "Yeah, but that's legal." And he said, "Yeah, I know; can I bring Salvadorans who are undocumented to your church?" I said, "Gee, Jim, I don't make the decisions around here, the elders of my church do. You'll have to ask them."

And we did. The elders and I sat down and spent about four hours discussing that question. I was real clear with them, "If the government catches us doing this, it's five years in prison for every refugee we bring in this church." They voted to do it.

Some of the refugees would come to worship on Sunday, and I'd introduce them to the congregation as we introduce all guests, and tell their story briefly, and say to the congregation, "Your government says that these people are illegal aliens. It is your civic duty when you know about their status to turn them in to INS. What do you think the faith requires of you?" We'd just leave that question hanging Sunday after Sunday.

The congregation would take people home after church for dinner, call me up later that afternoon and say, "People can't live in a church; that's not a decent place for this family to live. They're going to stay with us for a while."

By the time the next critical step came, I was driving some refugees from the border up, and so were other members of my congregation. Other church people were involved with that whole work that has since come to be called the "underground railroad."

But we were all a bunch of amateurs. My training is in Bible and theology, not smuggling and covert activities. We did all the things we saw on television that we thought we were supposed to do. We had codes and code words, and it never worked out. We got a telegram in code from Corbett in Mexico one time, sat down with a whole group of us, and couldn't figure out what he wanted us to do. It took us two hours.

We got a very clear and direct message from INS and the border patrol, delivered from an INS attorney to one of the paralegals who was working with us. It said, "Look, we know what Corbett and Fife are up to. You tell them to stop it, or we'll have to arrest them." We sat around my living room saying, "What do we do now?" I said, "I can see the headlines in the paper now—'Presbyterian minister indicted for smuggling illegal aliens.'"

We couldn't stop. We'd already made the decision when we got involved in that whole effort that the life-and-death needs of the refugees overrode any other set of risks that we might encounter here in the United States. The conclusion we came to is the only other option we have is to give public witness to what we're doing, what the plight of the refugees is, and the faith basis for our actions.

And then the question came, "Well, how do you do that?" Do you call a press conference and say, "Hey, we'd like to acknowledge that we've been smuggling people into this country for some time"? It didn't seem to make any sense.

Out of that discussion emerged the idea that what we're really doing is the ancient historic tradition of sanctuary in the church. We decided to publicly declare the church a sanctuary and publicly receive a refugee family into the sanctuary of the church. The only thing we could do was tell our story so that at least when they arrested us, they'd have to play on our turf. They would have to deal with the reasons why we did it. And the community and the church would have to deal with that too.

Then I left to make coffee, so they all decided that Southside Presbyterian Church ought to be the one to try it. But then we took about two months—December 1981 and January 1982—and we did Bible study, prayer, discussion, and agonizing over that two-month period. At a four-hour congregational meeting, we took a vote by secret ballot so nobody felt intimidated by anybody else. They voted to declare sanctuary. I think there were 59 affirmative votes, with two negative votes and four abstentions.

Somebody at the congregational meeting said, "Why don't we ask other churches to do it, too?" And I said, "That's a good idea! Great idea!" We wrote a bunch of letters to churches across the country and said, "We're going to publicly receive a family into the sanctuary of the church at worship, and we've decided to do that on March 24, 1982. It's the anniversary of [Archbishop Oscar] Romero's assassination, and the attention of the church is going to be at least partially focused on Romero and Central America.

Four other congregations wrote back and said, "Yes, we'll do it on the same day." They were First Unitarian Church in Los Angeles; University Lutheran Chapel in San Francisco; Luther Place Memorial Church in Washington, D.C.; and an independent Bible Church in Long Island, New York.

Because we were public, more refugees knew there was a place where they could get help. So we were swamped at the border, and at the same time we were getting requests for information on sanctuary from all over the country. One of the groups that called was the Chicago Religious Task Force, and that relationship developed, and the movement took off.

In 1982 I went to Central America for the first time and got converted. That's the only way I can describe it. I discovered a new way of reading Scripture, of seeing the community of faith under enormous pressure and persecution respond with courage and hope.

The refugees began to tell us about the *comunidades de base*, about their experience in the church in El Salvador and Guatemala and the new spiritual vitality and strength that was being given to the people in Central America through their faith. My first sermon to the congregation when I came back was, "This may come as a shock to you, but I have been converted to the Christian faith since I last was with you."

I think that part of what the sanctuary movement means in North America is that there are covenant communities, congregations who are being converted to the Christian faith, to that spiritual reformation that is now being brought to North America from Latin America and other parts of the world. I now am convinced that there is a genuine reformation, and it's going to change our world as much as the sixteenth-century Reformation changed our world.

You are all under indictment. What are your reflections now?

Merkt: These days are showing us more clearly what it means to be a faithful person. I think we're all aware of what the cost is, but the reality of that becomes a little bit clearer as days go on. What I have learned from the people of Central America is that I believe in a God of love and of life and of faithfulness, and that means that I live each day, come what may.

I think so far as the sanctuary movement goes, everyone has been up front in saying that this [the indictments] can only strengthen and galvanize the response of everyone to meet the needs of the refugees both in El Salvador and here in the United States. I have also become aware that the "subversiveness" of the church that we have experienced through the eyes of the refugees from El Salvador has become more clearly what is happening here in the United States.

I also have been asked about the fears that one individually might have being in this seat. We as people of faith need to examine our fears in light of the stories of why the refugees come to us. If we don't take that small step and act regardless of our fears and regardless of whether or not we have courage, we'll never know what courage is. It is step by step and inch by inch that we struggle in our process to live out our faith.

In contrast to that word "fear," I try to look at hope. We are a community of people that God has mandated to act in a certain way—for the best interest of others and also to proclaim that we are a faithful people. Those are pretty powerful things.

Willis-Conger: For me it's been a deepening of faith and conviction. I know what's right, and I started in the right direction, and it's the faith that keeps me going down the road that I've already started on.

The way that the government is going about attacking the church and attacking the refugees, they're making it easier for people to understand—by the fact that they infiltrated a church and that they've deceived us as to how they would deal with us. I think it means that the church under persecution is going to respond, and it means a lot of organizing and educating. The religious community—including the Jewish faith and people of conscience who wouldn't even consider themselves religious—is going to respond, and is going to rise to the challenge. I see it happening already.

Corbett: We very quickly discovered in the process of declaring sanctuary that sanctuary is not a place, but that it's the protective community of a congregation of people with the persecuted. It has infinite dimensions.

What we're doing is called for in large measure by our place here on the border. There are all kinds of sanctuary congregations around the country who are discovering new dimensions of sanctuary outreach, of what is most appropriate for them in the way of entering into a protective community with the persecuted.

What will be your response in light of the infiltration and deception of the government?

Fife: The refugees have set the agenda; their needs have set our agenda continuously since 1981, and I suspect that they will continue to do that. Depending on what our government decides to do in Central America, depending on what the death squads decide to do in Central America, and depending on what immigration officials decide to do on the border and in Tucson—that will set our agenda, and we'll just have to walk into it one day at a time. We have to struggle in the midst of those things that are out of our control to discover what it means to be faithful from day to day. I now understand that spiritually and emotionally.

I think the other thing we've discovered over the last three years is that we serve refugees more effectively the more we "testify to our faith" publicly. Clearly the government would like through intimidation and harassment, indictments, arrests—now through placing spies and agents inside church worship services and Bible study groups with wire taps and bugs—to drive us more and more into ourselves and our own little "trusted," close-knit organizations. I think we've got to resist all that. I think we've got to be more and more welcoming and open in our invitation to people to join us as a covenant community, and we have to be more and more public in our testimony and in our witness to what our faith is and what we believe.

And I think we need to understand what resistance is these days. We have to be more and more creative in finding ways in which the church community can actively resist the evil that is so pervasive around us. Central America and Central American refugees are only one facet of the call to resistance at this point, and *Sojourners* has helped us to understand that calling.

Willis-Conger: My concept of sanctuary is not just resisting, but a forward-moving, positive kind of thing where we're going out and doing justice as a community. And the reason we've survived here in Tucson is because we've been able to take the initiative instead of just resisting what the government's doing.

Corbett: We're discovering that while as individuals every one of us can make that choice to resist, if we are going to make that choice to do justice, we have to come together in community—and sanctuary takes that step. It's not a step that allows us to avoid that decision between resistance and collaboration, but it's a further awareness— that as communities provide sanctuary, or enter into protective community with the persecuted, the poor, the marginalized of the world, it may result in our becoming "illegals" along with the refugees.

Fife: I think we've all grown in understanding that sanctuary is what God created this world to be. Reverend Marta Benavides [of El Salvador] first told me what we really need to do is work with them to make Central America a sanctuary for Central Americans. Nuclear freeze people have come to me and said what we really need to do is make this earth a sanctuary from nuclear armaments.

I think sanctuary is beginning to capture people's spirits and imaginations. It is the way the church community can really be a covenant community and a way we can understand ourselves and our faith and our role in this world. I'm looking for the whole community gathered to put our souls to work in discovering just what that symbol can mean and how it can explode in our consciousness and lead us into all kinds of creative pilgrimages.

Beyers Naudé

Breaking Ranks

He was born into the inner-most sanctum of Afrikaner nationalism. His father was a hero of the Boer War (1899–1902), one of the stubborn handful who refused to surrender to the British, and a founder of the Broederbond, the secret society that conceived and manipulates South Africa's apartheid system of white supremacy.

He was the youngest person ever to join the Broederbond, rising quickly through the elite ranks of white South African society and the Dutch Reformed Church to become, like his father, a preacher and protector of the Afrikaner faith. Many said that one day he would be prime minister of South Africa.

But something happened to Beyers Naudé. It can only be fully understood by comprehending the true meaning of Christian conversion. Like Saul on the road to Damascus, the journey of the young South African was interrupted and his course irrevocably changed by an encounter with a loving God.

This much-favored Afrikaner son would become the most implacable foe of apartheid that his people ever produced and, even more significant, the white South African most trusted by black South Africans.

Beyers Naudé knew the Afrikaner community and code of loyalty as well as anyone in South Africa. He knew what the cost would be of stating his new convictions to his own people, and it made him "terribly afraid."

"They warned me," recalls Naudé, "'Beyers, you're playing with fire. Do you realize if you start stating these convictions, your whole future is destroyed. There will be no acceptance within the Afrikaner community. You will be totally ostracized, pushed out, and left in the cold.'"

In 1963, the deep ties that bound Beyers Naudé to the Dutch Reformed Church were formally severed, and he preached his farewell sermon, titled "Obedience to God."

Naudé soon became the director of the Christian Institute, a multiracial ecumenical body that so effectively challenged the moral basis of apartheid while promoting Christian unity and social justice that it was outlawed in 1977. Beyers Naudé was himself banned and would remain so for seven years. When his banning order was lifted in 1984, he succeeded Archbishop Desmond Tutu as general secretary of the South African Council of Churches. His clarity of voice and courage of action once again bore public testimony to the truth and power of the gospel.

At one of the massive funeral services that became powerful symbols of black pain, protest, and hope, Beyers Naudé was carried high on the shoulders of the crowd, a rare tribute to a white South African.

Naudé says of the experience, "I realized that as far as white people were concerned, if I still needed a final kiss of death, that was the final one. But I also realized that as far as the black community was concerned, this is a singular honor; never exploit it as long as you live."

Beyers Naudé (who died on September 7, 2004) was interviewed by Jim Wallis in November 1987.

I'm greatly intrigued by your conversion, because conversion is the core of our Christian faith. Many of us in the United States are on the journey of conversion. There's so much from your history that bears upon ours and that helps shed light on our experience.

I was particulary intrigued by your response when asked sometime ago about your conversion—how and why it happened and what was behind it. You said, "I read the Bible. That's all."

I think I should start by saying that I am an Afrikaner, born in a deeply religious Afrikaner home that was very conservative politically, with a father who fought in the Anglo-Boer War on the side of the Boers and who deeply loved the Afrikaner people.

After four years of academic study, I continued with four years of theological study. During all those years, the question of apartheid being biblically unjustifiable never arose. Apartheid was simply taken for granted: The Bible supported apartheid, the Bible blessed it, and the Bible sanctioned it. And I never questioned this in any way critically, because I'd assumed that it was something that had been properly thought through.

I served a number of white congregations in South Africa until 1949, when I was called to become what you call here a "university chaplain" of the Dutch Reformed Church at Pretoria University. During that period I began to look at what was happening in Africa and realized that the period after the Second World War, with decolonization taking place in the vast continent of Africa, would deeply affect the life of the Christian churches, especially of the Dutch Reformed churches.

In the course of that thinking, the questions arose about apartheid, and voices of dissent and rejection of apartheid increased on the part of other churches, especially in South Africa. So eventually I decided that I would undertake a self-study on the biblical justification for apartheid, which I did between 1955 and 1957.

I came to the conclusion that my own church's attempt at justifying apartheid on biblical grounds was simply not tenable. Although it may have been sincerely intended, in fact it had no proper, valid, biblical, or theological grounds. And for me that was a shattering discovery, because the whole moral basis of ministry with regard to the apartheid relationship between whites and blacks was removed. That was the first experience, or the first phase, in the process of conversion.

How is it that a church that no doubt prides itself on its biblical fidelity did not ask in a biblical way a question about something as fundamental as apartheid in South Africa? And how is it that you began to ask that question, when probably no one else around you did?

I think it came about because of the fact that the Afrikaners were of a deeply religious background. They simply took for granted the belief that in a special way they were a part of the elect nation of God. They believed they were called upon to evangelize and Christianize the heathen community of South Africa. They believed they had a divine mission and a divine charge given by God.

But because of the outlook of the Afrikaner people—their understanding of their divine calling and their deep-rooted, unconscious prejudices toward people of color—they did not realize to what degree they were deliberately or unconsciously distorting passages of the Bible simply to fit with their political and ideological or their racial outlook. And with church leadership giving full justification, with universities offering no critical approach, with the Afrikaner society being so totally isolated, it was very easy to present that ideology.

What happened in your life that led you to question whether the apartheid system was justifiable biblically?

The first thing was that I was mandated by the church in 1953, together with another minister, to undertake a study tour of church youth work. I was elected as the first chair of a national church youth society, which I was instrumental in forming. We undertook a six-and-a-half-month intensive study tour through Europe, the United States, and Canada. A number of these questions about apartheid arose during that tour.

The second phase of my conversion was during the period I was acting moderator of the Transvaal Synod. A number of young white ministers who were serving black congregations—that means congregations of Africans, Indians, and those people of mixed descent called "colored" in South Africa—were confronted by members of the different congregations. In the suffering that they were experiencing as a result of apartheid, they challenged the ministers, asking, "How can you justify this suffering on the basis of the gospel? What kind of a faith is this?"

The ministers called me in because of their deep concern and asked for advice. My first response to them was, "I can't believe what you are telling me is happening," because I was living in a happy, white, privileged ghetto of Afrikaner life in South Africa. When eventually I got the opportunity, I went out of my way to visit the parishes, the areas concerned. I discovered for the first time in my life what was happening, and I was shattered! To discover what apartheid was doing to human beings created in me a tremendous moral crisis.

The third and final phase was the event of the Sharpeville Massacre on March 21, 1960, when sixty-nine people who were protesting peacefully were simply shot, most of them in the back as they were running away. That was a moment in my life when I just felt I could not allow this situation to continue any longer.

You have said, "I just had to see for myself. I had to go where I'd never been before. And just seeing it was a shattering experience." Most people have never had the occasion to cross the barriers and boundaries that circumscribe their lives. Your experience raises the question, not just in South Africa but here or anywhere, of whether we can even understand the meaning of our faith if we can't break through those barriers.

I fully agree. The problem in my country is that the church in the past has made a very serious mistake by presenting the Christian faith as primarily a rational belief based on a certain theological or theoretical understanding and interpretation of the gospel. Another mistake was not realizing that faith is meaningless unless it becomes contextualized.

If you talk about hunger, go and see where hunger is. If you talk about injustice, go and view what kind of injustice. If you talk about human dignity, go and see where human dignity is being violated. If you talk about racial prejudice, go and meet with the people who know themselves and experience themselves to be the victims of that prejudice.

Unless you are willing to do that, you can never discover the full truth of the gospel. That was the example of Jesus himself. But it's much easier to sit in your study and to preach about it. Or to be in your theological school and theologize about it. Or to have academic, theoretical discussions and even write a book about it.

Dare yourself to be challenged by a faith that is real. Then go out into the highways and byways and say, "I want to be there when it happens. I want this to be part of my whole understanding of the Christian life and its challenge." But it's painful, because once you've set your foot on that new road it is a continuous process of conversion.

What makes that road so threatening to many people is that you never know where God is going to lead you next, what new challenge lies ahead, what new sacrifice, what new problems may arise. How will your Christian faith be able to meet that? To what degree does this require a greater form of sacrifice from yourself and your family? I suppose all of us are afraid to go that way, because we don't know the cost of going along that road.

There is a place in South African society, as there is in the United States, for a kind of liberal position or stance that is concerned and aware. But you have broken through that, in a way most whites in South Africa haven't, and indeed as most white people in this country haven't yet either, to a radical stance. How do you stay on this road and not get diverted to observing the conflict and being a voice of reason and not really going where you need to go or taking sides with the people who are in fact really suffering?

I don't know what happens to other people. I can only describe what happened in my own life. First of all, I felt that if I wanted to commit myself to the truth, and therefore to an expression of the real love of Christ toward all human beings, I had to make myself open to others' feelings, concerns, pains, suffering, and joy. In order to do that, I had to set aside the time in order to make myself available to them, to move into where they are.

We must open our hearts and our minds and our whole beings to others' needs, and absorb and allow the Spirit of God to interpret to us what is happening and what should be our message and our response. In that sense it is a process of continuous conversion of our own lives, and also of a deepening commitment all the time.

And what is helpful is if we specifically request those who suffer to challenge us and to indicate to us where they feel that our understanding is incomplete, where they feel that our commitment is not real or sincere, and where they feel more is demanded. It is the moment that we become willing to open ourselves to them, and therefore enable them to assist us, that there is growth. It's the spiritual and the political and the social growth and understanding that are required.

But if you're not prepared to do that—out of fear that it may cost too much, the sacrifice may be too great, and the dangers could be very, very serious—then that process of growth is stalled. It does not go any further.

That's when we become stuck in a rut, or a position, or a career that we maintain. But when we've stepped off or detoured from that road, then we can be on a path to a deeper involvement with suffering people.

That is true. But that is where the question of material security plays a very important role, because you can feel that there is so much at stake. From the viewpoint of material privilege and security, you find it becomes much more difficult to even risk the possible loss of these things.

But if you know there is very little to lose, because whatever you have you have committed to God, then you can say, "Well, it's not mine. I share this with whomever may wish to have this." Then there is an inner freedom that comes about as a result. There is also, therefore, a liberty that you experience of being available to people in their need. That's a tremendously enriching experience.

The Observer, a British newspaper, said in 1984 that yours was "the longest journey of any South African of any colour," from where you came from to where you are now. People have said of you, "He could have been the prime minister of South Africa." But instead, you were banned for seven years. All that you gave up, all that you've sacrificed, all that you could have had but have turned away from—yet, you are not a person who acts as if you have sacrificed or lost the great things in life. It seems that you have gained, somehow, more than you've lost.

Oh, there's no doubt about it! What I've gained is so much more. I would never exchange this for all the positions in the world, all the possible situations of popularity that I would have had in South Africa. There's no question about it. I've gained an inner freedom and an inner peace of mind. I've also gained the ability to continue to love when others hate, to forgive when others would wish to enter into a situation of revenge.

Because of my experience, I've been able to tell other white Afrikaners, who despise me or have rejected me and feel that I'm a traitor to their cause, "I pity you, because I feel that you, in fact, have become the victims of your own imprisoned philosophy of life. And therefore you cannot be free. You cannot be free to love people of color deeply and sincerely. You cannot be free to look at the future of South Africa outside the confines of your present political viewpoint. You cannot be free to think of a church that operates in a totally different way. You cannot be open to the concept of Christian community with Christians of all denominations around the world. And therefore, as a result of those things that you have imposed on yourself, your vision is limited."

But there is a cost. I have a feeling that one painful place in your heart must be how much love you have for the church of your birth—a church that has so lost its way that it's labeled you traitor and heretic and worse. A break with the church is not painful if one doesn't love the church, but if one does, it's always a painful thing.

That is true. I think that was the most painful decision I had to make—to terminate my membership with the white Dutch Reformed Church. But the moment had to come when I made the decision and eventually said, "I'm sorry. I cannot, with a truthful conscience, remain a member of this church any longer." I can only hope that the day will come when the Dutch Reformed Church will understand and will realize that my motivation was one of deep concern and love for a church which, to my mind, has betrayed the essential calling of being the church of Christ.

In the United States, people sometimes have difficulty understanding the relationship between the system of apartheid and our own system, or the global system under which apartheid exists. They say things like, "South Africa has a problem of racism now just like we had in the 1960s." The problem is not seen systemically by many people, and some people use apartheid's existence to focus energy on a problem "out there" rather than dealing with problems here. What are your systemic, theological reflections on this?

First of all, it's important to realize that the challenges to our faith and to our understanding of the responsibility that we have toward each other are basically the same, whether you deal with them in the United States or South Africa.

Certainly we have a racial problem, but we have much more than a racial problem. We've got a problem of social justice; we've got a problem of different classes; we've got a problem of some people living on a First World standard and some on a Third World standard; we've got a problem of wealth and poverty; we've got a problem of a much higher and a much lower quality of education being given to different people.

So basically it is a problem of what we are willing to do and how far we are willing to go to share our lives, our opportunities, and our privileges with those who don't have those things. In that sharing there will be, first of all, a tremendous transformation of all people concerned. There will also be an enrichment of our culture and our society. There will be a new possibility of making that available to all those around us.

South Africa is often described by journalists as one of the more hopeless situations in the world today. And yet you don't come across as a hopeless person, but as a person with a deeper theological kind of hope. What do you have to say to those of us in the middle of the same struggle, or in our own latest struggles, about hope and perseverance and how to sustain one's life in the midst of lengthy struggles?

Well, it is true that, on the face of it and for the foreseeable future, our situation in South Africa is bleak and certainly presents very little grounds for hope. I agree with that. But I think that is a superficial analysis; there's much more to it.

It is important that we constantly remind ourselves and others who believe that they are on the side of truth that we must not only maintain but also increase the demand for truth and seek to implement it in a spirit of love and understanding. The openness that you have toward other people, including your most bitter opponents, once you have discovered that truth, is a source of continuous strength and hope, because you know truth will eventually prevail. I think it is very important that we never forget that.

Second, if we believe that we are dealing with a God of justice and love, a God who wants to see the Kingdom become a glorious reality, then we know that whatever we are doing through God's grace is part of that process of renewal. It takes time. I may not be able to see it all happen, but I know with the strength of my faith and my convictions that moment will come.

Those of us who are suffering in South Africa are aware of the fact that the struggle may be a long one; but we know with a deep inner certainty that the day of liberation will come. Our people and our country will be free. We realize that sacrifice is needed. We realize many of us may not be able to see the eventual realization of freedom. But we know it will come.

Third, if you are involved in the struggle, you are constantly encouraged by the incredible commitment on the part of people, the quality of their leadership, the willingness to sacrifice time, energy, and life in order to attain that goal. That is a continuous source of inspiration.

I'm thinking, for instance, of young people who have been detained. How do they feel when they come out of jail? Are they willing to continue? With an immediacy and a deep sense of conviction, they say, "The period of detention, even the torture, has strengthened us. It has made it possible for us to move out with a greater commitment in order to obtain what we believe is the goal of a just society and a free South Africa."

Therefore, if you ask me whether there is hope for South Africa, I say, without any doubt. Tremendous potential exists in our country, but not only by way of the material riches that we can share; there is also tremendous potential for re-creating and transforming this evil, immoral, and totally objectionable system of apartheid and building something new: a society where there is the possibility of all of us— people of all colors, all religions, all classes—being able to live and work together. And to do so on the basis of our past experiences—our sufferings, the injustices of the past—to see that through God's grace they will not again occur.

Do you have advice, encouragement, or practical suggestions that have been helpful to you over the years to offer to those engaged in the struggle?

I would say, first of all, ensure that your understanding of faith, of the gospel, of the message of Christ's liberation is clear, relevant, and comprehensive of the whole of humankind. That's number one. Make your Christian faith real, meaningful, vibrant, and relevant.

The second piece of advice is to realize that this can never be done in isolation. God wants us to be Christians and to be human beings in community. You can never be fully human unless you've discovered the humanity in other human beings. You become human through him or her. Therefore the building of the sense of community, of mutual responsibility, of the sharing of joys and sorrows, of the need to grow together, is a vitally essential element in our life.

Third, stretch out your hand and discover those communities, areas, and countries where there is suffering, injustice, or a system of oppression. Discover to what degree there are similar patterns of life and suffering being enacted and being experienced in your own country. Don't close your eyes to the injustices of your own country by trying to solve the injustices of another country. That's an evasion of Christian responsibility.

Instead, see in the light of that discovery what is needed at home. Then begin to share, in the deep and meaningful sense of the word, by going out to Christians and others saying, "We are one with you. We are one in the realization of our weakness. But we are also one in the realization of the tremendous potential for change that God has given to all of us. Let us build together so that we may truly make this world God's Kingdom."

Brian Willson

Standing for Truth

On September 1, 1987, Brian Willson, a Vietnam veteran, was participating in a vigil on the train tracks at the Concord Naval Weapons Station in Concord, California. The Concord installation is the starting point for the shipment of millions of dollars worth of bombs to Central America, and two groups—Nuremburg Actions and Veterans Peace Action Team—had decided to fast and vigil on the tracks for forty days in an effort to stop, or at least delay, the trains carrying bombs.

On that day, their first, a Navy munitions train struck Willson and dragged him 25 feet, severing his right leg, mangling his left, and severely injuring his skull. Holley Rauen, his wife of eleven days and a licensed midwife, saved his life by using her skirt to stop the flow of blood. Willson was in surgery for nine hours, and doctors had to amputate his left leg. He walks now on artificial legs, aided by two canes.

Brian Willson was interviewed by Vickie Kemper in January 1988 when he was in Washington, D.C., for a fast on behalf of Central America on the steps of the U.S. Capitol. In the summer of 1990, Willson and four other peace activists accepted an out-of-court settlement of $920,000 in damages from the U.S. government and the Navy.

*What are the events and forces that have taken you from Vietnam
and a very conservative background to the Veterans Fast for Life and
then to Nicaragua and the Concord Naval Weapons Station and back
to the Capitol steps?*

The first time in my life that I asked any questions at all was when
I was at a conservative Baptist college. And my questions were really
only related to the nature of Christianity. I had decided I wanted to
become a minister, so I wanted a Christian education before I went to
seminary. All of a sudden, almost without warning, I was asking questions about the church and the rules I had been raised to believe were
part of Christianity.

I started asking the second level of questions when I was in law
school in '65 and '66. I was getting a master's degree in corrections
and a law degree, and I became very interested in criminal law. So I
lived in this jail for 10 months. I decided that jail was counterproduc-
tive to helping people who commit crimes get straightened out.

And then I was drafted in '66, out of law school. I was in the Air
Force for four years, and I went to Vietnam in '69. During the training at an Army base before arriving in Vietnam, something else happened in me. Part of the training was to bayonet these dummies and
shout, "Kill! Kill!" and I found myself unable to do that. I had never
thought about it before. It never occurred to me that I might find that
offensive.

I was 27 when I went to Vietnam. There I was, exposed to attacks
and being very aware of the bombing missions and how many people
were being killed. I became incredibly aware of what I now think of as
the American lie.

It wasn't just the lie about the war, it was a lie about much of what
I had been taught about life. It all seemed suspect. The whole notion
of how one lives their life in this country. I was questioning the whole
system. I had a major transforming experience.

For many years after Vietnam, I was relatively successful in following a fairly normal professional life. But I was very restless, and I
never lost a sense that something was fundamentally wrong in my
country. But I just put it aside.

From 1970 on, I was steadily employed in some fashion, either in a
private business or with an agency or organization that enabled me to
work at something that I really believed in and that was somewhat
harmonious to my own evolution. I was a consultant on prison issues
to the Cincinnati, Ohio, city council, and later a dairy farmer for two
years in upstate New York. For two years I was a legislative aide on
prison issues for a state senator of Massachusetts, and then I was vice
president of my own dairy company, manufacturing all-natural dairy
products. After that I was director of a Vietnam veterans outreach
center for two years.

Then around '81 I began having some vivid memories of Vietnam. And I think there were two factors contributing to that. One was a beginning awareness of U.S. policy in El Salvador and Nicaragua. Then I witnessed a fight that really brought it all back.

I wasn't particularly a Rambo, but I had plenty of retaliation in me. So I started going to veterans rap groups to get out my rage, and then I started with some other vets something called Veterans Education Project. We started going into high schools, talking with students about war and peace. I started going to rallies speaking out against the war in Central America. But I wasn't a member of any peace group; I was just a vet coming out.

I also had become very intellectually curious about nonviolence—to find an alternative way of talking about peace other than through the just war theory. I couldn't see how we could get anywhere with military solutions.

So I was looking for an alternative, which I discovered initially in Tolstoy. That led me to Gandhi, who had been motivated by Tolstoy and Thoreau. And Gandhi led me to King and A.J. Muste.

And then in the '80s, I began to feel complicit. I had felt complicit from Vietnam, but in some ways I had worked through that. But I was feeling this constant responsibility, "Oh my God, I'm a citizen of this country. And even though I don't agree with the policies of my government, how do I take responsibility for policies that are done in my name?"

I started thinking about how we could begin to express ourselves as citizens in more clear and demonstrative ways, and Gandhi and King have given me clues. I guess it was to withdraw consent, to commit civil disobedience. I've never even been arrested for doing civil disobedience.

All this didn't start meaning much to me until about four years ago. I started thinking a lot more, and I concluded, "I need to withdraw my consent from the government. And I want to do it in ways that are very meaningful to me."

I'm not much of a bandwagon joiner. I really have to think things through. I'm a very conservative person. It takes me a long time before I feel clear that I'm at a place that's right for me.

I also realized that we have a code of law [the Nuremberg Principles], established after World War II, that pertains to individual responsibility. The ultimate enforcer of the violation of international law is the citizen of each country. I realized working at the veterans outreach center that the Vietnam experience was very profound because the war was a policy of this country and not a policy of individual veterans.

How could we explain the lessons, the insanity of Vietnam, to people who had supported the war but had not experienced the insanity of it? Society had detached itself from the meaning of Vietnam, and we veterans felt very alone. This nation wasn't able to deal with why we spent $400 to $600 billion dollars in Vietnam over 10 years; and I realized that if we couldn't deal with that issue, we couldn't deal with anything.

I didn't know where to turn. I could just talk about the truth of my own feeling, but most people couldn't respect or understand that. I began to wonder how war could continue if we didn't consent to it. Why weren't we chaining ourselves to the front doors of the offices of the members of Congress who vote for war?

Well, maybe it's because people live their own private lives, and what's most important is their careers and their families and their reputations. But I saw veterans who were becoming homeless, drug addicts, and alcoholics because the issues were so profound and they had no paradigm or frame of reference to turn to for hope. I began finding my hope in nonviolence.

What was the next step for you?
At the end of '85, I resigned from the veterans outreach center and said, "I want to go to Nicaragua to see for myself." The first week I was there, the contras hit on the outskirts of Estelí and killed 11 people. I could hear the machine-gun fire three nights in a row.

I was furious. I told the Nicaraguan woman with whom I was staying, "This is my money and it's killing people and it's for a lie. I've been through it before, and I won't go through it again. I'm going to be a spokesperson somehow with my life for the truth."

I came back from Nicaragua after two months, and I went into seclusion for a month because I was so affected. I just had to come to grips with all my feelings.

So I read and read, and I typed my thoughts out. I started talking about the revolution in my own consciousness and the need for a revolution in the consciousness of my country.

Then I went back to King's speeches, and he was right there. And that confirmed for me that I was not crazy. But it's hard work; society's almost more entrenched now than it was in '67. Yet I believed that we were at this extraordinary time in history in which peacemaking and an alternative way were the only things that made any sense.

I asked myself, "Am I up to it?" I wasn't alone, but I felt alone at the time. And I thought, "I don't have any alternative. This is not only intellectually honest, but it's what my heart is saying." I prayed for help, that I would have the courage to speak my heart through my brain with my life to the world, and that I would find others who were doing the same thing.

And, of course, I did find others. There were three others in the veterans peace movement who wanted to fast. I said to them, "I'm prepared to fast to the end if I have to, to awaken the consciousness of my country." And it wasn't done with despair or depression; it was done with incredible affirmation.

I had no interest in dying. I went to the steps of the Capitol with a desire to affirm life in the most profound way I could, by saying, "I'm willing to put my life on the line for life."

After the Veterans Fast for Life, I felt really liberated and went immediately to Nicaragua. I spent a lot more time there traveling around the country, meeting people, and then working on putting together these veterans teams to go into the war zones. I met Holley, now my wife, in Managua during that trip.

The first Veterans Peace Action Team went to Nicaragua last spring. We spent two weeks in the war zones, and everywhere we went, we were either just ahead of the contras or just behind them. The contra atrocities were occurring almost in front of our eyes every day—mortar fire and bridges being mined.

When we returned to Managua, we decided to plan a walk from Jinotega to Wiwili. There were 11 of us, unarmed and undefended, who walked the 73 miles on a road that had previously been ambushed and mined. It was the road where the Pantasma land-mine explosion occurred in October 1986. Fifty-five people were blown out of the truck; 11 ultimately died, six immediately and five later.

On that walk we prepared ourselves for losing our legs. We went through role playing, through medical procedures for how to stop the blood flow. And Holley, being a midwife, was our medic. She carried all our bandages and medical supplies.

We met the amputees from the Pantasma mine explosion—12 in all. Then we went to all the hospitals in the country. I personally visited more than 400 amputee victims, and I cried a lot.

I think I grieved over the loss of so many legs in Nicaragua that I had already grieved over the loss of mine. I believed that at some metaphysical level, their legs and my legs became the same, and that their legs were no less valuable than mine. I was not articulating that consciously, but I really think that was happening inside me.

When you returned from Nicaragua this time, you began vigiling outside Concord Naval Weapons Station. What moved you to begin thinking about another fast there, and possibly blocking the trains?

I had seen the munitions trains all summer. And all I could see in my mind were bodies in those boxcars, because they were loaded with bombs and rockets. The first two days I saw the munitions trains, I just broke down. And I said, "Well, I'm going to begin blocking these trains, but I'm not ready to do it yet. I don't have the strength mentally."

Other people started blocking munitions trains right away, but I spent 60 days preparing for September 1. What happened September 1, I think, has to be considered providential.

Why do you say that?
Well, first of all, I survived. And second, it's such an extraordinary event in history that it couldn't have been conceived in advance. It was such an unbelievable thing that happened. And yet I believe these kinds of things are going to happen if we're going to stop the violence. In other words, we're going to have to start taking risks to stand up for the truth. Those of us who are speaking truth are going to be intimidated, jailed, injured, killed. But when you start living the truth, and what you really believe in, the risks don't matter anymore. It's not that you do stupid things—in fact, you do things even more thoughtfully and carefully—but you are going to push the system. You are going to give those in power an alternative, which to them is perceived as a threat to their national security. But their national security is a threat to my personal security, and the world's security.

And so the train running over me was something people could relate to. It represented our standing up to the madness, and it had an empowering effect. I know this from reading my letters. People say, "Your blood is our blood, and I haven't recovered from it yet. And I don't know what it means, but I know it means something very significant for my life."

I was just there on the tracks; I didn't have anything to do with the train moving over me. But it's so powerful, it's just way beyond me and all of us why this happened, how it happened.

Jim Douglass, from the Ground Zero Community in Washington, came down and said, "I really believe, Brian, that you were the right person to be on the tracks at this moment in history, because the train ran over you, and yet you survived and came out of it with a vision that doesn't involve retaliation."

I'm just a normal person like all of us, and I've just chosen to follow the truth of my heart, which everybody can do. And that's what happened on September 1. People said, "My God, he's just doing something extremely natural and rational. He's stopping the death trains. And they had the audacity to run over him! That tells us a lot about our government and about the ethic of the society, the insanity." I think it has helped people to realize that the power is in themselves and not in these people on the trains. Where do we turn for our expression? Well, we've got to turn to each other now and build a new society that withdraws our consent from the government, that resists through an alternative of affirmation.

We resist, not because we like to resist, but because we love life ar we must resist policies that destroy life. No government can funct' without consent of the people—through taxes, through participation, through complicity, through silence.

The events of September 1 have been a real watershed for the peace movement in this country. It has inspired and motivated people. Has it been that watershed in your life? How has it changed you?

I'm still coming to grips with what it all means. This kind of celebrity status I now have is very unnatural to me. I don't feel comfortable with it. I'm just trying to surrender in a way to the truth of the moment and say, "God help me. I don't know how to do it, I don't know how to be, except just to fall back and be myself."

I'm amazed that people look to me as much as they do. I'm just a normal guy; I just happened to be the one the train ran over. I don't have any special wisdom. I just have a commitment that I'm not going to continue supporting the madness.

Probably a third of my mail calls me a hero; and I worry about it, because I didn't do anything except walk out and sit on the tracks and say, "You're not going to kill any more people in my name without at least dealing with my body."

Now, anybody can do that. It didn't take any skill. I understand it takes an evolution of your consciousness, but it doesn't take any skill at all. None. It doesn't require any special preparation outside your internal process of consciousness. We all can do this.

You can define the train, and your track, however you want, but we all need to be participating now in a new society. And each person's heart will tell them what their role is and what their truth is.

That's part of what I see as the revolution of consciousness—that people take their own power, and listen to themselves, to the intuitive self, the inner voice, the higher self, whatever you want to call it. The answers are there.

You know, people get irritated at me sometimes for not telling them what they should do. I say, "I just encourage you to listen deeply as to what you think is the truth. Do you think killing mothers and fathers and children is wrong? Do you realize that you're paying taxes to support that policy? Do you believe that you might be able to express yourself in some way you haven't before? The answer is in yourself as to how to do that."

We all need to do it, we all need to start thinking about whether the solution is in the political structures, or within our hearts and our collective energies. It's very simple if you understand that the government can't function without the consent of the people.

Besides being a celebrity of sorts now, you have also caught the attention of the government, which is now monitoring your activities. How does that make you feel?

I was shocked when I saw I was on the government's terrorist list. How did I find out? I was in the ABC-TV studio here in Washington in December. They asked me to come in for an interview, and they showed me the documents and said, "We want your face on camera looking at these documents." I didn't know anything about it until then.

I'm in a position now where I feel incredibly liberated because I've been put on the terrorist list. They've monitored all my mail and phone calls for the past 14 months, they've taken off my legs, they've fractured my skull, and they've threatened to put me in jail for tax resistance. They can do whatever they're going to do, and I'm going to keep doing what I'm doing because I believe in it. And if I'm in jail or dead or have my arms taken off, I feel like I've found a place in the universe that's whole and feels clean.

I think of Nelson Mandela, who had been in prison for 25 years for what he believes in; and he always talks about his spirit, his indomitable spirit. That's what I cherish more than anything—having an indomitable spirit that can withstand what is in the way of the truth. I can confront it and walk through it.

My prayer every morning is that I'll be open to the infinite wisdom and truth of the universe that can be embodied in me and that I'll have the courage to follow what my inner voice is saying. I sometimes say, "Hold my hand because I don't know how to do it."

I don't know how to set up a peace force in Nicaragua, but I'm committed to it. I didn't know how to fast, and I didn't know how to create a Veterans Peace Action Team with other people. And then all of a sudden, we were doing it.

Do you believe there was an order for the Concord munitions train not to stop? Did you believe that all along?

Well, others believed it more than I did. From the beginning a lot of people came up to me and said, "You know this can't happen without it having been designed and intended to be this way." I'm not a very conspiratorial-thinking person, nor particularly a paranoid person. I'm kind of naive.

But when I came to the congressional hearings last November 18, that's when I started thinking differently, because Navy officials admitted that they knew all about me. Navy Captain S.J. Pryzby told the congressional committee, "Oh, yes, we knew all about Mr. Willson, about his fasts, his trips to Nicaragua, and his being on the tracks since June 10, and that he was a man of his word." And I'm sitting there thinking, "They knew that I wouldn't get off the tracks."

That was the first moment I thought that there was attempted murder. Then I found the notes of the unsanitized Navy report that had not been made public lying on the table in the room next to the hearing room. I started reading them and said, "My God, this is in the original report that they didn't release to the public." I put them in my briefcase, and I didn't even read them through for another month.

Also, I just got a copy of the local sheriff's report, which was not included in the Navy report. It contained the interviews with the train engineer, who said he was under orders not to stop the train.

So I'm still coming to grips with what all of it means—metaphysically, spiritually, and in terms of the realities of what my own government will do to its own citizens.

I don't hear any bitterness or anger or resentment in you.
Well, I don't have bitterness or anger or resentment that I'm aware of. I might be in denial. I haven't had any depression or grief either over the loss of my legs. So it's possible I'm in denial, but I don't think so.

I worked hard to rid myself of retaliation. It was all part of the development of nonviolence for me. I worked this through in therapy dealing with my father, who I hated. Working through that was a big breakthrough in my personal nonviolent development. Not my intellectual commitment to nonviolence, but my deep emotional commitment to nonviolence, my ability even to grasp it.

I also learned from the Nicaraguans who, when they saw one contra dead, grieved over the loss, saying, "If we'd only had five minutes with this contra, we could have convinced him to be part of the revolution." And I said, "You know this is really the gospel in action, or love in action."

So it's not that I don't have moments of anger, and even rage, but I choose not to act out of anger and rage anymore. There are moments when I'm feeling anger and rage, and I cannot relate to somebody. For example, I may get to the point with a police officer at Concord, where I recognize, "I'm not at a good place right now, and I cannot offer this person an alternative of love." So I will not participate at that point.

What are your feelings toward the operators of the Navy train that ran over you?
I have a lot of empathy for the train crew, and I'll tell you why. First of all, they're all living the way I used to live; they're brainwashed like I was. I really can identify with that. Second, they probably do have traumatic stress, which is what they're suing me for, because I think they're caught between following their orders and following their conscience.

So they are living with a tremendous conflict. And third, they're caught between a rock and a hard place. They're on the lower end of the totem pole of a chain of command that's involved with a criminal policy—madness. And they're the grunt men like we were in Vietnam.

My offer to them is that the solution to their stress is within them-selves, not in suing me. But if they are going to sue, they should sue the Navy, which has money and gave the order.

I condemn their action. I just plead with them to be open to trans-formation, which is the only way to heal their stress, and to tell the truth about who gave the order.

What are the lessons we should learn from all of this?
All these decisions that are being made by the policy-makers should reveal to the people of the United States that our solution is not here in Washington. This realization represents a paradigm shift that's happening in the country. It's empowering, it's liberating; but first you have to walk through an emotional minefield, come to grips with your own power, and realize that we can assert our power.

By being here, fasting on the steps, we're beating the policy-mak-ers' delusions. They really are our employees, yet we've let them become our masters. That's why I don't like the lobbying any more. The most I could see myself doing now is fasting, which most people don't think much of, but it helps me to reflect and become clear.

There is hope—tremendous hope—but it's not in Washington, and it's not in our political structures. It's in the consciousness of human beings, which, for me, has come through liberation theology. I'm very hopeful that people are beginning to sense that the solution is within each of us, as we work with one another.

There is no security without justice. I'm interested in promoting the security of the world which comes from everybody working for justice. That's what I'm into, a revolutionary consciousness for North America.

So I'm hopeful. I had a political conviction, a political channel to begin working. I became very non-ideological and said, "I'm going to reconstruct my heart as a human being." Now I know that my power is not in Washington; my power is in my heart.

Pedro Arrupe

Finding God in All Things

by Joe Nangle, OFM

To be the only Basque elected superior general of the Society of Jesus since Ignatius of Loyola would have been notable enough when Father Pedro Arrupe, S.J. (1907-1991) assumed that post on May 22, 1965. But the parallels between the lives of the first and the 28th leader of the Jesuits go much further.

Both men first embarked on careers well outside religious life: Ignatius as a soldier, Arrupe as a medical student. Each experienced a remarkable conversion that led him to pursue a radically different pathway in life. Both Ignatius and Arrupe left their Basque homeland in search of the best way to serve God—the former in the Middle East, the latter in Japan. Each served the Catholic Church during turbulent times in that communion's history; each had his difficulties with the ecclesial institution. Both made indelible marks on the Society of Jesus.

So it is that the lives of these two giants of the Jesuit Order are increasingly linked. Indeed the appellation "refounder" or even "second founder" of the Jesuits is heard more and more in reference to Don

Joe Nangle, OFM, is a Franciscan priest who today serves as Co-Director of the Franciscan Mission Service.

Pedro, as he was called. None of this should surprise us when we look at the wealth of experience that Arrupe brought to his 18-year ministry as superior of the Jesuits, and when his impact on the order and the church is considered.

Pedro Arrupe became a Jesuit in 1927. After priestly ordination in 1936 he was granted his wish to serve as a missionary in Japan. He arrived in that country in 1938 and began learning the Japanese language and culture, accomplishments that he cherished until the end of his life.

On August 6, 1945, Don Pedro was serving as director of Jesuit novices in Nagatsuka, six kilometers from the center of Hiroshima. He saw and felt the impact of the world's first nuclear bombing and described it in these words: "I was in my room with another priest at 8:15 when suddenly we saw a blinding light, like a flash of magnesium. . . . As I opened the door that faced the city, we heard a formidable explosion similar to the blast of a hurricane. At the same time doors, windows and walls fell upon us in smithereens."

Arrupe went on to describe his and his companions' attempts to enter the destroyed and dying city, initially prevented because of the procession of dazed and wounded people emerging from Hiroshima. Arrupe's medical training enabled him to help out with the overwhelming number of people needing attention.

In telling of those endless days and nights during August and September of 1945, Arrupe mentions celebrating the Eucharist, though his description is not greatly detailed. One can only speculate on the depth of his reflections, as he offered the bread and the cup over a broken city, as he celebrated the paschal mystery of resurrection in a place surrounded by death. It must have been a powerful, searing preparation for the work that lay ahead in his life.

In 1958 the Japanese mission of the Jesuits was raised to the status of a province and Pedro Arrupe became its first superior. His task was to mold into an effective evangelizing body the 300 Jesuits from 20 different countries working in Japan at that time. His position as provincial superior in Japan made it necessary for him to travel worldwide in search of additional personnel and funds for the fledgling province. Thus by 1965 and his election as the new superior general, Arrupe was a familiar figure in most parts of the Jesuit world.

Accounts of Don Pedro's personality by those who knew him reveal a thoroughly contemporary man, possessed of deep spiritual convictions, enormously interested in people. In addition to his duties as superior general of his order, Arrupe was elected to five three-year terms as president of the Union of Superiors General of Catholic orders worldwide.

To these tasks he brought the ability to inspire those he was called to lead, especially younger members of his own order. His travels all over the world of the Jesuits—a departure from the custom of his predecessors—made of Arrupe a connector of Jesuits everywhere.

It was in small groups of his brothers that Arrupe was said to be at his best. The story is told of a car trip in Egypt during which Arrupe was engrossed in conversation about the order and its ministries there. An aide tried to point out the beauty of the pyramids as they passed them on the road. Arrupe paused for a moment, nodded in appreciation and plunged back into his conversation.

As provincial in Japan, Arrupe's travels had taken him to various parts of the underdeveloped world. These journeys, together with his momentous experience at Hiroshima, forged in the future superior general the conviction that the pursuit of justice was integral to life in Jesus. He saw this integration as a unifying force for the life and ministries of the Jesuit Order in modern times. It became the great gift of Arrupe to the Society of Jesus.

What is more, the justice he saw as being needed in the world was as much on the level of societal structures as in personal relationships. His travels and conversations with oppressed peoples and those ministering to them convinced Arrupe that justice meant structural change in every aspect of human life.

Ecclesial events around him served to reinforce this conviction. As the newly elected superior of the Jesuits, Arrupe attended the final session of Vatican II and witnessed the promulgation of the great document "The Church in the Modern World." Its opening sentence confirmed Arrupe's own sentiments: "The joys and the hopes, the griefs and the anxieties of the people of this age, especially those who are poor or in any way afflicted, these too are the joys and hopes, the griefs and anxieties of the followers of Christ."

In 1971 Arrupe attended the synod of Catholic bishops and witnessed the amazing declaration from that body: "Action on behalf of justice and participation in the transformation of the world fully appear to us as constitutive to the preaching of the gospel." Such statements and all that led up to them in terms of social analysis, pastoral concern, and biblical reflection reinforced Arrupe's own conviction that his order had to be about the work of justice in the name of the gospel. As one of his closest collaborators described it, Arrupe's dream was that there be one mission for the Jesuits—that of promoting justice—which would focus all of their apostolic energies.

This dream, articulated by Arrupe from the time of his election as superior in 1965, culminated in the 32nd Congregation, a meeting of representatives from across the Jesuit world, held December 1974 to March 1975. Under Arrupe's guidance this supreme gathering of the society stated in its famous "fourth decree" what was the modern-day vocation of the Jesuits.

The title says it clearly: "Our Mission Today: The Service of Faith and the Promotion of Justice." It went on to flesh out the concept: "Our faith in Christ Jesus and our mission to proclaim the Gospel demand of us a commitment to promote justice and to enter into solidarity with the voiceless and the powerless."

Prior to the promulgation of this breakthrough decree, Arrupe had prophetically warned his brothers of its consequences. He asked them to pray about what they, and he, were contemplating, stating that they would lose friends, be criticized, and suffer persecution. How right he was. Less than three years later, Don Pedro was writing a letter to the entire society about the five Jesuits who had already been killed for their pursuit of justice.

Much has been written and spoken about Don Pedro's other contributions to his order as its superior general, which include modernizing its internal structures, promoting its missionary endeavors, encouraging the prayer and community life of Jesuits. But even today, so shortly after his death, it seems clear that the great integrating vision of Arrupe—joining Christian faith and the service of justice— will mark him as the order's second founder.

As clear implementations of Arrupe's vision for his order, one can point to the University of Central America (UCA) in El Salvador and the Center of Concern in Washington, D.C. The first of these, under the leadership of the Jesuits during the Arrupe years, made an institutional option for the poor.

The rector of the UCA, Father Ignacio Ellacuría, offered the clearest explanation of this institutional option: "A Christian-inspired university focuses all its academic activity according to what it means to make a Christian preferential option for the poor. . . . The university should become science for those who have no science, the clear voice of those who have no voice. . . . Our university has modestly tried to adopt this difficult and conflictive course." (Ellacuría was murdered by elements of the Salvadoran military on November 16, 1989.)

This was precisely what Arrupe had in mind in the fourth decree of his 32nd Congregation, where it states: "Solidarity with men and women who live a life of hardship . . . should be a characteristic of the life of all of us as individuals and a characteristic of our communities and institutions as well."

Similarly, during the first part of Don Pedro's generalship, the Center of Concern in Washington, D.C., came into being. Originally a Jesuit initiative, directly approved and blessed by Arrupe, the center has since expanded to include men and women from many walks of life among its staff. However, it remains true to its original vision—a think tank, educational resource, and activist center offering alternative analyses of current economic and political issues, based on an option for the poor.

Inevitably, Arrupe's vision and its implementation throughout the Jesuit world drew criticism and opposition. Many of his own order felt that their leader, far from building up the society, was destroying it. They simply could not understand nor accept the great gift they had in this man. Those who knew Arrupe testify that he exercised great charity toward his brothers who disagreed with him. His constant theme was that they all had a right to express their opinions.

From the highest ranks of the Catholic Church as well came opposition. Pope John Paul II and to a lesser extent Paul VI found Arrupe too radical or too permissive. One can imagine the reaction of institutionally minded popes on hearing what Don Pedro had said in answer to a question about Jesuits in jail: "If it is necessary to give witness to injustice by going to jail, well, 'Welcome jail.'" A Jesuit who knew him well said that one of Don Pedro's dreams was to wake up one morning and not have on his desk a letter of complaint about a Jesuit from another ecclesiastical authority.

Most notable was Don Pedro's attitude toward the members of his order who stretched the limits—in some people's minds—of a "prudent" promotion of justice. A case in point is the conduct of the Jesuits in Nicaragua both before and during the Sandinista revolution.

Jesuits in the country felt that the nature of the changes taking place there had been badly misunderstood in the Vatican. To label them "Marxist" without any nuancing was for the Nicaraguan Jesuits incorrect and pastorally dangerous. This led to the accusation that they themselves were Marxist sympathizers. Arrupe countered the criticisms by saying that the Nicaraguan Jesuits were in constant communication with him, that they had done nothing without his knowledge and support, and that to attack them was to attack him.

Without doubt Arrupe on occasion had to call his Jesuit brothers to accountability for their mistakes. But even in these cases he showed utmost generosity and loyalty to the men.

One of his more famous quotes came out of the monumental debate over Pope Paul's letter on artificial birth control. Jesuits found themselves on all sides of the issue, and while Arrupe supported those who found the letter difficult or impossible to accept, he asked: "Please make it easier for me to defend you." He stated his overriding principle in taking responsibility for a large and activist order in a 1966 press conference when he said that the worst position would be to fold one's arms and do nothing for fear of making a mistake.

The final chapters of Pedro Arrupe's life began with his request to resign from the generalship in 1980. Though he was still in good health, he wanted to implement a decree passed at the general assembly that elected him in 1965, namely that the superior general could resign. Theretofore the Jesuit superior general had served for life. But Pope John Paul II refused to accept Arrupe's resignation.

Somewhat more than a year later, on August 7, 1981, Don Pedro suffered a disabling stroke. The pope appointed a personal delegate from among the Jesuits as interim superior of the order passing over the man whom Arrupe had designated as his vicar general.

Two years later, at the election of his permanent successor Arrupe tendered his official resignation. In a moving farewell message to the assembled group, Don Pedro, limited now to halting speech, had these words read: "In these 18 years, my one ideal was to serve the Lord and his church. . . . I thank the Lord for the great progress I have witnessed in the society. Obviously there would be defects too—my own, to begin with—but it remains a fact that there was great progress, in personal conversion, in the apostolate, in concern for the poor, for refugees. And special mention must be made of the attitudes of loyalty and filial obedience shown toward the church and the Holy Father, particularly in these last years. For all of this thanks be to God."

We can only speculate on the last, silent years of Arrupe's life. The man who perhaps knew him best, his vicar general, Father Vincent O'Keefe of the New York Jesuit Province, says simply: "From his resignation as general until his death on February 5, 1991, Pedro Arrupe's life was one of silent prayer and suffering, of utter dependence on others for daily and devoted care, and of waiting patiently for his Lord. His speech had become more and more difficult and limited, but he said a great deal with his eyes and his face. . . . The man himself was the most striking message."

History will pass judgment on Pedro Arrupe's ultimate place in the Jesuit Order. Still, it seems clear already that his niche will be found alongside the great ones of that remarkable group, even that of the founder himself, Ignatius of Loyola.

It is universally agreed that Arrupe demonstrated a serenity of spirit in the midst of enormous pressures from inside and outside the order during his generalate. Such equanimity speaks of a deep relationship with God and reliance on the Holy Spirit—hallmarks of true sanctity. Further, he remained true to his commitment of service to the institutional church, even when tried sorely by that very organization. Such steadfastness, too, bespeaks a life of trust in God at work in and through the church, despite its sins.

Above all, it appears that history will accord to Arrupe the title "refounder of the Jesuits" for his great vision that integrated faith and justice. It was Arrupe's call to articulate that vision and see to its implementation among his brothers. This he did in all faithfulness throughout his life as their superior.

Said another way, Don Pedro came to understand the Last Judgment chapter of Matthew's gospel in social and universal terms. The hunger, thirst, nakedness, loneliness, and imprisonment, and our response to them which Jesus declared in that gospel passage as the final judgment on our lives, Arrupe saw not only in personal terms but in a societal and global sense as well. He called himself and his entire order to analysis, concern, and action around the indignities suffered by the least of humanity. In this the Society of Jesus will never be the same again.

On February 5, 1991, the day God called him to give an account of his stewardship, Pedro Arrupe could say in the words of the first Basque: "Take, O Lord, and receive all my liberty, my memory, my understanding and my entire will. Whatever I have or hold, you have given me; I restore it all to you and surrender it wholly." Arrupe had done just this throughout his life, in and through the circumstances of his special time in history.

Penny Lernoux

A Journey of Trust

by Tom Fox

*To choose what is difficult
all one's days
as if it were easy,
that is faith.*

— *W.H. Auden,
from* For the Time Being

With these words Penny Lernoux concluded her monumental book *Cry of the People* in 1980. One decade later they serve to summarize more than the struggling Latin American church of which she wrote. They speak of her own life and the spirit she brought to her work.

Penny Lernoux was a Christian journalist until she died, October 8, 1989, one month after being diagnosed with cancer. Her career inspired a generation as she moved from observer-reporter through gradual awakening into conversion and on to become an impassioned advocate for the poor of Latin America. Penny was always a professional, and her work was a public faith journey influenced by and paralleling that of the Latin American church. Thus, she was able to share with her audience—as no other journalist could—both suffering lives and messages of liberation and hope.

Penny's death in a New York state hospital left many friends and colleagues stunned and mourning, but, beyond the shock, also express-

---

Tom Fox is the publisher of the *National Catholic Reporter*. This article appeared in the December 1989 issue of *Sojourners*.

ing gratitude for the gift she had been—and the awakening she had stirred. She wrote courageously of courageous people, seldom leaving her readers unmoved. Class conflict, she learned two decades back, was a pervasive, ugly reality throughout Latin America. And she took sides—with the poor. Always factual, always thorough, Penny did not apologize for her partiality. And she was good at what she did. The best.

Editors sought her out. She wrote for *Harper's, Newsday, The Nation, Newsweek, Sojourners*, and the *National Catholic Reporter*. Her books, jam-packed with facts, detailed the ways powerful people and institutions oppress the powerless of Latin America: *Cry of the People* documented U.S.-supported persecution, *In Banks We Trust* examined crime in the international bank community and the weight of foreign debt on the Latin American poor, and *The People of God* looked at recent Vatican policies and their spirit-depressing impact on the increasingly independent churches of Latin America.

"All we can do is trust in God," Penny said as she concluded her shocking telephone conversation September 7 from her home in Colombia, where she lived and worked for the past 15 years. She had just shared the news of her recent cancer diagnosis. "Trust in God," she repeated.

Her worst fears had been confirmed. A biopsy of her hip contained cancer cells. For five months, she said that day, she had been suffering severe back pains. Doctors had advised rest and exercise to rid her of stress. She tried to comply, but the pains persisted. The cancer diagnosis had been an unexpected and devastating blow. She and her husband, Denis Nahum, quickly decided to fly to New York for further diagnosis at the Sloan-Kettering Institute.

Responding to the moment, the Maryknoll sisters, whom Penny much admired, helped with arrangements, taking her into their community in Ossining, New York. Penny had been working for two years on a book about the history of the Maryknoll nuns. She had finished dozens of interviews and had written six chapters.

The news the doctors continued to tell Penny was not good. Further examinations showed her primary cancer was in the lungs, and it had spread into her bones and liver. Penny, who had faced injustices head-on many times before, decided to fight the disease. She began chemotherapy even as her physical condition grew quickly weaker.

From Maryknoll she wrote me a letter two weeks before her death, ending with these words:

> I feel like I'm walking down a new path. It's not physical fear or fear of death, because the courageous poor in Latin America have taught me a theology of life that, through solidarity and our common struggle, transcends death. Rather, it is a sense of help-

lessness—that I who always wanted to be the champion of the poor am just as helpless—that I, too, must hold out my begging bowl; that I must learn—am learning—the ultimate powerlessness of Christ. It is a cleansing experience. So many things seem less important, or not at all, especially the ambitions. Peace and love, Penny.

Many times in recent weeks my mind has wandered through those words, often lingering on the phrase "the ultimate powerlessness of Christ." Penny had long learned from the Latin American poor the presence of a tender and caring Christ in their midst, in their very powerlessness. It was a faith act and, ironically, an empowering realization.

Journalists are a schizophrenic lot. Often they become wrapped up in the lives of those of whom they write, but they are also, in their very act of writing, removed from those lives. When compassion and love are involved, the distance can be painful.

Penny had grown close to the Latin American poor. She knew, however, that she had power they did not. She could cry out about injustice. They were powerless to do so. And thus, a form of separation, until almost the end. Until Penny, suffering grave illness, was powerless, too.

I was blessed to be able to see Penny one more time at Maryknoll. She had grown very weak. We held hands, saying little, sharing much. It was decided the time was right to bring her daughter, Angela, 11, up from Colombia. Her mother and sister flew in from Los Angeles. She spent two days with them and then lapsed again. She was taken to a hospital and on Sunday, shortly after midday, October 8, Penny Lernoux, 49, completed her earthly journey.

Penny first went to Latin America in 1962 to work with the U.S. Information Agency, the year the Second Vatican Council in Rome was getting under way and getting set to turn the church on its head. The council would soon have an enormous impact on Penny's life, although she had no clue at the time. She soon left the information agency to join Copley News Service, where she worked for a decade, reporting from Caracas, Buenos Aires, and Bogotá.

Raised a Catholic, she was distancing herself from the church during those years, as she explained in a letter she wrote to the Maryknoll Sisters Central Governing Board in December 1987, asking for permission to write the Maryknoll book:

My reasons for wanting to write about Maryknoll are personal and have to do with my faith commitment. I admire women and men from other religious orders, but I owe a special debt to Maryknoll because it was through your missionaries in Chile that I regained my Catholic faith. Although I was educated in Catholic schools, I began to drift away from the church after I arrived in Colombia in the early 1960s, before [the impact of] Vatican II. The institutional church seemed so wedded to the upper classes, particularly the Conservative Party.

My experience of this near-feudal institution was so painful that, for years afterward, I was estranged from the church. But in the early 1970s I came in contact with Maryknoll missioners in Chile, who showed me a different church—the church of the poor. It was through them that I became aware of and entered into another world—not that of the U.S. Embassy or the upper classes, which comprise the confines of most American journalists, but the suffering and hopeful world of the slums and peasant villages. The experience changed my life, giving me new faith and a commitment as a writer to tell the truth of the poor to the best of my ability.

There is a saying in this church of the poor: "You make your path by walking it."

Penny began to walk "in solidarity with the poor," as she would explain to those who cared to ask. And she was not alone.

Speaking at the University of Notre Dame in March 1989, Penny further explained the beginnings of her Latin American faith journey:

I think my own journey in search of a different, more mature faith paralleled that of many Latin Americans who stumbled along the rocky outcrops of a strange, new landscape that took form after the Second Vatican Council in the 1960s—a place where, as we Christians say in Latin America, we had to make our path by walking it in solidarity with the poor. Many incidents and accidents occurred along the way, but as I look back along that road, I see the hand of God on every signpost. As the bishops in Latin America have often said, the Holy Spirit was evident in the long-awaited awakening of the Latin American church.

Penny's earliest encounter with that awakening church came in Paraguay, she recalled. That was where she found church leaders actively promoting peasant leagues and other socio-political organizations. She met some remarkable religious leaders, she said, including Bishop Ramon Bogarin, one of the Latin American church's early defenders of poor peasants and slumdwellers as well as a strong supporter of the Latin American church's new "preferential option for the poor," a phrase coined at the historic 1968 gathering of Latin American bishops in Medellín, Colombia. It was an unexpected turning point for the church, one Penny missed because she was not yet tuned in to what was going on in the church, she noted.

But if Paraguay was the beginning of Penny's discovery of a recommitted faith, Chile and some Maryknoll missioners were "the cause of conversion."

She recalled at Notre Dame that she, like most other North American journalists, was initially suspicious of the leftist President Salvador Allende government because it had expropriated copper mines belonging to the U.S. multinationals. However, she also recognized in Allende's efforts a laudable attempt to redistribute income to benefit the poor.

Like the bishops of Medellín, she had gradually faced up to the reality of "institutionalized violence" against the poor majorities by governments of and for the rich. Chile was typical of the greed of the upper classes.

This was the lesson taught her by the missionaries working in Santiago's shantytowns. They introduced her, she said, to the "sounds, smells, hopes, and sufferings" of the underworld poor. "You can look at a slum or peasant village, and I had seen enough in my reporting, but it is only by entering into that world—by living in it— that you begin to understand what it is like to be powerless, to be like Christ."

Powerless and Christ-like. It was a riveting faith insight, one she would continue to carry in her work. The poor were no longer simply the subjects of her writing, not the objects of charitable acts, but rather educators and preachers of the Word, carrying experiences and messages needing to reach wider audiences. Penny had connected the powerlessness of the poor with the power of the gospels. She would hold that connection to the end of her life.

> Chile not only radically changed my reporting, but also led to my conversion to the church of the poor—the church of Medellín. Something similar happened to the bishops, many of whom had signed the Medellín documents without understanding the implications of such a radical shift from rich to poor.

It was a shift that led to persecution of the church, so much so that by the end of the 1970s more than 850 bishops, priests, and sisters had been killed, exiled, arrested and/or tortured. But the blood of martyrs was also having a positive effect by helping to awaken a generation of North American Christians to the urgent need for social justice in Latin America.

Through her writings, Penny had become a critical link between the churches and peoples of North and South America. Every year or two, she would return to the United States for speaking tours, talking in church halls, classrooms, and informal gatherings, wherever interest in Latin America was shown. She seemingly had endless energy, though her work, no doubt, took its toll.

She frequently spoke about the journey of "the people of God," the *pueblo,* or *povo de Deus*—meaning, in Latin America, "the masses, the poor." Whereas the church had previously encouraged fatalism, she explained, the church after Medellín was teaching the poor they were equal in the sight of God and should take history into their own hands by seeking political and economic changes.

Penny once recounted a particularly telling story of a meeting she had with Father Leonardo Boff, the Franciscan liberation theologian from Brazil. In 1975, both attended a Brazilian conference on base communities to which peasants and farm workers from all over Brazil had come.

"The military believed the communities to be subversive, since poor people were not supposed to question the regime's semifeudal system and the communities kept insisting on their civil rights," she wrote. As expected, police arrived to break up the gathering, but the presence of religious leaders, including Boff, kept them from acting. The church, she said, was providing "protective space in which the communities could breathe and grow."

In the church's new role as servant of the people, Penny explained, religious leaders made no attempt to direct the agenda but rather listened to the communities' needs and agreed to support their priorities. Boff, who served as "animator" at the gathering, noted to Penny that one of the greatest challenges he initially faced was learning to listen to the people in their own halting language.

Penny recognized that it was Boff's ability to listen—and pick up the agenda of the people—that gave strength and credence to his theological writings. This was because, she noted, those writings came "from the heart of the Brazilian poor."

Penny, it seemed, had learned another lesson. As a result, her journalism was to grow in strength and credence, too. Her agenda had come "from the heart of the Brazilian poor."

In recent years Penny, sharing Latin American concerns, had become increasingly upset by the rightward shift in the church, primarily the result of Vatican episcopal appointments. Newly appointed bishops were no longer emphasizing peace and justice and, instead, were talking personal piety. But through the tears she often laughed it off, repeating that there is no turning back, that faith and history compel the church forward.

Echoing the words of Brazil's Archbishop Helder Camara earlier this year, Penny encouraged us to stay the course with the poor. Revealing characteristic confidence—confidence derived from the people of God, she stated:

I believe that those who seek a new path, whether in the church or secular society, should not expect roses but must be prepared to endure the prophet's life in the desert. Yet, as the archbishop [Camara] notes, "The desert also blooms"—as we have seen in Latin America. . . . Meanwhile those of us committed to the church of Medellín and to Vatican II must continue the struggle. Sometimes it is hard, as I know from my reporting on the church in Latin America, but I also believe it is the only way to remain steadfast to Christ's vision.

No, never easy, but possible—with faith.
Thank you, Lord God, who hears the cry of the poor, for the gift of Penny Lernoux.

VI

Blessed Are the Pure in Heart

Joan Chittister

The Fullness of Grace

Joan Chittister, O.S.B., is former executive director of the Alliance for International Monasticism and the author of many books on Christian spirituality. She was interviewed in March 1987 by Joyce Hollyday at the Mount Saint Benedict Priory in Erie, Pennsylvania, during her tenure as prioress there and as president of the Conference of American Benedictine Prioresses.

You are part of a tradition that goes back more than 1,500 years, and one of the major aspects of that tradition is the importance of community. Religious life has always taken the shape of community. Could you talk a little bit about why that is so?

The function of the Christian community in sharing the bedrock of Christian spirituality is the upbuilding, the co-creation of the kingdom; the bringing of the kingdom now, the bringing of now to the kingdom. So, like the community recorded in the book of Acts, the major witness of the new Christian community is the creation of an alternative way of life.

Benedict of Nursia, founder of the Benedictines, deepened his own spirituality to the point that he had a new vision of the Christian life. He looked around post-Constantinian Rome and saw a well established, politicized church. It was a church that had been made church

by virtue of the baptism of the emperor and his decree that all his subjects would likewise be baptized.

An analogy would be an emperor who was a basketball player
decreeing that basketball should be the only sport in the empire. So
everybody plays it; but that doesn't make everybody a basketball player. So the emperor decreed that everybody was Christian, but that
didn't make everybody a Christian. Benedict was immersed therefore
in a "pagan Christian" culture.

Although the Edict of Constantine in 313 liberated Christianity in
Europe, it also began the murky merger of the sacred and the secular.
And that's been as much a burden as it has been a blessing.

That's the environment which young Benedict of Nursia saw 150
years later in the late fifth century in Rome. He didn't attempt to convert Rome. We have no history of Benedict of Nursia preaching in the
streets, approaching the government, or going to church figures; he
simply left Rome to begin an alternative way of living.

He provided a sign and a choice—not an argument or a program.
And that sign and choice is the Christian community at the level of a
radical dimension of love.

What is the radical dimension of love? It is the sign that strangers
can become sisters and brothers in Christ.

And what's the power of this community today? We've never had a
more fragmented world, or a more pseudo-nationalistic world, or a
more chauvinistic world. And so if monasteries and convents and
intentional religious communities are a sign of anything, they're a
sign that you can transcend all the differences, all the barriers, all the
impossibilities, all the things that people say can't come together.

Monasteries are a collection of all the differences of the world made
one in Christ. And that's the nature of communal spirituality. It's
reflecting in the contemporary community, in the ongoing Christian
community, what was the sign and model of the community of Acts.

*Could you comment on the role of prayer in your community specif-
ically, and in the life of any community? How have you developed a
spirituality of community?*

We all, I believe, accept the notion that the function of prayer is not
to cajole God into saving us from ourselves. The function of prayer is
not magic. The function of prayer is not bribery of the Infinite. The
function of prayer is not to change the mind of God.

The function of prayer is to change my own mind, to put on the
mind of Christ, to enable grace to break into me. So, if you're going to
have a communal spirituality and witness, then you must have a
praying community.

The monastic community has a prayer life, developed around what
St. Benedict called the *opus dei* and what the churches traditionally

called the "divine office," what we now call the "liturgy of the hours." It's the speaking of the psalm life of the people of God for our own time.

The psalm life has three dimensions: personal, national, and global. The psalmist prays out of the struggles of the psalmist, out of the struggles of the people, and out of the consciousness of the cosmic, of the universal: "All nations shall stream to you"; "You shall see the poor"; "In you are all things." So, this prayer life of a Benedictine monastic community is equally conscious on all three levels.

I'm here as an individual intent on contemplative conversion, intent on developing in my life over a period and process of time the ability to see with the eyes of Christ, and to put on the mind of Christ. I'm here as part of a community that claims to be a Christian community, and therefore has to struggle with its interpersonal agendas, with the life needs of one another, with being something other than itself. In order to do something, I have to be something. In order to be for someone else, I have to be part of a group. And then finally, we're here praying out of consciousness for the whole global community, for all the people of God.

To some the notion of monastic life is a phenomenally well-institutionalized narcissism. It is precisely the opposite. If and when it ever becomes that, it's at its most decadent. When monastic life is life only for the monastics, then it ceases to be monastic life. That's the paradox of it. When prayer is privatized religion on a spree, it's not prayer.

What is the contemplative life? In the first place, "contemplation" and "enclosure" are not synonyms. Enclosed communities are not necessarily called to be any more contemplative than my own community. Enclosure is a vehicle for contemplation. But so is stopping by the beaten person on the roadside.

The oldest mystics that we have in organized religious expression— the fathers and mothers from the desert, the gurus of the Sufi tradition, the masters among the Hasidim—all have similar parabolic insights into contemplation.

There is a story about the master saying to the disciples, "Tell me how you know when it is dawn." And one disciple says, "Master, is it when we can tell the fig tree from the lemon tree at one hundred paces?" And the master says to the disciple, "No, that is not how you will know it is dawn." So a second disciple says, "Well then, master, is it when you can tell the sheep from the goats at fifty paces?" And the master says, "No, that is not how we shall know when it is dawn." Then the third disciple says, "Well then, master, how do we know that we have seen the dawn?" And the master says, "We will know that we have seen the dawn when we can see the face of Christ in the face of any brother or sister, no matter how near or how far."

That's contemplation. That's the fruit of the contemplative life. And unless you're putting on the mind of Christ, I don't know if you'll ever

see the face of the Christ in the other, or the face of the cosmic, or the
face of the people of God in the other. You may be a highly efficient
social worker or a marvelously compassionate do-gooder, but you will
not necessarily be a Christian contemplative.

*You have been at the forefront of issues dealing with women in the
church, and you've seen the role of women in the church go through a
lot of change through the years. But even though the understanding of
ministry for women is changing and expanding, women in the Catholic
church are still denied ordination. How do you think this situation will
be resolved?*

You cannot have a changed understanding of the notion of ministry
for women until you have a changed understanding of the notion of the
personhood of women. The question is simply, what is a woman for?

And the answer is not from biology. It's from Shakespeare. It's
Shylock's answer in *The Merchant of Venice:* "If you prick us, do we
not bleed? If you tickle us, do we not laugh? If you poison us, do we not
die?" The answer is, "I am fully human. Therefore, I am fully graced
by God. Therefore, I am fully called by God."

When they baptize a woman they don't say, "Now we pour this slightly diluted water on this slightly diluted creature who will give us slightly diluted Christianity—or ministry or service—back." When they bring
the girl up to confirm her, and she stands next to the little boy who is
her peer and colleague in this great Christian moment, they don't tap
him on the cheek and say, "You are confirmed to do battle for Christ our
Lord and the spreading of the faith," and then look at her and say, "You
are almost allowed to do battle for Christ our Lord in faith."

Someplace along the line, the effects of the sacraments are going to
have to be able to be manifested in the ministries, as much for a
woman as for a man. There's either something wrong with the present theology of ministry, or there is something wrong with the present
theology of all the sacraments. If women qualify for baptism, confirmation, salvation, and redemption, how can they be denied the sacrament of ministry?

*Can you say something about how women's understanding of spiri-
tuality is changing our understanding of God and our use of language?*

My professional background is in social psychology and communication theory. Ten years ago I wrote my first article on that subject and
called it "Brotherly Love in the Roman Catholic Church." What I tried to
point out in that article is the notion that language structures thought.

The basic principle is that what is not in the language is not in the
mind. So if you are ignoring women in church language, or lumping
women under a so-called generic term which is only generic half of the
time, then what you have done is erase half the population of the earth.

They can exist only when somebody else calls them into existence. So half of us are left to figure out when they mean us and when they don't.

That's why in the Hebrew tradition the idea of naming, of giving identity to, is a very important part of the theology. And we recognize it at that level. But we have failed to recognize it when we say, "Dearly beloved brethren, let us pray for the grace to recognize that we are all sons of God."

I never got that grace—that's how I'm sure that kind of intercession doesn't work. I remember from the time I was 5 years old, looking around the church, knowing that they had forgotten somebody; they'd forgotten me, and I was in the church. I was not a son of God. I was a daughter of God and very comfortable with that.

The whole notion that the language comes out of a woman's envy of men is ridiculous! It comes out of a woman's recognition of the greatness of the creation of womanhood. If God could afford to make us separately, then it seems somebody could talk to us separately.

As I read the tale, God addressed Adam and Eve separately. God didn't call up Abraham and say, "I just presume Sarah will get her part of the message." Throughout creation history there has been direct confirmation of the fact that God and a woman can have direct conversation and contact. We've lost that in our languages; and then we act as if it's not important.

Linguists can tell from a language what is important to a people. They may find archaeological elements they cannot account for in the language. They'll know that those elements were not important to the culture, and the people's way of thinking subsumed multiple things under other categories.

The Eskimos have 18 separate words for snow, because snow is central in Eskimo life. Americans have at least that many words for car. We call them hatchback and Taurus and Ford, Diplomat and Regal and Oldsmobile and Chevy. The language for car in this country is almost unlimited.

But when you ask for two pronouns for the human race, they tell you you're going too far! The only thing that a woman can conclude is that she is not as important as the multiple kinds of cars, and wood, and fishing poles in the world—let alone guns.

When you look at that from a broader theological construct, you begin to look at language about God. You cannot understand the problem about God language unless you are willing to realize that it is not that we are just discovering a feminine dimension of God; it is that the recognition of the feminine dimension of God, a cosmic dimension of God, has been suppressed.

It isn't that we shouldn't call God "Father." It is that we shouldn't call God only Father. It isn't that Jesus wasn't male. It is that Jesus was a great deal more than male.

The oldest, most basic, most traditional theologies I know do not claim that Jesus came to become male. Jesus came to be flesh. And when you subsume all of theological language, all God talk, in male terms, then you have lost a sense not only of who and what woman is, but who and what God is.

We are in a state of great linguistic, and therefore great theological, paucity. We have reduced God to one of the tiniest elements of creation. And we say that's everything God is. That is heresy raised to a fine art.

The new calf in the desert is maleness. While Moses ascends to do dialogue with the transcendent spiritual God, the people in the desert below turn God into a golden calf. And while we claim great spiritual insight and full revelation in the churches, and sophisticated understanding for our creative God, we have turned God into a male.

The scriptures don't do that. The oldest litanies of the church don't do it. Right up until the last century, God was multiple images. God was rock, God was mother, God was hen, God was creator, God was mighty, God was love, God was all of the divine praises.

I can remember having to stretch my little mind when we said great litanies in the Catholic school. I can remember being a third grader just unable to take in this God. I knew God was ineffable. Because when Sister prayed with us, she told us God was all these things.

Now if you dare to assume that "Sophia Wisdom," the feminine side of God, is still with us, you touch the raw edge of an insecure male church. And that's a shame, it's a great disservice to God.

Prior to the Babylonian captivity, we see many more images for God in scripture than we do afterward. Because apparently—and this is speculation by some of the historians—there was a great concern not to have Judaism confused with the pagan ritual and worship of the Canaanites.

Nevertheless, the notion of wisdom in the scripture was clearly recognized as the feminine side of God. In Proverbs, wisdom is always a female figure. For example, from Proverbs 4: "Get wisdom, get understanding, do not forget or turn aside from the words I utter. Forsake her not, and she will preserve you. Love her, and she will safeguard you. Get wisdom at the cost of all you have. Get understanding, extol her and she will exalt you. She will bring you honors if you will embrace her."

Isaiah also uses feminine references for God. Jeremiah uses feminine references. Jesus uses feminine references. And the church in its early litanies used cosmic references, or non-gendered references, always.

It's in our own time, in the attempt to keep women in their place, to make sure that the full creation does not break out in a woman, that language is used to keep reminding her that she is not as normative of

God as a man is—because God is Father, therefore God is male, therefore males are closer to God. Language is a key function in bringing women to the fullness of creation.

What is happening to women as they're rediscovering their closeness to God and the part of God within them, and as the language and women's understanding of their place in the church are changing?

I think a great new sense of grace is coming into women. I know people want to attach a secular language to it—that it is aggressive, or at least assertive, or it is uppity or out of line. But I think it's what happens to a person who comes face to face with the grace of God in life.

I think it's what happened to Mary the mother of God. I think you become capable of anything. And no system, no matter how sincere, can ever again convince you that your relationship to God must be mediated by a man, or that God doesn't want to deal directly with you. Or that God certainly doesn't want you to have the fullness of grace. Somehow you begin to know that what is going on inside you is of God. It's both a center and channel of grace. And that's extremely important.

And with that happening to women, there's also a wholeness that's coming to the church that hasn't been there in a long time.

I really believe that. I haven't seen anything yet that walks well on one leg. And I honestly believe that we're going to be a truer church when we recognize in one another, in *every* other, the call of God to total fullness.

It just has to happen, because we complement one another. But you and I complement one another as much as you and any male minister complement one another. We are all small pieces of the mind and face of God. And as long as we are erasing half of us, we're never going to get a full picture of God.

You have said that contemplation sometimes means binding up the wounded person along the road. Would you say more about what you mean by that?

If the contemplative life has to bring us to an awareness of the presence of God and a consciousness of the mandates of Jesus, how else can you purport to live a contemplative life? Contemplation is not an excursion into the "airy fairy."

Contemplation is an immersion into the mind of God and the life of Christ to such an extent that the way you live your own life can never again be quite the same. That's why people change. Because they're drawing from a different set of values and a different goal.

The goal is the building up of the kingdom where the widows are cared for, orphans are loved, the measures are equal, dreaming is possible, and everybody is brought to the fullness of life. If you're living the contemplative life, then eventually you have to come face to face with your obligation to be touched by all those dimensions.

That's why Thomas Merton had the most contemporary prayer life in the world. That's why you ought to be able to go to any enclosed monastery and get good counsel about your own life and the circumstances of the world you're living in.

There's a historian who said that the monastery confronts the castle with a question mark. The values that are derived from the contemplative life are the filter through which the contemplative sees the world. And they are consequently the critique that the contemplative brings to the constructs and institutions of a society. These values should never be "other than" or "out of" the world. The world should be seen through those values. And the contemplative speaks of the incongruity of those values.

As a result, you have to be part of the binding up of the wounds of the world. And you can do it in many, many ways. You can do it by critiquing the world, if you live in an enclosed community. You can do it by restructuring the world, if you live in an active community or a monastic community. You can do it by providing alternative models for the world. You can do it by working within the world. How you do it doesn't matter, but you must do it. It cannot *not* be done.

I have the sense that your community's prayer life and ministry life are very integrated, and that they grow out of each other. I often hear people who describe themselves as Christian activists ask, "Where do I find time for my prayer life, or how do I integrate prayer into ministry, or how do I find balance in my life?" Could you address that?

I certainly can, because if there's any question that we go through regularly, it is that one. In the first place, I can tell you that after years of experience of community living, and with all the change that came with renewal, and all the major issues that we are grappling with in this world, you do not *find* time for prayer. Nobody finds time for prayer. You either take time for it or you don't get it. If I am waiting for it to be given to me, it shall never be given.

I think if I reach that point I have begun the last trek down a very short road. Because the fuel runs out. The energy goes down. I become my own enemy. I can no longer remember why I ever decided to do this. And if I can't remember why I decided to do it, I can't figure out how I can go on with it. Because I'm tired, and the vision just gets dimmer and dimmer.

On days when I have worn myself out most in behalf of peacemaking and women, I have gone to bed knowing that when I get up the next day, we will still be a militaristic society, and sexism will still reign. So if I take an additional thirty minutes away from the problem, not only will the problem still be there, but I will probably be able to spend the next day on it, which I couldn't have done otherwise.

I had a spiritual director who used to say, "The empty vessel must be filled." And those of us who think we can go on forever pouring ourselves out without at the same time filling ourselves up need to read the seventh chapter of Benedict on the rule of humility. The first degree of humility is to allow God to be God. And we're just not going to be able to do it without becoming a more contemplative part of this ongoing cycle of development.

So, what does all that mean? It means that prayer, in my opinion, is absolutely essential both to consciousness and to serenity. And that our important work will be done with more impact and import if we bring to it our best selves. And our best selves come when we are calling ourselves to conversion in the scriptures, and constantly putting on the mind of Christ. Balance is something we have to achieve for the sake of the long haul.

You're talking about prayer mostly in terms of nurturing ourselves. But we are people who are very connected to the world's suffering and believe in a God who hears the cries of the poor and those who clamor for justice. And we believe that God hears our cries for justice as well. We offer petitions and intercessions. Can you talk about that kind of prayer in relationship to our ministry, in relationship to the suffering that we see?

The scripture tells us very clearly that God hears the cry of the poor. And God notes it and records it and watches. And on the basis of that hearing, God will someday judge what *we* did with the cries *we* heard.

Prayer asks for the strength to respond, for the insight to know, for the grace to do, and for the courage to endure. And I believe God gives us all those things. When we become conscious of those needs, we have the promise, "Ask and you shall receive," and the assurance of God's presence with us.

We're not talking to the great cornucopia God. If that were our theology, we would soon have to begin to doubt our God. The grace has come, the strength has come, the awareness has come, the courage has come, the repentance has come, both for us who are rich and for the poor who know that their ultimate salvation is in God. In the meantime, you and I are praying for the grace to get through our own smallness so that we too can hear the cry of the poor, and change our own lives accordingly, because God is hearing and God will judge on the basis of those cries.

I think many of us who are active in ministry and in touch with people's suffering find it easy to offer petitions and difficult to offer praise.

We have so many visions for change that it's difficult to see what we have and be thankful.

That comment is related to the place of joy in the Christian community and the notion of recognizing the signs of hope. Hope is a phenomenal Christian virtue. And not to be able to praise is not to be able to hope.

That's one of the ways in which the poor evangelize us to such a depth, because in many instances they're not complaining about the things we're complaining about for them. They know what the necessities of life really are. They know when they have them, and they know how demanding of praise those things become.

So if we lose sight of praise, either we are not seeing the presence of God in our world, we have failed to note the distinction between needs and wants, or we are on the brink of thinking that only what we call good is what God calls good. Or we've lost a sense of time. We want everything in our time instead of in the fullness of time.

Scripture says that the great good—Jesus—only came in the fullness of time. We don't know when the fullness of time is for anything. We must live in praise that we've done what we can to contribute to the coming of the fullness of time.

So, should there be intercessory prayer? You bet. And does God wait to hear or respond to the needs? Yes. And are we both breaking open ourselves and the consciousness of the cosmic in intercessory prayer? Of course. But we are also recognizing in praise that we've received a lot of things that we never thought to pray for, because God is God and loves us and continually builds up our hope in the fullness of time by the things we weren't even smart enough, holy enough, to recognize that we needed.

There's a great Sufi story about a seeker who was tramping around the world looking to find the true God. She was examining all religions and all communities and all manifestations of religion to determine when she had discovered that perfect manifestation of God in life. In one of her trips, she stopped at the monastery and she said to the monastic, "Tell me, does your God work miracles?" And the elder said, "Well, it all depends on how you define a miracle. Some people think that it is a miracle if God does the will of people. But here in this community, we think a miracle is when people do the will of God."

That's my theology in a nutshell. Of course we cry out to God with what we believe are our needs, knowing that God will always respond to our needs. But the question is, what do we really need?

The purpose of that is not to rationalize suffering. And it is not intended to deter us from dealing with suffering on the human level. On the contrary, we deal out of our concern for the fullness of the kingdom, knowing that the fullness will come in God's good time.

Elias Chacour

Beyond All Boundaries

You won't find it on the map of Israel unless the map is a remarkably good one, but if you draw a line between Haifa and the western bulge of the sea of Galilee, Ibillin is a quarter of the way from Haifa. This village of 5,500 Palestinians is atop a mound that, were you to dig through it layer by layer, would tell the story of life and faith in this contested land back to very ancient times. But the face of the past is largely buried, apart from a bit of a Crusader castle wall that was unearthed a few years ago when the villagers were building a community center.

Yet there are living monuments: the olive trees with their silvery gray-green leaves and gnarled, cratered trunks. Some on the hillside just south of Ibillin are more than 2,000 years old. It may be that Jesus, his family, and disciples ate olives from these ancient trees that, well-tended across the centuries, are still producing fruit.

Ibillin is a Christian and Moslem town. Two thousand of the villagers are Moslem, 3,000 Greek Orthodox, and 500 Melkite (Roman Catholics of the Eastern liturgical rite). The Melkite priest, a man well known throughout Galilee, is Fr. Elias

Chacour. He is a gray-robed man in his middle years with a thick, jutting black beard, piercing gray eyes, and a contagious energy.

Chacour doesn't fit either Christian or Palestinian stereotypes. A Palestinian who well understands the anger that occasionally leads to violence on the part of the Palestinian minority in Israel, an anger he shares, Chacour is a pacifist. Again and again he draws attention to a talk given some centuries ago on a hillside not far from Ibillin—the Sermon on the Mount.

A Catholic priest of tremendous dedication, Chacour is impatient with Christians' preoccupation with their differences and their shrines—"holy stones and holy sands," he says with impatience. His attention is entirely with living people. To the occasional bewilderment of his fellow Christians, including members of the hierarchy, Chacour has devoted himself to founding community centers, libraries, and kindergartens, in addition to his parish responsibilities. He organizes summer camps for Palestinian villagers in Galilee which are used by everyone—Moslem, Druze, Catholic, and Orthodox. This interview was conducted in Galilee in June 1980 by Jim Forest.

When did you first encounter the Israeli government?

I think I was six years old. My father told us—we were six children—that in a country called Germany there had been "a cruel Satan killing Jews." Of course we knew little about faraway places. We Palestinians had come out from under the slavery of the Turks, and then the British Mandate, ignoring almost everything else in the world. But nobody could ignore Germany, even if that nation was at the end of the earth.

Father said there were Jewish soldiers who had escaped from Germany and that they would be coming to our village, Ba'ram, in the north of Galilee. He said some of them wanted to settle near us. As Christians, he said, we must welcome them, help them, and give them food and drink.

When the soldiers came, he told us they would need to sleep in our beds, and he asked us to sleep on the roof. And we children gladly accepted this—it was fun to sleep on the roof! We thought of the soldiers as our guests. For the first time in my life I saw father slaughtering a sheep to prepare a feast. It was like this throughout the village, and the soldiers stayed in every house. It was the consensus to accept them.

But a few days later, the keys to the doors were collected by an officer. For security reasons, he said, we must all leave for a few days. He would be guardian for our village. Then we could come back.

We accepted this. People like my father never thought our guests could play an ugly game with us. So we left and for several days lived in the open, under olive trees. I remember it was very, very cold at night. Then my father managed to find us a cave. After that we went to an abandoned village, where our whole family lived in one room of a deserted house.

What was to be a few days became weeks and then months and now it is thirty years.

And now Ba'ram is only ruins. How was it destroyed?

When the elders realized the Israeli army had fooled us, when we saw that all our furniture had been taken away and that we were expelled—such a reward from our guests!—we applied to the Israeli Supreme Court of Justice in Jerusalem, and at last we won the case.

But when we asked the army to implement the court's order, the soldiers refused. Their own court! We applied to the court a second time, and in 1951 we won again. When this happened, the Prime Minister, Ben Gurion, ordered the destruction of the village. On Christmas morning it was bombed, and then bulldozers swept away what was left.

When those in your family realized they could not soon return home, where did you go?

To Gish, also in the north of Galilee. My parents are still there and many others of Ba'ram. From there I was sent to a boarding school in Haifa.

And your education after that?

Then a secondary school in Nazareth. Later my archbishop sent me for studies in Paris: philosophy and theology in preparation for ordination to the priesthood. In 1965, I was ordained in Nazareth. Afterward I went to Jerusalem and studied Bible and the Talmud at the Hebrew University. Finally, I went to Geneva, where I spent a year with the World Council of Churches completing a doctorate in ecumenical studies.

Have you had other childhood experiences which have shaped your understanding of belonging to a minority?

There is one event I can never forget. I was perhaps ten or twelve at the time. There was a telephone wire running on the ground in Gish. One morning it had been cut, and a section of it was missing. Soldiers came and accused some of the children, including myself.

They took us, and then gathered our parents and grandparents, our entire families. Then they said horrible things: "You are worth nothing, your children are worth nothing, you are doing underground work, your children are thieves and you are the teachers of theft. . . ." Words like these.

Then, before our elders, the soldiers beat us with sticks. Our parents did not dare interfere. At the end, a soldier said to me, "Now bring that piece of wire to me." I went to my father and asked. "Father, where should I go?" Then the soldier thought my father must have the wire, so he began to curse and accuse him.

But to whom could I go and ask this question? I was innocent, but even my mother did not know what to believe. The next day my father and I were taken to a police station in a Jewish town, and they threatened us with prison if we did not confess and return the wire.

When we returned, I remember mother made a few sweets for me, saying, "If you took it, tell me where it is." But I didn't know! A week later it was discovered that the wire had been cut by a bus. The soldiers got the wire from the driver who had taken it back to his home in another town. But for us in our village there was never an apology. Why? Because we were just Arabs.

Experiences like this must be rather common. And the effect must be deeply embittering.

It is amazing. You will not believe it. While of course some grow an attitude of revenge—to do it back to the other, to do it worse—others become disgusted and do not want to see these things done again. They try to act in the opposite way.

Many of us Palestinian Arabs do not allow ourselves any feelings of hatred, although we will never give up our rights, and we question many things.

We will even turn to God and ask, "How can you allow this to happen?" It is understandable. Our people have always trusted God in everything that happened. "Why now do you mislead us?" we ask. Yet even now there is this effort not to hate, not to take revenge.

Every year people come to Israel—the Holy Land—and yet seem unaware of the people who live here today.

Yes, they come to see the holy stones and holy sands. They do not care much for the people. We have many basilicas to take their time, and even now there are new ones being built. It reflects a church mentality of triumphalism, a priority in the churches for stones and antiquities.

On the other side, there are the tourists and pilgrims who are much more interested in the phenomenon of the Jewish state. It's new. It has something to do with Europe. There is the guilt complex of the European Christians about what has been allowed to happen to the Jews. There is a wish, mainly in Germany, that Israel do what Europe was unable to do. And to these visitors the Arabs within Israel do not exist except as *enfants terribles*, as terrorists. We do not exist.

Speaking of terrorists, it is remarkable that so far this morning there have been no jets flying over the Galilee to drop bombs in Lebanon. There have been many the last few days. Do you get used to this?

At first it was terrible. Now it is our daily bread. We know these are bombs for our heads. For Palestinians. With these jets they can kill more innocent people in a single day than all the Palestinian soldiers kill in a year. Yet it is the Palestinians alone who are said to be terrorists.

One thing strikes me about the Palestinian people. We have never been colonizers. We have been satisfied with our land. We have never wanted to conquer any other nation, although others have always tried to conquer us. Yet not once have the conquerers stayed. Not one has remained forever here. Egyptians, Romans, Greeks, Babylonians, Assyrians, Crusaders, Turks, British: they all came, and they all have disappeared.

Yet Palestinians seem very new to nationalism.

Nationalism in the Middle East began with the end of World War II and the dismemberment of the Ottoman Empire. The Arab states were stubborn and resisted Jewish existence here, and this did much to help the Jews found their separate state. Then in reaction to Jews becoming so radical, so fanatical, so Zionist in the negative sense, the Palestinians became more and more radical and nationalistic.

It is true there was little Palestinian national expression forty years ago. We were part of the Middle East. But this does not mean that today Palestinians have no right to a state, to nationhood, to existence on their own land.

What of the Jewish religious claim to the land?

Many Jews truly believe they are fulfilling God's will, that they are fulfilling ancient prophecies: "God gave us the land thousands of years ago, and we are coming back. These ugly Palestinians have no right to be here." They forget we gave our name to the land of Palestine even before the Jews came. And they forget that the Holy Land was promised to Abraham and his descendants—all of them. If [Israeli Prime Minister Menachem] Begin is one of the descendants of Abraham because he is a son of Isaac, I too am a descendant of Abraham because I am a son of Ishmael. We are all Abraham's children.

What makes the Palestinian children of Abraham so sad is the realization that we are being made to pay the cost of what other people, not we, have done to the Jews. We have felt solidarity with the Jews because we are both people who have been often persecuted. And now we, not the Europeans, become the victims of the children of the martyrs of Auschwitz.

What do you see in the future regarding relations between Palestinians and Jews? Is healing possible?

I don't believe it is impossible. But Zionist ideology does not allow another people within Israel equal footing. It is not an ideology of tolerance, or equality. This is troubling.

The Palestinian Charter can be criticized, but its basic idea is to have a democratic, secular state with no official religion and no raising of one people over another. The idea of a Jewish state in which others are barely tolerated, this must be changed. Otherwise, as they say in the Talmud, we non-Jews will have a *britah*—a footnote in the margins about how to deal with us.

We in the West have little sense of connection with Palestinian or Arab culture. Through films, books, and personal encounters, we feel connected with Judaism and Israel as a Jewish state. But there is no Palestinian equivalent to The Diary of Anne Frank *or* Leon Uris' Exodus. *Instead, all we have is a terrorist image of Palestinians, or perhaps an idea of people who lived on a land but neglected it.*

Why are the Jews so well known in your countries? Because for two thousand years they were there, in the Diaspora, while we Palestinians were at home. The Jews are well known because they have had a strong, effective lobby in the United States and Europe.

And, to speak plainly, they have benefited because Europe has wanted to get rid of the Jews and, since Hitler, the remnants of the Jews: "Go away, wherever you want, and you will get from us all kinds of help. You can have weapons. You can steal warships from France. You can have heavy water for nuclear reactors from Belgium. Anything you want. But go away." This Western "sympathy" for Jews is another way of getting rid of them.

I remember a Swiss professor who was angry at a PLO attack on a Swiss Air jetliner. "You Palestinians are welcome to throw bombs in Tel Aviv and Haifa and Jerusalem, but in Zurich, in a Swiss airplane, no!" I told that Swiss friend, "I prefer that every Swiss airplane, if they are empty, be exploded rather than one Jew or Palestinian be wounded. The airplanes are not worth a single drop of human blood."

How do you humanize the Palestinian image so that there is more in the Western perception than a political killer? It seems to me every PLO raid that kills more children or bystanders only reconsecrates the terrorist image.

The image can be changed in two ways. One is the way of the Sermon on the Mount of Jesus Christ, which, let us admit, is a slow way, a way many, including most people in the West, do not think is efficient. The other way, sadly enough, is the violent way, which is also used in your countries.

And I have to ask you: Without those bombs and terrorist actions, would the world acknowledge any right of the Palestinian people? Would you notice that we even exist? Would we be anything but poor refugees? What else has made you look at us?

It is true in every country that one person with a bomb can draw more attention in five minutes than a thousand unarmed people in a month. But is not the Israeli government glad that the Palestinians are noticed only as a people of violence? The Israeli counterviolence, even if it kills many more people, then only seems part of the game.

Ask why! What is on your TV, what is in your newspapers? Is it our fault you see only the killing? Until a few years ago, you were unable to say, "I saw a good Palestinian on television."

In 1974, a Dutch television station made a program about how we Palestinians in Israel were organizing kindergartens and libraries despite the complete lack of public help. The program never mentioned discrimination or the problems between Jews and Palestinians. But one letter protested the program as Nazi because it dared to give a positive impression of the Palestinians.

I think your libraries and kindergartens are far more threatening to some than guns and dynamite.

You are not the first to say that. The prime minister's adviser on Arab affairs once said, "It is more dangerous to give Fr. Chacour the opportunity to provide Arabs with books than to give him a bomb to throw in a Jewish shop." He's definitely right. With a bomb you kill. With books you can make people aware of their own responsibility. But perhaps he thought of that only as leading toward vengeance. Responsibility can also lead people toward forgiveness.

Why have you spent so much time founding libraries?

Three-quarters of our young people are under twenty-eight. Our future depends on the opportunities they have. I did some research earlier and discovered that every young person here, and it is true in other villages of Galilee, has six to eight empty hours a day—sitting on street corners, playing with stones, waiting for nothing—growing bitter thinking of the opportunities young Jews have in neighboring villages raised on confiscated lands.

I wanted to find an alternative for this empty time. Each time a young person accepts a book, you have given meaning to twenty hours in his or her life, and perhaps have done more than that. In this one small village, we have every day one hundred twenty to one hundred fifty persons taking books home from the library.

I remember what my father said when he realized it was a trick and that we had been driven from our village. "Don't forget to return, even if at the end of your life, but to do that never use the same means that were used against us."

I believe that that foolish man of Galilee, Jesus Christ, had something to tell us, to tell me. Not considering his existence here, I would immediately go into despair. Immediately. And forgetting him, I would first despair of the institutional church and its hierarchy and only later, of the Jews.

We have tried violence. We have tried wars. We are sure that wars will bring wars. I am sure that the attempt to kill the Arab mayors on the West Bank in early June will bring more killings of Jews. I am sure. It's a vicious circle. It's the logic of violence.

We know where violence leads. Even if we are not certain where we are going with nonviolence, let us try it. At least that. At least we can be sure with nonviolent action that, even if we are destroyed ourselves, we will not destroy any other person.

You said that, if you despaired, it would be first with the institutional church. Why?

It is painful to say, but we clergy, if we read the New Testament at all, read it only as an instrument of instruction for the people, not to be instructed ourselves. You know the churches here in Israel are the most wealthy churches in the world. At the top. But there is a divorce between the institution and the people. The people get very little from the wealth of the church. Where all that huge amount of money goes, only God and the hierarchy know.

What, in general, is your advice to the traveler in Israel?

Do not suffice yourself with holy antiquities. Jesus is not in Jerusalem. He is not there, he is risen. The Holy Sepulcher is only a reminder of a person who is not there. To touch Jesus Christ, to have contact with him, is only possible through his living brothers, his living sisters, the community.

We Christians in Galilee have a vocation to behave beyond all confessional and denominational boundaries, to try to behave as Christ behaved, to represent the living, risen Christ to all who come searching for him. We do not have to show you that we are reformed, or re-reformed, or not-yet-reformed, or Roman Catholic, or Orthodox. That should mean nothing to us here in Galilee. What means something is that the man of Galilee is risen and is still alive.

What is it, in working for peace here, that you, a Palestinian Christian priest, hope to say to your Jewish neighbors?

I want to say: You can take our lands, you can take our houses, you can kill us. But you cannot take our hearts with violence. Impossible! I hope you will try to have our hearts in the way described by Antoine de Saint-Exupéry in *The Little Prince*—"to tame each other"—not with bombs, but with silence, contemplation, and one's own conversion. We have to tame each other. There is no alternative if we are to survive. We go on killing until there is no one left, or we choose to survive together.

Howard Thurman

In Love with Life

by Julie Polter and Marvin Chandler

Howard Thurman, minister, theologian, and teacher, was a spiritual commentator on a wide range of issues—segregation and racism, relationships between religions, the nourishment of the inner life, and God's special word to the outcast, to name but a few.

Although he was a revered mentor to many in the civil rights movement, and a source of wisdom and inspiration for both contemplatives and activists of numerous creeds, Howard Thurman remains remarkably unknown to many others in the church. This is a great loss, for his story and his words provide rich food for the soul and mind.

Born in 1900, Howard Thurman was raised in the close-knit black community of segregated Daytona, Florida, by his mother and grandmother (his father died when Thurman was a boy). Despite the barriers put up by racism and the lack of funds, he passionately pursued his education, graduating from Atlanta's Morehouse College and then Rochester Theological Seminary.

Thurman was ordained as a Baptist minster, but he only served two years in that denomination before pursuing what would be a life spent in many different faith settings. During his far-flung career he served

---

Julie Polter is an Associate Editor of *Sojourners*.
Marvin Chandler, a workshop leader and lecturer, is the retired pastor of the Church for the Fellowship of All Peoples in Indianapolis.

as dean of the chapels at two major universities, co-founded an inter-racial, interfaith church in San Francisco, and was named an honorary canon of the Cathedral Church of St. John the Divine in New York City. Along the way he wrote many books and founded the Howard Thurman Educational Trust.

That there is a fundamental unity to all life—in all of creation, and certainly within the seemingly fragmented human race—was a guiding conviction for Thurman. He saw the alienation that people forced on one another as an affront to this deep truth, whether it was the soul-distorting structures of segregation, the often bloody competition between different faiths, or the chasms between rich and poor.

This conviction had its roots in Thurman's childhood. His experience of segregation was balanced by an intensely nurturing African-American community and the personal refuge he found in the companionship of nature—the Atlantic Ocean, a favorite oak tree, the river, the night sky. Time spent studying Western mysticism and its ethical implications with Quaker philosopher-mystic Rufus Jones in 1929 helped to "frame in meaning" what Thurman's life had shown him thus far.

But the analyses of faith and social relations that Thurman drew from his experience and study were profoundly confirmed in the mid-'30s, when he and his wife, Sue Bailey Thurman (his partner in his many endeavors, an accomplished musician, and leader in her own right) were invited on a friendship delegation of African-American Christians to India, Burma, and Ceylon (now Sri Lanka). India was in the midst of the struggle to throw off British colonial rule.

Thurman was deeply struck by the painful similarities between the treatment of the Indians by the British and his own experience as an African American in a segregated society. And, as he wrote in his autobiography *With Head and Heart*, he was repeatedly challenged by Indian students. "If Christianity is not powerless, why is it not changing life in your country and the rest of the world?" they would ask. "If it is powerless, why are you here representing it to us?"

These were questions Thurman had asked himself. Indeed, he had initially refused the invitation to the delegation because he did not want to be seen as a defender of "American Christianity." He had agreed to go only when assured that he would be free to speak from the truth of his own life. As he told one student, "I think the religion of Jesus in its true genius offers me a promising way to work through the conflicts of a disordered world. [But] I make a careful distinction between Christianity and the religion of Jesus. My judgment about slavery and racial prejudice relative to Christianity is far more devastating than yours could ever be."

The culmination of the journey through India was a meeting with Mahatma Gandhi, who eagerly questioned Thurman about the struggle of African Americans. Gandhi noted that it might be through the

African Americans that the "unadulterated message of nonviolence" would be delivered to people everywhere.

Thurman left India resolved to proclaim specifically the message that Jesus had for those who were without power in the world and to work to overcome racial barriers in bodies of faith. He was also moved by his encounters with Hindus, Moslems, and Buddhists to search for the common ground of religious life. He held in tension throughout his life the particular and the universal—searching for ways to, as Vincent Harding describes it, "manifest the essential unity of human life and commit ourselves to it on more than sentimental and verbal levels."

Howard Thurman died on April 10, 1981, in San Francisco. Late in his life he was quoted as saying, "I have always felt that a word was being spoken through me—and that three-fourths of the time I didn't get it right." Perhaps that is true, but he leaves behind a legacy of changed hearts and lives that stands testimony to the power of the other fourth of the time.

— JULIE POLTER

Although I had known of Thurman for a number of years, our first meeting took place in San Francisco in 1977, when he invited me to his home. We became friends immediately, our contacts becoming more sustained as I became a staff member at Fellowship Church, then executive director of the Howard Thurman Educational Trust.

When we were together, it was always lively because there were so many facets to his person: large expressive eyes that conveyed that they had seen much of life; a face that reflected presence without intrusion—lighting up with impish joy at the slightest provocation; a voice that was commanding but never demanding. He was a joyous man who had suffered much and had learned through his suffering, a person alive and in love with life.

He loved nature, especially the ocean, and we used to go down to the pier at San Francisco's Fisherman's Wharf to watch the waves come in. The cries of the gulls, the restless skies, the playing people, all so immensely alive—he delighted in the whole thing, feeling total congruence with it.

He spoke about the scene in a way that seemed to permeate his understanding of all creation: Creation is a continuum, rather than a hierarchy with humanity at its acme. All of life moves toward realization, and every form of life is to be respected.

This complex but fundamental order in life implies, but does not prove, the existence of a Creator, such affirmation belonging to the province of faith, which comes from One who is self-revealing and mysterious. Humanity's response to this Presence is worship (awe and ritual) and work (social responsibility). (Thurman laid great emphasis on the experiential quality in life, not discounting that which is rational, but insisting that experience must be affirmed beyond logic and science.)

Truth cannot be the captive of any enterprise, even religion. ("Truth is in a religion because it is true, not because it's in a religion," Thurman wrote.) Spirituality is a fundamental aspect of existence, to be experienced and explored by all, not by a few in some esoteric manner.

A central issue for Dr. Thurman was the meaning of Jesus, whom he loved. He had questions: Had Christianity made a fetish of Jesus, ignoring the religion that Jesus embraced? Yet, he would profess that "Jesus was about all you were going to get of God." Jesus was Savior because he made the nature of the eternal real. Jesus made love, truth, and life real, and wherever and whenever these abstractions are brought to life the incarnation takes place.

Often Thurman spoke of his encounter with a rough-talking, roughly dressed "Good Samaritan" at a railroad station in his hometown— a black man whose help literally made possible his entry into the academy, a man who went on his way after his unheralded deed, never to be seen again. I believe that this kind of action is significant to Thurman's ideas on incarnation.

After six months at Fellowship Church, I had a question for him: How does one maintain the integrity of one's particular religious beliefs and tradition while, at the same time, truly recognizing the validity of others' religious experience? It would seem to be a serious issue since religion, by definition, is a matter of ultimate concern.

After a moment's silence, he threw back his head, laughing, eyes alit with humor: "I've been trying to figure that out for at least thirty years!" His advice was, "Don't remove your neighbor's landmarks."

Thurman *lived* what he spoke and wrote. Immense integrity and self-possession came from his faith in the One who created him. Toward the end of his life, when physical pain and weakness challenged him each day, he once said to me, "Death will come, but I'm not going to open the door for it."

Soon after his death, I was asked to write a statement about him. I close with it:

Howard Thurman was a child. Of God. Notwithstanding the fact that he was a man. His keen intellect, his enormous sense of responsibility, his wisdom born of experience, his mature judgment were the unmistakable marks of a man. However, those qualities were matched by a childlike wonder and delight of life, a simplicity which needed no status symbols, a penetrating candor that went to the very core of issues concerning the human spirit, a sense of humor that lit up large eyes and carried a touch of profundity and had its genesis in a clear recognition of the tragi-comedy of existence.

He sought to demonstrate that the *experience* of struggling with issues was of immeasurable value to personal growth, meaning as much or more than the intellectual exercise, moving to depths beyond those of intellectual reach.

He loved God, and saw in Jesus of Nazareth the fulfillment of God's will for humankind in a special way; but he loved other great religious leaders also, and did not discount the integrity of their understandings. For him, Buddha, Tagore, and Gandhi were vessels through which the rich flow of life came as well. His religious experience was the experience of the substance without form; the antithesis of form without substance.

His lack of concern for his own authority, reputation, and power was obvious. He disdained being seen as a "guru," a mystic, or a saint. Yet he held tremendous power to draw others to him to find the strength in themselves to live life unto God. He did not seek status, yet his name is known among ordinary and extraordinary people in many places around this Earth. He laid no claim to ownership of the Truth; rather, he invited others to join him in his search so that they might claim their own truth. And as a poet he articulated, in the language of beauty and clarity, the unspoken revelations of the hearts of all of us. He was our spokesperson.

His spiritual journey was never finished. He never claimed to have "arrived" at that place we all seek; rather, he had an appealing hunger of spirit that yearned, as we all do, to return again to the wellsprings of the presence of God. His struggle, in those final days, was to make sense out of the event of his dying. He never quite resolved that, which is as it should be. It was a reflection of his determination not to cooperate with death. At one point, when his physical condition would not seem to permit it, he spoke with fierce intensity:

"Marvin, Life shall have dominion!"

Now I must say it. Howard Thurman is dead. But our belief in his immortality is demonstrated by us. For as long as we show integrity of spirit, honesty of conviction, and love of heart, his immortality is assured. And so is ours.

— Marvin Chandler

Dom Helder Camara

Hope Against Hope

by Vickie Kemper and Larry Engel

On a muggy July afternoon in 1977, Dom Helder Camara, the beloved archbishop from Brazil, came to Washington, D.C. Seeing the poverty in the neighborhood that was the home of Sojourners Community, and observing the displacement of those who are poor by the wealthy, this humble prophet who has taken on Brazil's power structure commented, "It's the same all over the world." Later, Dom Helder held out the promise to the gathered community, "I think that together we can help construct a more just world." A decade later, *Sojourners* dedicated its December 1987 issue to the life of this saint and servant of God. The following article was written by Vickie Kemper, then *Sojourners* news editor, with Larry Engel, then West Coast field representative for the National Catholic Conference's Campaign for Human Development.

Just as Judas was paid in silver to deliver Jesus to his murderers, a Brazilian man had been hired by his country's rich and powerful to kill yet another religious troublemaker. Already this instigator had been silenced and warned and threatened, his house shot at, his followers and co-workers jailed, tortured, and murdered. Yet his work continued, his movement flourished. And with it grew the anger of rich landowners and the frustration of the military dictatorship.

And so the time had come to kill this man. The assassin was hired, the money was paid, the deed was planned. All that remained was to carry it out.

His heart hardened and his trigger ready, the executioner walked through the small flower garden belonging to his intended victim, his marked man: his excellency, the Roman Catholic archbishop of Recife and Olinda in northeast Brazil. Unmoved by the well-tended appearance of the garden or the stark simplicity of the house, the experienced assassin proceeded according to plan, knocking on the plain wooden door.

A very small, frail-looking man opened the door.

Speaking with authority, the visitor said he wanted to see Dom Helder Camara.

"I am Dom Helder," replied the little man at the door.

His plan disrupted, his image of the archbishop instantly shattered, the assassin stammered, "*You* are Dom Helder?"

"Yes," answered the "red bishop," as many called him. "What do you want? Come in." After showing his guest into the house and giving him a chair, Dom Helder asked him, "Do you need me for anything? What do you want?"

"No, no," said the assassin, clearly flustered. "I don't want to have anything to do with you because you are not one of those that you kill."

"Kill? Why do you want to kill?" asked Dom Helder.

"Because I was paid to kill you, but I can't kill you," the assassin answered.

"If you are paid, why don't you kill me?" the archbishop reasoned. "I will go to the Lord."

"No," said the assassin, "you are one of the Lord's." And he got up and went away.

It is a story almost as famous as the man himself, but the incident was not at all surprising to those who know Dom Helder Pessoa Camara.

"He has disarmed soldiers with only his words," says one friend, adding, "he's a little pipsqueak of a guy, but he radiates energy."

"No one can be indifferent in his presence," relates another friend and former co-worker. "You are always affirmed and challenged."

If an almost 79-year-old man standing just over five feet tall can be called powerful, his is not the power of physical stature or ecclesiastical position. Rather his capacity to dissuade would-be assassins, confront military dictatorships, shape the priorities of the world's largest church, endure intense persecution, and empower and mobilize millions of poor people comes from within himself.

That capacity, that gift, comes from his relationship to God. It is cultivated in daily prayer and meditation between the hours of 2 and 4 A.M., and it is expressed in love, hope, and compassion through his unwavering commitment to the poor, to nonviolence, justice, and the liberation—through faith, education, and development—of all human beings.

But neither a sensitive profile of Helder Camara's uniquely Christ-like spirit nor a routine listing of his many singularly important accomplishments can fully convey the extraordinary influence this one small man has had on twentieth-century Christianity and, consequently, the faith and lives of millions of people around the world.

"He is one of those seminal figures," says Thomas Quigley, adviser on Latin American affairs to the United States Catholic Conference. "He turns a page in history."

One of the words used most often to characterize Dom Helder is "prophet." His was a voice crying in the wilderness, the shaping force behind so many pivotal concepts and methods that now are commonly accepted and practiced: the identification of corporate sin and structural injustice, the church of the poor, active nonviolence, liberation theology, base Christian communities, genuine human and economic development, and the importance of struggling and hoping against all hope.

"He drew attention to the need for structural change, the need for both personal and corporate conversion, in a way that was very striking," Quigley says. "Dom Helder was able to speed up an inevitable process because he had the grace that allowed people to see things in a different light."

From the very beginning, the forces shaping Camara's own life were his personal relationship with God, the Roman Catholic Church, and his own experiences with poverty and oppression in one of the poorest and most underdeveloped countries in the world. But as his relationship with God deepened, he realized that those forces were not working together; his church was not addressing the needs and realities of his people.

Helder Pessoa Camara was born in the seaport city of Fortaleza, Brazil, on February 7, 1909, the twelfth of thirteen children. His father worked as a bookkeeper and part-time journalist, and his mother taught grade school in the front rooms of the family's house. While Camara's parents were able to provide their young son with a solid education and to support his dreams of becoming a priest, they could not shield him from hunger and hardship. During an epidemic of the croup, five of the family's children died within twenty-nine days.

Ordained to the priesthood in 1931 at age 22, Camara's role within the Catholic Church of Brazil developed quickly. But his years in seminary had given him no social vision, and his superiors in the church trained him to represent and advance the church's social and political authority. Like other good Brazilian Catholics, Camara saw communism as "the evil of evils. To accept and defend the established 'order' and authority seemed to be my duty as a man and as a Christian," Dom Helder has said of his thinking at the time.

While the United States was in the throes of the Great Depression, Benito Mussolini was ruling Italy, and Adolf Hitler was gaining power in Germany, Brazil launched its own fascist movement. The Brazilian Integralist Party sought to unite the country under the motto of "God, Country, Family." Helder Camara was recruited into the movement and with his bishop's blessing stayed for two years, organizing electoral campaigns for party candidates.

The governor of Brazil's northeast province, impressed by this young priest-political organizer, named Camara as state secretary of education in 1934. In 1936, after some political skirmishes with the governor and his bishop, Camara moved to Rio de Janeiro, Brazil's capital at the time. There he worked in both public and religious education.

Meanwhile, Camara longed to return to pastoral work. He left his educational positions and began ministering among the desperately poor four million inhabitants of Rio's many *favelas*, or slums. There Camara began to realize that the church's greatest enemy was not communism but the social conditions that drove the masses to personal and political despair. And seeing the disparities between the needs of the masses and the programs and priorities of the church, Camara began to explore how he could bridge the gap.

For Camara, such work was the direct and obvious extension of his love for God. "The protests of the poor are the voice of God," he would later write. But young Camara was still decades ahead of most church authorities and theologians, and his efforts to open the ears and hearts of the church to the cries and needs of the poor would require years of deliberate, unprecedented, and often costly action.

At the time, vast geographic distances between archdioceses in Brazil and a poor communications system made decision making within the Brazilian church quite difficult. As a result, the church had no comprehensive program for addressing the problems of poverty, underdevelopment, illiteracy, and social injustice that threatened to tear the church and the nation apart.

Camara, using the skills he had gained as a political organizer, began lobbying church authorities in Brazil and the Vatican for the creation of an organization that would both strengthen the Brazilian church and better enable it to meet the needs of the people. In 1952, shortly after his consecration as a bishop, Camara formed the National Conference of the Bishops of Brazil (CNBB) and was named its secretary general, a post he would hold for twelve years.

The CNBB soon became the leading force for social change in Brazil. The CNBB also became a focus for conservative backlash as it advocated controversial political and social remedies, particularly land reform. But Dom Helder's heart and vision extended far beyond Brazil; he imagined an organization that would bring together the bishops of all of Latin America. In 1955, the same year Camara was named auxiliary bishop to the archdiocese of Rio de Janeiro, the first Latin American Episcopal Conference (CELAM) was convened in Rio. Camara would serve as its vice president from 1959 to 1965.

As auxiliary bishop of Rio, Camara engaged the church in grand social programs for the poor. He planned and coordinated the construction of apartment buildings, churches, schools, and the creation of parent-teacher associations and residents' councils. Within three years, nearly 1,000 families had been housed in new apartments and more than 600 children were in school.

But Dom Helder soon realized that working *for* the poor was not enough; the church had to work *with* the poor, empowering them to work for themselves. Studying the scriptures, Catholic social teachings, and the writings of Gandhi, Camara began to emphasize the dignity of the human person and the role of humanity as co-creators with God of the world and its human structures. The full development, or "liberation," of the human person—mind, body, and soul—became his passion. "Conscientization," a pedagogical method of consciousness-raising developed by Brazilian educator Paulo Freire, became Dom Helder's chosen method.

So in 1961, Dom Helder, with the cooperation of the Brazilian government, established the Movement for Grassroots Education (MEB), which worked both to wipe out illiteracy and to "conscienticize" poor Brazilians to their situations. The MEB broadcast its classes over radio, and with the help of 7,500 instructors some 180,000 Brazilians were soon listening to programs broadcast over 15,000 "receiving stations" located in 7,353 schools.

Through conscientization, the people of Brazil were learning that it was not God's will that they be poor and oppressed. They became aware of their basic dignity, asked questions about the injustices in their lives, and were encouraged to become active agents of social change.

In 1962, Pope John XXIII called the world's Catholic bishops to the Second Vatican Council. The pope had already begun to change the church's direction by declaring housing, education, and political participation as basic human rights, but the presence at Vatican II of some highly vocal Third World bishops, led by one Dom Helder Camara, was to radicalize the church even further. Camara and other bishops were calling for a worldwide "church of the poor."

Dom Helder's meditations from that time, written in the middle
hours of the night, reflect his sense of mission in carrying the needs of
the Third World to what was, at that time, a church very much of the
First World. On August 29, 1962, he wrote:

> I pray incessantly
> for the conversion
> of the prodigal son's brother.
> Ever in my ear
> rings the dread warning.
> The one has awoken
> from his life of sin.
> When will the other
> awaken
> from his virtue?

Meanwhile, on April 1, 1964, a military coup led by Arturo de Costa e
Silva overtook the Brazilian government. One of the new military government's first actions was to jail the leaders of the MEB, trade
unions, and other citizens' organizations. It was in the crucible of this
turbulent political environment that on April 12, 1964, just days after
the coup, Dom Helder Camara was installed as archbishop of the
archdiocese of Recife and Olinda in northeast Brazil.

Dom Helder wasted no time in using his new position to confront
the new government. Speaking at his installation, he said, "We are all
convinced that freedom is a divine gift which must be preserved at any
price. Let us liberate, in the fullest sense, every human creature in
our midst." Within four days of his arrival at Recife, Dom Helder
issued a statement along with sixteen Brazilian bishops calling for
justice and the release of the jailed leaders. The next day, government
soldiers raided the episcopal palace.

Dom Helder still remained a powerful force at Vatican II. In
November 1965, at the council's fourth session, he shared his vision of
church with the world's Catholic bishops: "Perhaps I am completely
deceived," he said. "But it seems to me that communism will disappear in a remarkable manner when spiritual leaders are moved, not
by secret ambition or Machiavellianism, but by the crisis of humanity, to take up the defense of the human person. Then, ecumenically
united, they can lead the world to harmonious and integral development under the banner of peace based on justice."

A month later, as he entered a period of long and intense conflict
with the Brazilian government, Dom Helder issued a warning to those
who would take up his call: "Whoever decides to awaken the masses
to the absurd, sub-human level of their existence; whoever rises up
and demands human and social advancement, which implies a reform
of structures, let him prepare himself for slander campaigns, let him

expect with certainty to be considered and opposed as a subversive and a communist."

Despite this warning, the church continued to move forward under Dom Helder's leadership. A 1966 declaration formulated by Dom Helder and signed by 15 bishops from developing countries, and the documents from meetings at Medellín, Colombia, in 1968 formalized the Latin American church's "preferential option for the poor" and its commitment to "liberating education."

But Brazil's military dictatorship had no patience with the "church of the poor." By 1967 the government was systematically torturing, imprisoning, and murdering "political dissidents," many of them priests and lay workers. Greatly pained, Dom Helder continued to speak out against the government's actions, and soon he, too, was subjected to government persecution.

Still, Dom Helder only escalated his call for nonviolence. "My personal vocation is to be a pilgrim of peace," he said. "Personally I would prefer a thousand times more to be killed than to kill anyone. . . . We need only to turn to the Beatitudes—the quintessence of the gospel message—to see that the option for Christians is clear. We, as Christians, are on the side of nonviolence, and this is in no way an option for weakness and passivity. Opting for nonviolence means to believe more strongly in the power of truth, justice, and love than in the power of wars, weapons, and hatred."

On October 2, 1968, the 100th anniversary of Gandhi's birthday, Dom Helder launched, with the backing of the CNBB and CELAM, the movement Action, Justice, and Peace. The movement stated as its goal "the humanization of all those who are subhumanized by misery or dehumanized by egoism," through the change of economic, political, and social structures throughout Latin America. The movement committed itself to nonviolence, which it described as "positive action, daring and courageous assertion of nonconformity" with unjust structures.

In response to such opposition from the church and other quarters, the Brazilian government grew only more repressive. It closed the national congress, suspended civil rights, destroyed the MEB, and terrorized leaders of Action, Justice, and Peace. As a final blow, the government silenced Dom Helder Camara; he was banned from public speaking in Brazil for thirteen years. From 1968 to 1977, Brazilian newspapers could not even print his name, and he was banned from radio and television.

Never one to be dissuaded by great odds or dangerous obstacles, Dom Helder and the base community movement he inspired weathered twenty-one years of military dictatorship. Now retired as archbishop, Dom Helder continues to travel the world as an "itinerant apostle of human rights, social justice, and peace."

But Dom Helder has never expected social change to come quickly or easily. "We must have no illusions," he has said. "We shall not walk on roses, people will not throng to hear us and applaud, and we shall not always be aware of divine protection. If we are to be pilgrims for justice and peace, we must expect the desert."

Dom Helder believes justice and peace will be achieved through the faith, hard work, and persistence of small groups of people, those he calls "Abrahamic minorities," who are willing to take great risks in the face of tremendous odds. "Today, as always," he says, "humanity is led by minorities who hope against all hope, as did Abraham."

Truly great people are measured not only by their large-scale impact on history—through positions held, organizations created, documents written, and movements established—but also by the smaller, yet often more important, influence their lives have had on other people. Some achievements go down in history while other moments and anecdotes are forgotten by all but a few people. Often it is those personal stories and memories that create the most accurate picture of a historical figure.

Denis Goulet, for example, speaks of Dom Helder's "huge impact" on the one hand, and his simple humility on the other. Goulet, a development specialist who now teaches at the University of Notre Dame in South Bend, Indiana, worked with Dom Helder in Brazil for many years.

"He's had a huge impact," Goulet says of Dom Helder, "first in raising high the banner of 'true' development that benefits human beings. And for a whole generation [of Brazilians], he was one of the only flames that kept the fire lit, that kept alive the hope that it was worth struggling against the government."

Goulet and others cited as one of Dom Helder's greatest assets his desire and ability to be one with the people. Goulet recalls seeing Dom Helder several years ago at a conference in Senegal where Dom Helder was the keynote speaker. Organizers of the conference had provided Dom Helder with a car and driver, but he chose to ride the bus across town with everyone else.

After Vatican II the archdiocese of Detroit initiated a relationship with Dom Helder's archdiocese of Recife. The Detroit archdiocese has sent numerous priests and women religious to work among the poor in Recife. John Cardinal Dearden, who was archbishop of Detroit at the time, speaks of celebrating Mass with Dom Helder in Recife.

"It was interesting to see the response that his presence among his people called forth," Dearden remembers. "He is a man who is very close to his people. He moves about them as one of them. It was a very moving experience for me, to see him living out what he's been talking about."

Other stories reflect both the boldness and, some would say, eccentricity of Dom Helder. Tom Quigley recalled that at the closing session of Vatican II Dom Helder proposed that all the bishops take off their pectoral crosses, most of which were made of gold or silver, and symbolically lay them down at the feet of the pope. The Vatican could then melt down all the crosses and give the money to the poor. Dom Helder also suggested that, after their crosses of precious metal had been melted down, the bishops adopt wooden pectoral crosses, such as the one he himself wears.

"He didn't get very far with that idea, but he gave it a good try," Quigley said.

On a lighter note, Quigley points out Dom Helder's custom of speaking to virtually everything—plant, vegetable, or mineral. It is a habit that has earned him the nickname "St. Francis." Even while riding in a car, Dom Helder will, as if without thinking, greet an airplane passing overhead.

"Once we were driving in the Washington area and we passed by the Pentagon," Quigley remembers. "I pointed it out to him and he waved his hand at it. I guess he figured that it, like everything else, could use his blessing."

Dom Helder's friends and co-workers often cite his gentleness, his humility, his compassion, his commitment to nonviolence, and his unflagging efforts for justice. "He summons me not to give up on things," Goulet says. "He helps people realize that they should respond to their best selves regardless of the obstacles."

But perhaps Dom Helder's greatest and most influential characteristic is his love. Sister Carol Quigley, now president of the Servants of the Immaculate Heart of Mary, worked in Recife from 1967 until 1975 as a missioner from Detroit. She worked in a local parish for a year or two and then was named to Dom Helder's pastoral team for evangelization.

"He really does practice universal love," says Carol Quigley. "He loves *everybody*. Even those people who persecuted him, even the oppressors of the world, he tried, in love, to call them to love, to be the best in themselves."

Dom Helder's life is one of constant prayer, and he often prays the prayer of Cardinal Newman. "Lord, Jesus," he prays, "don't extinguish the light of your presence within me. O Lord, look through my eyes, listen through my ears, speak through my lips, walk with my feet. Lord, may my poor human presence be a reminder, however weak, of your divine presence."

For those few blessed to have known and worked with Dom Helder, for the millions touched by his life and work, and even for those who know him only through his writings and his legacy, it is a prayer powerfully answered in the life of Dom Helder Camara.

[Postscript: Dom Helder Camara died in 1999.]

Athol Gill

A Follower of Jesus

by David Batstone

The chief of El Salvador's national police stares intently across the table. Though the mere mention of the colonel's name strikes fear into the heart of many a Salvadoran activist, at this particular moment he is looking rather perplexed and unsure of himself. For seated on the other side of the table is Athol Gill, who, having just introduced himself as a Bible professor from Australia, continues to explain that he has traveled from the other side of the globe to find out why the national police have tortured and imprisoned a local Baptist pastor.

The colonel's confidence waxes while announcing that the pastor is a communist, then wanes again as the calm Aussie asks if serving the poor is always a crime in El Salvador. By the end of the hour, the colonel is signing a declaration that the Salvadoran Baptist community will be permitted to continue its ministry with the poor without fear of reprisal.

As incredible as it may seem in view of the final result, only two hours before Athol and I had sat in a hotel room in San Salvador with virtually no idea what we might say to the colonel. We had hopped on

David Batstone, who lived in the House of the Gentle Bunyip from 1980–81, is now Executive Editor of *Sojourners*. This article appeared in the June 1992 issue of *Sojourners*.

a plane and headed directly for El Salvador within days of hearing of the arrest and brutal treatment of the pastor. Yet that was the easy part. Now we were faced with the daunting task of how, with mere wit and moral suasion at our disposal, to battle forces that were armed with arrogance and impunity.

We could only come up with one strategy: Athol would negotiate with the colonel while I would take my time translating messages between them, thus buying Athol precious time to think on his feet. As we then looked at each other nervously, he remarked with a wily smile, "We will make the road as we walk it."

For Athol Gill, that seemingly shaky proposition was not merely born in the moment of desperation. It was a gospel basis for a messianic, vulnerable lifestyle. When Jesus calls, this New Testament professor never tired of saying, we must abandon everything and follow him on the road that leads to Jerusalem, the way of the cross.

Perhaps that message itself is not overly unusual to us, particularly when it is comfortably couched in the religious language of personal spirituality. What is truly startling, however, is to encounter someone who is willing to apply it to his or her way of life.

In fact, it was that very dichotomy between believing and acting that brought Professor Gill to a major turning point in 1971. He had just returned from Switzerland to his native Australia after finishing a doctorate under the tutelage of renowned New Testament scholar Eduard Schweizer. He was to take up a teaching post at the Baptist Theological College of Queensland. His humble, rural roots and work as a retail store manager left far behind, Dr. Gill was now seemingly set for a prestigious career in the seminary academy.

But before he even had time to settle into his new position, two students arrived at his office to throw their professor a serious challenge: His teachings were impossible to put into practice in the existing church. They boldly declared that either he stop educating them for frustration, or take responsibility to help them create a place where people would be encouraged to live out the radical commitment of the gospels.

Concluding that the "call to teach" did not preclude the "call to put it into practice," Athol and nearly twenty of his students soon opened a coffee house situated near the center of Brisbane's nightclub district. The coffee house provided a forum for religious, social, and political issues as a point of contact and dialogue with Australia's growing countercultural movement. Eventually, several of the staff organized a communal residence, and before long the wider group began talking about themselves as an intentional community.

Though these developments were exceptionally exciting for the theological students, they were not warmly received by the largely con-

servative seminary faculty and administration. After several turbulent years in Brisbane, it was clear that Professor Gill was no longer
a welcome presence and would be pushed out of the seminary. The
maturing community decided that Athol should accept an offer to
teach at the Baptist seminary in Melbourne, provided that he and his
wife, Judith, initiate a community in their new locale. Though they
were to leave Brisbane, the community they left behind, the House of
Freedom, has continued for nearly twenty years to celebrate life
together as a people committed to common life and works of justice.

Upon their arrival in Melbourne, the Gills discovered that an
alarming number of inner-city churches were shutting down as their
members fled "urban blight" and headed for the suburbs. In opposition
to the cultural trend, Athol believed that this would be the perfect
location to establish a community church.

Along with several theological students who had followed him to
Melbourne from Brisbane and Sydney, a small community was formed
in 1975 that began to operate out of the near-defunct Clifton Hill
Baptist Church. Shortly thereafter, the community began to organize
training workshops, called "radical discipleship weekends," through
which mission teams were recruited to become involved in inner-city
programs for youth, the elderly, and the homeless.

In order to strengthen these workshops, Athol produced a multiple
series of "discipleship studies" that related gospel texts to following
Jesus, living together in community, and working for justice. Gospel
stories, once thought to be solely proof-texts of Jesus' divine nature
(miracles, authority, sinlessness, etc.), came to life in Athol's studies:
They now beckoned one to radical and complete conversion. In his own
unique style, Athol encouraged the reader that "[Jesus] comes time
and again and calls us to follow him, offering us a fresh start in the
life of discipleship. The options don't vary, but the choices continue."

The discipleship studies were disseminated via crude, mimeographed sheets that were passed the length and breadth of Australia,
while eventually making their way even to intentional communities in
the United States that utilized them to deepen their own vision and
commitment. Copyright and royalties were never an issue; it was not
until 1989 that they were finally published in a book titled *Life on the
Road: The Gospel Basis for a Messianic Lifestyle.*

The Melbourne community landed on a rather unique name, House
of the Gentle Bunyip. Weary of British and U.S. imperial dominance
within their culture, the community wanted an Australian name that
would convey a true incarnation of the gospel within the roots of their
own soil. They chose the image of a bunyip.

A bunyip is a mythical Australian animal that comes from the
"dream time" in aboriginal culture. A well-known Aussie children's

story relates how the bunyip was rejected by everybody, both animal and human. However, he finally finds his own true identity and dignity when he encounters another bunyip who was rejected just like himself. The simple story of the bunyip's search for identity is tied to the discovery of corporate identity. As Athol often said, "The search for identity is the quest for community."

The House of the Gentle Bunyip over the last seventeen years has enjoyed a rich and varied history. At its peak it included seventy members and associates, all living in communal homes within walking distance of the community center. The Bunyip also organized an impressive array of service projects: a short-term accommodation for street kids, a crisis-care program for those suffering from schizophrenia, a food cooperative, a youth center, a lunch program for the elderly, an alternative primary school, an adult arts and crafts school, and a peace and disarmament group.

But the story of the community is not one of unmitigated success. During the last five years, membership has dropped dramatically and many of the programs have been forced to close. Mirroring the burnout, overstress, and disintegration of many intentional communities in the United States, Europe, and Australia, the Bunyip fell on hard times.

As leader and pastor, Athol realized that many mistakes had been made: High ideals and vision had led them to take on too much all at once. Consequently, all too often the community was fed by immature expectations, hurtful relationships, and weary souls.

"If we hadn't been so stupid—or perhaps simply so human—we may have done a lot better," Athol once lamented. "But, then, perhaps we would not have learned just how much Christian community is a life of grace and that God continues to call us to journey together, through our failures and successes."

Yet the Bunyip's own history is really only a limited reading of its broad impact on envisioning a new shape for the Western church. Interns, visitors, and ex-members of the community are working in inner-city programs and peace and justice communities throughout Australia. Others are leading voices in the social service sector of local and national religious and political structures. Some members of the community left to work in Sri Lanka, the Philippines, the Dominican Republic, and El Salvador. Four U.S. interns who made a yearlong stay at the Bunyip in 1981–82 returned to establish a community in downtown Oakland, California; they later collaborated with Athol to establish Central American Mission Partners (CAMP), an aid, development, and human rights program with offices in El Salvador, Oakland, and Melbourne.

This thumbnail sketch of Athol Gill's life and wide influence suggests the reason behind the shock, sadness, and deep sense of loss that the news of his sudden death by heart attack brought to so many "radical disciples" around the globe on March 9, 1992. The road to Jerusalem seems treacherous and lonely enough without losing an experienced traveler who helped us to read the maps so that we might not lose our bearings along the way.

For those of us who walk around with "messianic complexes" on our sleeves, the message of the gospels is clear: We are not called to save the world. Nor should we expect others to do so for us. The call to discipleship is much simpler and, for that reason, perhaps even more daunting.

We are to live our existence in communion with the Spirit of God as it has been revealed to us in the life of Jesus and as it is celebrated in the lives of our sisters and brothers whom we have joined on the journey. The specific commitments, activities, movements, and structures will be brought forth by the changing historical moment.

In that sense, we must say in regard to our dear brother Athol that his life was indeed "finished." We do not measure his life so much by his successes (though there were many) or failures (though we share the scars of those, too), but above all we recall the clarity of his vision and commitment. He demonstrated to so many of us the contours of a messianic lifestyle in our own time and place.

It is Athol who once wrote:

> *The stranger of Galilee promises a new future as he leads the way towards a new humanity. We will have done our work if we simply resist the temptation to settle down and reap the temporary pleasures of the materialistic society. We will have done our work if we simply continue to follow him towards the city with a firm foundation, whose architect and builder is God. The journey has really only just begun.*

Indeed, we look forward to meeting up with you once again, Athol, "on the way."

VII

BLESSED
ARE
THE PEACEMAKERS

Daniel Berrigan

The Push of Conscience

On September 9, 1980, Daniel Berrigan, Philip Berrigan, Dean Hammer, Molly Rush, Carl Kabat, Elmer Maas, Anne Montgomery, and John Schuchardt entered the General Electric plant in King of Prussia, Pennsylvania, where they hammered on the nosecones of two Mark 12A nuclear warheads. In March 1981, in their trial in Norristown, Pennsylvania, they were convicted on eight of thirteen counts. The final legal consequences of their action were held up for a decade by court procedures and appeals.

On April 10, 1990, the final pronouncement on their sentence was made. After listening to more than three hours of compelling testimony, Judge James E. Buckingham announced to a packed Norristown courtroom that "further incarceration in this case wouldn't do much good" and sentenced each of the defendants to time served.

During the decade of waiting, most of the defendants participated in other acts of civil disobedience. Others, following their example and the biblical call to "beat swords into plowshares," took part in similar Plowshares actions all across the country.

Below is the text of Daniel Berrigan's responses to Anne Montgomery's direct examination in their original trial, in which the defendants served as their own attorneys.

Father Berrigan, I'd like to ask you a simple question: Why did you do what you did?

I would like to answer this question as simply as I can. It brings up immediately words that have been used again and again in the courtroom—like conscience, justification. The question takes me back to those years when my conscience was being formed, back to a family that was poor, and to a father and mother who taught, quite simply, by living what they taught. And if I could put their message very shortly, it would go something like this: In a thousand ways they showed that you do what is right because it is right, that your conscience is a matter between you and God, that nobody owns you.

If I have a precious memory of my mother and father that lasts to this day, it is simply that they lived as though nobody owned them. They cheated no one. They worked hard for a living.

They were poor, and, perhaps most precious of all, they shared what they had. And that was enough, because in the life of a young child, the first steps of conscience are as important as the first steps of one's feet. They set the direction where life will go.

And I feel that direction was set for my brothers and myself. There is a direct line between the way my parents turned our steps and this action. That is no crooked line.

That was the first influence. The second one has to do with my religious order. When I was eighteen I left home for the Jesuit order. I reflect that I am sixty years old, and I have never been anything but a Jesuit, a Jesuit priest, in my whole life.

We have Jesuits throughout Latin America today, my own brothers, who are in prison, who have been under torture; many of them have been murdered.

On the walls of our religious communities both here and in Latin America are photos of murdered priests, priests who have been imprisoned, priests under torture, priests who stood somewhere because they believed in something. Those faces haunt my days. And I ask myself how I can be wishywashy in face of such example, example of my own lifetime, my own age.

This is a powerful thing, to be in a common bond of vows with people who have given their lives because they did not believe in mass murder, because such crimes could not go on in their name.

Dear friends of the jury, you have been called the conscience of the community. Each of us eight comes from a community. I don't mean just a biological family. I mean that every one of us has brothers and sisters with whom we live, with whom we pray, with whom we offer the Eucharist, with whom we share income, and in some cases, the care of children. Our conscience, in other words, comes from somewhere. We have not come from outer space or from chaos or from madhouses to King of Prussia.

We have come from years of prayer, years of life together, years of testing—testing of who we are in the church and in the world. We would like to speak to you, each of us in a different way, about our communities; because, you see, it is our conviction that nobody in the world can form his or her conscience alone.

Now, perhaps I don't even have to dwell on that. Most of you who have children know the importance of others—not just parents, but friends, relatives, those who are loved and who love, in helping us come to understand who we are.

What are we to do in bad times? I am trying to say that we come as a community of conscience before your community of conscience to ask you: Are our consciences to act differently than yours in regard to the lives and deaths of children? A very simple question, but one that cuts to the bone.

We would like you to see that we come from where you come. We come from churches. We come from neighborhoods. We come from years of work.

We come from America. And we come to this, a trial of conscience and motive. And the statement of conscience we would like to present to you is this.

We could not *not* do this. We could not not do this! We were pushed to this by all our lives. Do you see what I mean? All our lives.

I would speak about myself, the others will speak for themselves. When I say I could not not do this, I mean, among other things, that with every cowardly bone in my body I wished I hadn't had to enter the G.E. plant. I wish I hadn't had to do it. And that has been true every time I have been arrested, all those years. My stomach turns over. I feel sick. I feel afraid. I don't want to go through this again.

I hate jail. I don't do well there physically. But I cannot not go on, because I have learned that we must not kill if we are Christians. I have learned that children, above all, are threatened by these weapons. I have read that Christ our Lord underwent death rather than inflict it. And I am supposed to be a disciple. All kinds of things like that. The push, the push of conscience is a terrible thing.

So at some point your cowardly bones get moving, and you say, "Here it goes again," and you do it. And you have a certain peace because you did it, as I do this morning in speaking with you.

That phrase about not being able not to do something, maybe it is a little clumsy. But for those who raise children, who go to work every day, who must make decisions in their families, I think there is a certain knowledge of what I am trying to say. Children at times must be disciplined. We would rather not do it.

There are choices on jobs about honesty. There are things to be gained if we are dishonest. And it is hard not to be.

Yet one remains honest because one has a sense, "Well, if I cheat, I'm really giving over my humanity, my conscience." Then we think of these horrible Mark 12A missiles, something in us says, "We cannot live with such crimes." Or, our consciences turn in another direction. And by a thousand pressures, a thousand silences, people can begin to say to themselves, "We can live with that. We can live with that. We know it's there. We know what it is for. We know that many thousands will die if only one of these is exploded."

And yet we act like those employees, guards, experts we heard speak here; they close their eyes, close their hearts, close their briefcases, take their paychecks—and go home. It's called living with death. And it puts us to death before the missile falls.

We believe, according to the law, the law of the state of Pennsylvania, that we were justified in saying, "We cannot live with that"; justified in saying it publicly, saying it dramatically, saying it with blood and hammers, as you have heard; because that weapon, the hundreds and hundreds more being produced in our country, are the greatest evil conceivable on this earth.

There is no evil to compare with that. Multiply murder. Multiply desolation. The mind boggles.

So we went into that death factory, and in a modest, self-contained, careful way we put a few dents in two missiles, awaited arrest, came willingly into court to talk to you. We believe with all our hearts that our action was justified.

You mentioned work. Could you say something about how your work in the cancer hospital in New York influenced your decision?

Sure. I wouldn't want the jury to get the impression we are always going around banging on nose cones. We also earn a living. I have been doing, among other things, a kind of service to the dying for about three years now in New York. And I would like to speak shortly about that, because I come to you from an experience of death—not just any death, but the death of the poor, death by cancer.

I don't know whether you have ever smelled cancer. Cancer of the nose, cancer of the face, which is the most terrible to look upon and to smell, cancer of the brain, cancer of the lungs: We see it all, smell it all, hold it all in our arms.

This is not just a lecture on cancer. It is a lecture on those Mark 12A missiles, which make cancer the destiny of humanity, as is amply shown. This is another aspect of our justification.

We know now that in Hiroshima and Nagasaki, those who did not die at the flash point are still dying of cancer. Nuclear weapons carry a universal plague of cancer. As the Book of Revelation implies, after one of these missiles is launched, the living will envy the dead.

I could not understand cancer until I was arrested at the Pentagon, because there I smelled death by cancer, in my very soul. I smelled the death of everyone, everyone, across the board: black, brown, red, all of us, death by cancer.

So I talk to the dying. I take a chance on the dying, those that are still able to talk. And I say, "Do you know where my friends and I go from here?" Some of the patients know; and some of them don't. Some had read of our act in the papers. Some hadn't. I would talk about what I can only call the politics of cancer. The service the dying were rendering me was this: With their last days, their last breath, they helped me understand why I had to continue this struggle; because in them I was seeing up close the fate of everyone, and especially the children.

I have seen children dying of cancer. And we will see more and more of that as these bombs are built.

Justification and conscience. Could I mention briefly also that for two semesters I have been teaching at a college in the South Bronx, a college for poor people? It's a unique place, because only poor people who cannot pay are admitted. We have some one thousand students who are finishing degrees. You have undoubtedly seen pictures of the South Bronx; Jimmy Carter and President Reagan have visited there. It's a required campaign stop by now; and when pictures appear one thinks of a president stepping on the moon, a lunar landscape, a landscape of utter desolation and misery and poverty and neglect.

This is also to our point of justification, because I have been led to ask, "Why are people condemned to live this way in a wealthy country?" Where is the money going? Why is there a culture of poverty? Why are people born into it? Why do they live outside the economy, never have a job, have no future, live and die that way, hundreds of thousands in the South Bronx?

I don't know what to call our college. It is like a center for survivors. I look at the faces of these marvelous people, my students. And I think with sorrow in my heart that for every one who sits in that room, twenty have died on the way, or are in prison or are on drugs or are suicides, have given up.

And I was led to ask, "Why must this be?" So the cancer hospital and the college lead me to the Pentagon. I discussed freely in class, why are we so poor? Where is the money? General Electric costs the poor three million dollars a day, not for housing, not for schooling, not for neighborhood rehabilitation, not for medical care—for Mark 12A;

three million dollars a day stolen from the poor. A larceny of world-wide proportions. This is our justification. We could not be indefinitely silent.

The hospital, the college, and the Pentagon, this is the circuit of my life.

In each of these places I learn more about the other two. At the Pentagon I understand why cancer will befall everyone, and why so many are destitute now. Among the poor, I understand why the poor die in such numbers of cancer. And at the hospital I smell the death that is planned for all.

Getting to the King of Prussia action itself, would you describe something of the preparation for it?

I'm sure, dear friends, that others will speak of the great import to us of the spiritual life, our lives in God. I want to tell you a little about the immediate days preceding this action; indeed, about days that have preceded every arrest we have undergone.

We have never taken actions such as these, perilous, crucial, difficult as they are, without the most careful preparation of our hearts, our motivation, our common sense, our sense of one another. We have never admitted any person to our group whom we could not trust to be nonviolent under pressure of crises.

This is simply a rule of our lives; we don't go from the street to do something like the King of Prussia action. We go from prayer. We go from reflection. We go from worship, always. And since we realized that this action was perhaps the most difficult of all our lives, we spent more time in prayer this time than before.

We passed three days together in a country place. We prayed, and read the Bible, and shared our fears, shared our second and third thoughts.

And in time we drew closer. We were able to say, "Yes. We can do this. We can take the consequences. We can undergo whatever is required." All of that.

During those days we sweated out the question of families and children—the question of a long separation if we were convicted and jailed.

I talked openly with Jesuit friends and superiors. They respected my conscience and said, "Do what you are called to."

That was the immediate preparation. And what it issued in was a sense that, with great peacefulness, with calm of spirit, even though with a butterfly in our being, we could go ahead. And so we did.

This enters into my understanding of conscience and justification, a towering question, which has faced so many good people in history, in difficult times, now, in the time of the bomb. What helps people? What helps people understand who they are in the world, who they are in their families, who they are with their children, with their work? What helps?

That was a haunting question for me. Will this action be helpful? Legally, we could say that this was our effort to put the question of justification. Will our action help? Will people understand that this "lesser evil," done to this so-called "property," was helping turn things around in the church, in the nation?

Will the action help us be more reflective, about life and death and children and all life?

We have spent years and years of our adult lives keeping the law. We have tried everything, every access, every means to get to public authorities within the law. We come from within the law, from within.

We are deeply respectful of a law that is in favor of human life. And as we know, at least some of our laws are. We are very respectful of those laws. We want you to know that.

Years and years we spent writing letters, trying to talk to authorities, vigiling in public places, holding candles at night, holding placards by day, trying, trying, fasting, trying to clarify things to ourselves as we were trying to speak to others; all of that within the law, years of it.

And then I had to say, I could not not break the law and remain human. That was what was in jeopardy: what I call my conscience, my humanity, that which is recognizable to children, to friends, to good people, when we say, "There is someone I can trust and love, someone who will not betray."

We spent years within the law, trying to be that kind of person, a non-betrayer.

Then we found we couldn't. And if we kept forever on this side of the line, we would die within ourselves. We couldn't look in the mirror, couldn't face those we love, had no Christian message in the world, nothing to say if we went on that way.

I might just as well wander off and go the way pointed to by a low-grade American case of despair: getting used to the way things are. That is what I mean by dying. That is what we have to oppose. I speak for myself.

The Jesuit order accepted me as a member. The Catholic Church ordained me as a priest. I took all that with great seriousness. I still do, with all my heart. And then Vietnam came along, and then the nukes came along. And I had to continue to ask myself at prayer, with my friends, with my family, with all kinds of people, with my own soul, "Do you have anything to say today?" I mean, beyond a lot of prattling religious talk.

Do you have anything to say about life today, about the lives of people today? Do you have a word, a word of hope to offer, a Christian word? That's a very important question for anyone who takes being a priest, being a Christian, being a human being seriously, "Do you have anything to offer human life today?"

It is a terribly difficult question for me. And I am not at all sure that I do have something to offer. But I did want to say this. I am quite certain that I had, September 9, 1980, something to say.

And I will never deny, whether here or in jail, to my family, or friends, or to the Russians, or the Chinese, or anyone in the world, I will never deny what I did.

More than that. Our act is all I have to say. The only message I have to the world is: We are not allowed to kill innocent people. We are not allowed to be complicit in murder. We are not allowed to be silent while preparations for mass murder proceed in our name, with our money, secretly.

I have nothing else to say in the world. At other times one could talk about family life and divorce and birth control and abortion and many other questions. But this Mark 12A is here. And it renders all other questions null and void. Nothing, nothing can be settled until this is settled. Or this will settle us, once and for all.

It's terrible for me to live in a time where I have nothing to say to human beings except, "Stop killing." There are other beautiful things that I would love to be saying to people. There are other projects I could be very helpful at. And I can't do them. I cannot.

Because everything is endangered. Everything is up for grabs. Ours is a kind of primitive situation, even though we would call ourselves sophisticated. Our plight is very primitive from a Christian point of view. We are back where we started. Thou shall not kill: we are not allowed to kill. Everything today comes down to that—everything.

I thank you with all my heart for listening.

George Zabelka

Chaplain for Peace

In August, 1945, Fr. George Zabelka, a Catholic chaplain with the U.S. Army air force, was stationed on Tinian Island in the South Pacific. He served as priest and pastor for the airmen who dropped the atomic bombs on Hiroshima and Nagasaki.

He was discharged in 1946. During the next twenty years he gradually began to realize that what he had done and believed during the war was wrong, and that the only way he could be a Christian was to be a pacifist. He was deeply influenced in this process by the civil rights movement and the works of Martin Luther King, Jr., and Mahatma Gandhi.

In 1972 he met Charles C. McCarthy, a theologian, lawyer, and father of ten. McCarthy, who founded the Center for the Study of Nonviolence at the University of Notre Dame, was leading a workshop on nonviolence at Zabelka's church. The two men fell into the first of several conversations about the issues raised by the workshop. Some time later, Zabelka reached the conclusion that the use of violence under any circumstances was incompatible with his understanding of the gospel of Christ and began giving workshops on nonviolence himself. The following interview with Zabelka was conducted by McCarthy in 1980.

Father Zabelka, what is your relationship to the atomic bombings of Hiroshima and Nagasaki in August 1945?

During the summer of 1945, July, August, and September, I was assigned as Catholic chaplain to the 509th Composite Group on Tinian Island. The 509th was the atomic bomb group.

What were your duties in relationship to these men?

The usual. I said Mass on Sunday and during the week. Heard confessions. Talked with the boys, etc. Nothing significantly different from what any other chaplain did during the war.

Did you know that the 509th was preparing to drop an atomic bomb?

No. We knew that they were preparing to drop a bomb substantially different from and more powerful than even the "blockbusters" used over Europe, but we never called it an atomic bomb and never really knew what it was before August 6, 1945. Before that time we just referred to it as the "gimmick" bomb.

So since you did not know that an atomic bomb was going to be dropped you had no reason to counsel the men in private or preach in public about the morality of such a bombing?

Well, that is true enough, I never did speak against it, nor could I have spoken against it since I, like practically everyone else on Tinian, was ignorant of what was being prepared. And I guess I will go to my God with that as my defense. But on Judgment Day I think I am going to need to seek more mercy than justice in this matter.

Why? God certainly could not have expected you to act on ideas that had never entered your mind.

As a Catholic priest my task was to keep my people, wherever they were, close to the mind and heart of Christ. As a military chaplain I was to try to see that the boys conducted themselves according to the teachings of the Catholic Church and Christ on war. When I look back I am not sure I did either of these things very well.

Why do you think that?

What I do not mean to say is that I feel myself to have been remiss in any duties that were expected of me as a chaplain. I saw that the Mass and the sacraments were available as best I could. I even went out and earned paratroop wings in order to do my job better. Nor did I fail to teach and preach what the Church expected me to teach and preach—and I don't mean by this that I just talked to the boys about their sexual lives. I and most chaplains were quite clear and outspoken on such matters as not killing and torturing prisoners. But there were other areas where things were not said quite so clearly.

The destruction of civilians in war was always forbidden by the Church, and if a soldier came to me and asked if he could put a bullet through a child's head, I would have told him absolutely not. That would be mortally sinful. But in 1945 Tinian Island was the largest airfield in the world. Three planes a minute could take off from it around the clock. Many of these planes went to Japan with the express purpose of killing not one child or one civilian but of slaughtering hundreds and thousands and tens of thousands of children and civilians,—and I said nothing.

Why not? You certainly knew civilians were being destroyed by the thousands in these raids, didn't you?

Oh, indeed I did know, and I knew with a clarity that few others could have had.

What do you mean?

As a chaplain I often had to enter the world of the boys who were losing their minds because of something they did in war. I remember one young man who was engaged in the bombings of the cities of Japan. He was in the hospital on Tinian Island on the verge of a complete mental collapse.

He told me that he had been on a low-level bombing mission, flying right down one of the main streets of the city, when straight ahead of him appeared a little boy, in the middle of the street, looking up at the plane in childlike wonder. The man knew that in a few seconds this child would be burned to death by napalm which had already been released.

Yes, I knew civilians were being destroyed and knew it perhaps in a way others didn't. Yet I never preached a single sermon against killing civilians to the men who were doing it.

Again, why not?

Because I was "brainwashed"! It never entered my mind to publicly protest the consequences of these massive air raids. I was told it was necessary; told openly by the military and told implicitly by my Church's leadership. To the best of my knowledge no American cardinals or bishops were opposing these mass air raids. Silence in such matters, especially by a public body like the American bishops, is a stamp of approval.

The whole structure of the secular, religious, and military society told me clearly that it was all right to "let the Japs have it." God was on the side of my country. The Japanese were the enemy, and I was absolutely certain of my country's and Church's teaching about enemies; no erudite theological text was necessary to tell me. The day-in-day-out operation of the state and the Church between 1940 and 1945 spoke more clearly about Christian attitudes toward enemies and war than St. Augustine or St. Thomas Aquinas ever could.

I was certain that this mass destruction was right, certain to the point that the question of its morality never seriously entered my mind. I was "brainwashed" not by force or torture but by my Church's silence and whole-hearted cooperation in thousands of little ways with the country's war machine. Why, after I finished chaplaincy school at Harvard I had my military chalice officially blessed by Bishop Cushing of Boston. How much more clearly could the message be given? Indeed, I was "brainwashed"!

So you feel that because you did not protest the morality of the bombing of other cities with their civilian populations, that somehow you are morally responsible for the dropping of the atomic bomb?

The facts are that seventy-five thousand people were burned to death in one evening of fire bombing over Tokyo. Hundreds of thousands were destroyed in Dresden, Hamburg, and Coventry by aerial bombing. The fact that forty-five thousand human beings were killed by one bomb over Nagasaki was new only to the extent that it was one bomb that did it.

To fail to speak to the utter moral corruption of the mass destruction of civilians was to fail as a Christian and a priest as I see it. Hiroshima and Nagasaki happened in and to a world and a Christian church that had asked for it—that had prepared the moral consciousness of humanity to do and to justify the unthinkable. I am sure there are church documents around someplace bemoaning civilian deaths in modern war, and I am sure those in power in the church will drag them out to show that it was giving moral leadership during World War II to its membership.

Well, I was there, and I'll tell you that the operational moral atmosphere in the church in relation to mass bombing of enemy civilians was totally indifferent, silent, and corrupt at best—at worst it was religiously supportive of these activities by blessing those who did them.

I say all this not to pass judgment on others, for I do not know their souls then or now. I say all this as one who was part of the so-called Christian leadership of the time. So you see, that is why I am not going to the day of judgment looking for justice in this matter. Mercy is my salvation.

You said the atomic bombing of Nagasaki happened to a church that "had asked for it." What do you mean by that?

For the first three centuries, the three centuries closest to Christ, the church was a pacifist church. With Constantine the church accepted the pagan Roman ethic of a just war and slowly began to involve its membership in mass slaughter, first for the state and later for the faith.

Catholics, Orthodox, and Protestants, whatever other differences they may have had on theological esoterica, all agreed that Jesus' clear and unambiguous teaching on the rejection of violence and on love of enemies was not to be taken seriously. And so each of the major branches of Christianity by different theological methods modified our Lord's teaching in these matters until all three were able to do what Jesus rejected, that is, take an eye for an eye, slaughter, maim, torture.

It seems a "sign" to me that seventeen hundred years of Christian terror and slaughter should arrive at August 9, 1946, when Catholics dropped the A-bomb on top of the largest and first Catholic city in Japan. One would have thought that I, as a Catholic priest, would have spoken out against the atomic bombing of nuns. (Three orders of Catholic sisters were destroyed in Nagasaki that day.) One would have thought that I would have suggested that as a minimal standard of Catholic morality, Catholics shouldn't bomb Catholic children. I didn't.

I, like the Catholic pilot of the Nagasaki plane, "The Great Artiste," was heir to a Christianity that had for seventeen hundred years engaged in revenge, murder, torture, the pursuit of power, and prerogative violence, all in the name of our Lord.

I walked through the ruins of Nagasaki right after the war and visited the place where once stood the Urakami Cathedral. I picked up a piece of a censer from the rubble. When I look at it today I pray God forgives us for how we have distorted Christ's teaching and destroyed his world by the distortion of that teaching. I was the Catholic chaplain who was there when this grotesque process that began with Constantine reached its lowest point—so far.

What do you mean by "so far"?

Briefly, what I mean is that I do not see that the moral climate in relation to war inside or outside the church has dramatically changed much since 1946. The mainline Christian churches still teach something that Christ never taught or even hinted at, namely the just war theory, a theory that to me has been completely discredited theologically, historically, and psychologically.

So as I see it, until the various churches within Christianity repent and begin to proclaim by word and deed what Jesus proclaimed in relation to violence and enemies, there is no hope for anything other than ever-escalating violence and destruction.

Until membership in the church means that a Christian chooses not to engage in violence for any reason and instead chooses to love, pray for, help, and forgive all enemies; until membership in the church means that Christians may not be members of any military—American, Polish, Russian, English, Irish, et al.; until membership in the church means that the Christian cannot pay taxes for others to kill others; and until the church says these things in a fashion which the simplest soul could understand—until that time humanity can only look forward to more dark nights of slaughter on a scale unknown in history. Unless the church unswervingly and unambiguously teaches what Jesus teaches on this matter it will not be the divine leaven in the human dough that it was meant to be.

"The choice is between nonviolence or nonexistence," as Martin Luther King, Jr., said, and he was not, and I am not, speaking figuratively. It is about time for the church and its leadership in all denominations to get down on its knees and repent of this misrepresentation of Christ's words.

Communion with Christ cannot be established on disobedience to his clearest teachings. Jesus authorized none of his followers to substitute violence for love; not me, not you, not the president, not the pope, not a Vatican council, nor even an ecumenical council.

Father Zabelka, what kinds of immediate steps do you think the church should take in order to become the "divine leaven in the human dough"?

Step one should be that Christians the world over should be taught that Christ's teaching to love their enemies is not optional. I've been in many parishes in my life, and I have found none where the congregation explicitly is called upon regularly to pray for its enemies. I think this is essential.

I offer you step two at the risk of being considered hopelessly out of touch with reality. I would like to suggest that there is an immediate need to call an ecumenical council for the specific purpose of clearly declaring that war is totally incompatible with Jesus' teaching and that Christians cannot and will not engage in or pay for it from this point in history on. This would have the effect of putting all nations on this planet on notice that from now on they are going to have to conduct their mutual slaughter without Christian support—physical, financial, or spiritual.

I am sure there are other issues which Catholics or Orthodox or Protestants would like to confront in an ecumenical council instead of facing up to the hard teachings of Christ in relationship to violence and enemies. But it seems to me that issues like the meaning of the primacy of Peter are nowhere near as pressing or as destructive of church credibility and God's world as is the problem of continued Christian participation in and justification of violence and slaughter. I think the church's continued failure to speak clearly Jesus' teachings is daily undermining its credibility and authority in all other areas.

Do you think there is the slightest chance that the various branches of Christianity would come together in an ecumenical council for the purpose of declaring war and violence totally unacceptable activities for Christians under all circumstances?

Remember, I prefaced my suggestion of an ecumenical council by saying that I risked being considered hopelessly out of touch with reality. On the other hand, what is impossible for men and women is quite possible for God if people will only use their freedom to cooperate a little.

Who knows what could happen if the pope, the patriarch of Constantinople and the president of the World Council of Churches called with one voice for such a council? One thing I am sure of is that our Lord would be very happy if his church were again unequivocally teaching what he unequivocally taught on the subject of violence.

[Postscript: George Zabelka died in 1992.]

Peacemakers

An Endowment of Courage

With a common faith and dedication, Marion and Ernest Bromley and Maurice "Mac" McCrackin became close friends in 1950. For 40 years, they have worked together and supported one another in countless struggles for peace and social justice.

In the 1950s, they worked tirelessly, faced jail, and risked their lives in the ultimately successful efforts of the Cincinnati Committee on Human Relations to integrate the local amusement park, music schools, and other public facilities. They joined other members of Peacemakers, a movement committed to radical and personal pacifist action which Marion and Ernest helped to found in 1948, to create Operation Freedom. They made repeated trips to the Deep South with material and emotional support for families who lost jobs and homes as a result of their involvement in the civil rights movement.

Through the 1960s and early '70s, they continually broadened Peacemakers' draft and war tax resistance efforts and served as a vital communications and support center for war resisters and their families across the country. In the latter half of the 1970s, Ernest and Mac were involved in work with prisoners in the Ohio state prison system.

Marion is an active member of the Cincinnati Friends Meeting and is involved in issues of feminism and nonviolence. Mac continues his pastoral work and has been the catalyst in the development of Cincinnati's first neighborhood community land trust and low-income housing project. Ernest, joined by the others, has been actively opposing draft registration and participating in the various actions of a peace movement which they have all helped to strengthen and to shape, including January 1981 demonstrations at the Pentagon which brought them to Washington where they were interviewed by

Chuck Matthei, then-director of the Institute for Community Economics in Boston.

How did you get involved in your work for peace?

Marion Bromley: I was a secretary for the Firestone Company in my hometown of Akron, Ohio, until 1942. I began to be dissatisfied working there, especially as Firestone started to take on more military contracts.

I went to a local meeting of the Fellowship of Reconciliation (FOR) and heard A.J. Muste speak. He needed a secretary for the FOR in New York. I didn't think that I could take such a cut in pay and leave behind so many things, including my airplane.

But I walked away from Fire-stone after thirteen years there, with never a backward glance. The change has been a blessing. I went to New York and met a whole community. That's how I had my own little revolution.

Ernest Bromley: I grew up around Boston and then did seminary work at Duke in North Carolina beginning in 1939. I intended to do rural ministry there in the Methodist Church, but I was caught by World War II.

I recognized that I was a pacifist, which was a new term to me. At that time each driver of an automobile had to display a sticker on the windshield saying that he or she had paid a government tax. It was the first federal tax since Pearl Harbor, and had been enacted in Congress in preparation for the war. I refused to buy the sticker and was interrogated. The process ended in a federal court with my getting sixty days in jail.

After I got out of jail, I continued to use my car until gas rationing was put into effect and a driver had to display the sticker to get gas ration stamps. Then I put up my car and used a bicycle, which was pretty hard since the churches I was serving were spread over forty miles. I had four churches.

Marion: And well-developed calves.

Ernest: The hierarchy of the Methodist Church was opposed to my refusal to pay taxes for war. I withdrew from my pastorate in 1947 because of the church's attitude toward war and went to New York to work as a youth secretary with the FOR, where I met Marion.

We moved from New York right after we were married in 1948 to a little town in Ohio called Wilmington, about fifty miles from Cincinnati. We had heard about the integration and pacifism work of the minister of a Presbyterian Episcopal church in Cincinnati. That pastor was Maurice McCrackin. We became quite well acquainted.

In 1950 Marion and I and the one child we had then moved with three other people to the edge of Cincinnati to form a small community in the Peacemaker orbit.

Is it true that the Internal Revenue Service took away your house?

Marion: In 1975 it almost succeeded. The house we had moved into as a community had become a Peacemaker headquarters. We edited a newsletter there and maintained a fund which sent out monthly checks to families of imprisoned war resisters who needed financial support.

The IRS, during the period when it had a "special services staff"— which nobody knew about until after the exposés during Nixon's latter years in office—went to the Peacemaker bank account without our knowledge and came up with an assessment of something like $25,000 against us.

We had support in Cincinnati and carried on daily leafletting at the federal building downtown, holding off for several months a public auction by the IRS on our house. We had a stroke of good luck in that the Senate committee that Sam Ervin headed disclosed the secret political audits that were going on, including an attack on us. We won our struggle.

But the IRS went ahead with the auction. We had quite a demonstration and by the time the whole thing was over the man who won the property didn't want it. He knew that when it would come time to take possession in a hundred and twenty days, we'd be wall-to-wall people demonstrating.

The head of the local IRS, a personal friend, called some of the people who were on the steps of the federal building one day to come into his office. So they went on in with mops and pails and signs that said, "We're cleaning up the IRS." He explained that the IRS was now in a position and was going to reverse the sale. It had to pay the man the amount of the sale, plus interest.

Mac, when did your involvement begin?

Mac McCrackin: I'm an ex-Presbyterian minister. I hasten to say that some of our best friends are still Presbyterian. I spent five years in Iran after graduating from McCormack Seminary in 1930, then came back and served as a minister in the Midwest.

I heard about two churches in the west end of Cincinnati which had decided to work together, and I moved there in 1945. This was an ecumenical project in a racially mixed neighborhood.

Other churches, who supported our project, would send toys down to our children for us to distribute come Christmastime. I'd pull out all the toy tanks and guns, figuring the children shouldn't play with them and that they had enough education along that line in other places.

I remember right where I was standing in the office the day a friend came in and said, "Mac, did you ever think that every year when you pay your income tax, you're buying live guns to kill people with?"

So I withheld my 1948 tax return—my first withholding. If I had been of an age to register to fight, I would have refused that too. I thought then: The thief holds you up in the alley and says, "Your money or your life"; the Pentagon doesn't give that option—it says, "Your money *and* your life." And unless we can withdraw our money and refuse to give our lives, there's going to be total disaster. I still believe that, and I've been believing it more as the years have rolled on.

When did the church give you your walking papers? Was it over the tax issue?

Mac: Well, it wasn't over what they said it was. I'd been in federal prison for nonpayment of taxes. When I got out, I was brought to judicial trial in the Presbyterian Church.

With what did they charge you?

Mac: Let me see now . . . Disobeying the ordinance of God, disturbing the external peace of the church—I thought it was the inner peace that I ought to have been—and was—disturbing.

I think the thing that really gave them the fuel to get me out of the church was the fact that I wouldn't say that I wasn't a communist. I had connections with Highlander Folk School, an institution committed to racial equality which was accused of being a communist training school.

When asked if I were a communist, I responded, "I will never answer that question." It's a hysterical question.

There was a cadaverous-looking picture of me in the newspapers, which had stamped across it, "He doesn't know. He won't say." So the hierarchy of the presbytery called me in. I thought I was going to be out of the denomination in maybe a few days; I didn't know how slow the ecclesiastical wheels grind.

In 1963 the final separation took place—best thing that ever happened to me. I was so involved going to meetings, classes, with United Appeal. I've been just as busy, but now it is a selective busy-ness.

I'm a pastor of a non-denominational community church. It began with eighty members of my former church. We've all been together since 1945. After I left the Presbyterian Church, I took them all with me to another building about three blocks down the street. And every reporter in town said, "You're going to open up that church right here in the neighborhood?"

I said, "Well, that's where my people are, my friend."

You had a recent experience in prison.

Mac: At the Ohio penitentiary in Lucasville where I had been working with prisoners, the guards had been violently mistreating them. Three escaped and came to me, telling me that I would have to consider myself a hostage, but assuring me that I would not be hurt. They fled in my car. One was later killed, the other two captured.

In January of 1979, the court ordered me to come and testify that I had been kidnapped. I made it clear that I didn't want to add any more years to what I know the prisoners put up with in Lucasville. I refused to cooperate. So I was arrested for contempt and put in jail for four months.

Over the years, the world situation has not improved; in fact, it has worsened. How do you persevere without visible signs of success?

Marion: I remember what I.F. Stone said at a memorial service for A.J. Muste. He mentioned that A.J. had worked many years very effectively. But he said he doubted if all A.J.'s great work had made a bit of difference. "And yet," he said, "who the hell wants to be on the other side?"

So I can't conceive of giving up any of my ideas, no matter how grim the chances of success. It's a matter of integrity.

Mac: Someone once said, "Blessed are the peacemakers, for they shall never run out of work."

It is deep relationships with people that sustain you. Such community extends into whatever situation of conflict or pressure you may get yourself into and gives you reason and foundation not to let yourself down.

Everyone has fears; courage is not letting those fears control you. The world has made so many mistakes that if people don't have a place where they can be deeply rooted in nonviolence, they will have a tendency to ask themselves why they shouldn't just join the insanity like everybody else.

I was thirteen years old when the First World War was over, but I was old enough to remember the slogans: "The War to End All Wars" and "Making the World Safe for Democracy." Of course, all the war made the world safe for was Hitler, and later Stalin.

The more war goes on, the more vindictive it becomes. The means we use determine the ends we reach, and nothing has proven that so much as war. If you are for defending human rights and life, then you shouldn't get into a situation where you will destroy life. Not only will you fail to destroy the enemy of life, you will yourself become life's enemy.

The tragedy now is that there are very few people who are willing just to stand up for what they know to be true. I'll never forget something A.J. Muste said. Jesus, he noted, was a completely free person because he was not afraid of losing his possessions, prestige, job, or his life. Until there are enough people who think there are values more important than material and physical survival, we won't be able to change the course of things.

Ernest: As time goes on, you become aware that things are not going to change very fast. The idealism and energy of your youth begin to fade. Then you have to accept that even if you don't change the world, at least you don't have to let the world change you.

How has your faith affected your ability to persevere?
Mac: I've never been able to cooperate in anything that I think is violating the moral absolutes to which I hold. There comes a time when you have to act on those absolutes, when you can no longer stay in a state of suspended moral animation. Of course, when you choose to act, you risk being wrong; but I've heard many times that it's better to be inconsistently good than consistently bad. And sometimes the only way to clarify truth is by acting on it.

I have tried to live my life in light of my commitment to Jesus and to his way of life. He was concerned about people and helped them without judging them. He never asked a creed of people; he just said, "Follow me." And then they made up their own creeds as they discovered truth about themselves and their world.

Jesus did two things: He condemned the system by confronting groups like the Pharisees, but he also knew and responded to individuals within that system like Nicodemus and Joseph of Arimathea. He spent his time doing good for people individually but also trying to change the conditions under which they lived. His love for people was unconditional.

Those who were with Jesus were inspired and encouraged by his joyful, loving spirit. The more they were with him, the more they came to test and measure their lives by his life and teachings.

Jesus told his followers, "I, if I be lifted up, will draw all people unto me." If we lift up his matchless love in our lives, his loving concern for others, the great spirit of forgiveness, if we lift this life up before others, they will be drawn to Jesus. People can't be driven into the kingdom. They are wooed, attracted, and drawn into it.

It's tragic that the organized church has lost these roots, which were evident in the early church. The early church was forgiving, loving, and nonviolent.

We live in a time when many people fear destruction by nuclear or ecological disaster. Where do you see signs of hope?

Marion: You younger people who have rearranged your lives so as not to participate in the system—you are signs of hope. But you must organize others; only then will you have a movement.

Ernest: You must do all you can, give your whole life, to avoid being persuaded by feelings of despair. People don't want to live long lives so much as they want to live full lives. The individual is the highest of God's creation. So if you are living for others, you are living for the highest there can be.

Do you have any other advice that you can pass on to us from what you've learned over the years?

Mac: At all costs, preserve a sense of humor. Someone once said, "It is our responsibility that we are to take seriously, not ourselves." We must deal as gently with the faults of others as we do with our own. We should speak the truth as we see it plainly and clearly, but with such love that those listening will weigh what we have to say with an open mind and an open heart.

Marion: The last fifty years of my life—that is, the most recent fifty years—have affirmed nonviolence as the key to the good life. Nonviolence is based on a commitment to the sanctity of all life and to the conviction that there is a basic equality among human beings, that we are all part of a whole, and we are all equally precious, equally worthy, within that whole.

I accept life as a gift; I gladly accept the beauty of the earth and of life, not feeling that I have to pay any dues for it, or that I owe something to the society into which I was born.

This probably affects my attitude toward government and the laws of government. I know I do not belong to the state where I happen to be born or where I live. I will decide how much loyalty and obedience I will offer to any government.

Ernest: Obedience to higher laws often demands disobedience to some of the lower ones. The New Testament talks much of obeying the law of the kingdom.

If we conform to mediocre standards and moral values, no way remains by which to transform ourselves or be an example to others. The New Testament exhorted, "Come out from among them" and "Do not conform to the world, but become transformed."

Mac: The greatest social evils of our time are war, poverty, and the criminal justice system. We don't know when these evils will be abolished, but we do know that there are people suffering whom we can help. There are those who will hold onto hope because we care.

To the question, "When will injustice cease?" someone replied, "Injustice will end when those who are not injured are as indignant as those who are." To become indignant is to become involved. To become involved is to become the friends of some of the greatest and bravest people in the world—people who suffer mistreatment and injustice without bitterness, and who, though the odds are stacked overwhelmingly against them, keep their faith and hope alive.

[Postscript: In December, 1990, Ernest and Mac were arrested for climbing over the fence at the White House (aided by a ladder) to protest the Persian Gulf war. Marion died in 1996. Ernest and Mac died in 1997.]

Thomas Merton

A Noisy Vocation in the Silent Life

by Jim Forest

"Paradox" was a word Thomas Merton appreciated and often used, perhaps because there were so many paradoxes within his vocation. He was, for example, a monk belonging to a religious order with a particular tradition of silence—and yet millions of people were to become familiar with his life and convictions. He had a noisy vocation in the silent life. It was a paradox he often wished would end, in favor of silence, but it wouldn't.

In an existential and temperamental sense, Merton was one of the most committed pacifists I have ever met. He saw war as one of the clearest examples of human estrangement from sanity and from God. He was appalled by war in an intense and personal way and saw response to war as a major element in the religious life. Some of the most lethal irony to be found in his writings is reserved for the subject.

Jim Forest, Secretary of the Orthodox Peace Fellowship, lives in Alkmaar, Holland. This article, which appeared in the December 1978 issue of *Sojourners*, was adapted from an essay in *Thomas Merton: Prophet in the Belly of a Paradox*, edited by Gerald Thomey (Paulist Press). Forest's book, *Living with Wisdom: A Life of Thomas Merton*, was published by Orbis Books.

So deep was his revulsion regarding war and its premeditated terrors and cruelties that, when World War II was bursting its European seams and men like Merton's brother were volunteering for the Royal Air Force, Merton was one of the rare Catholics to declare himself a conscientious objector. At the time, Catholic bishops in the United States, England, and Germany were as busy as other religious leaders in offering their unqualified support for lay compliance with "legitimate authority," including military service and killing under orders. Merton, though a thoroughly devout Catholic, marched to the beat of a different drummer away from battlefields and into a weaponless Trappist monastery.

Twenty years later, increasingly conscious of the monk's responsibility for the world rather than against it, he established deep and continuing ties with several strongly pacifist groups, including the Catholic Worker, the Fellowship of Reconciliation, and the Catholic Peace Fellowship.

It was while visiting the Catholic Worker's New York house of hospitality, St. Joseph's, that my own friendship with Merton began. I was still in the Navy, freshly a Catholic, still too fragile in my newly acquired pacifism to have begun finding a way out of the military and into a vocation that had something to do with the peace of God. But I was looking. Hence my inquiring presence at the Catholic Worker, a religious community whose commitment to nonviolent social change was an outgrowth of its hospitality to social rejects.

Merton's letter, arriving just before Christmas, 1960, began with a reference to the Catholic Worker's main peace witness in those years: its annual refusal to take shelter in the subways as a compulsory dress rehearsal for nuclear war with the Soviet Union. It was, really, a bad joke, as the subways offered protection only from conventional weapons; but the ritual had the effect of making nuclear war seem realistic and even survivable. Dorothy Day, the Catholic Worker founder, had been imprisoned several times for her civil disobedience, until the crowds that gathered with her in City Hall Park became so large that the war game was abandoned. But that end was still not in sight when Merton wrote:

> I am deeply touched by your witness for peace. You are very right in doing it along the lines of *Satyagraha* [literally "truthforce," Gandhi's word for what Western people often call nonviolence]. I see no other way, though of course the angles of the problem are not all clear. I am certainly with you on taking some kind of stand and acting accordingly. Nowadays, it is no longer a question of who is right, but who is at least not a criminal. If any of us can say that anymore. So don't worry about whether or not in

every point you are perfectly all right according to everybody's
book; you are right before God as far as you can go, and you are
fighting for a truth that is clear enough and important enough.
What more can anybody do? . . . It was never more true that the
world cannot see true values.

I don't suppose anyone can readily appreciate the value of this and
similar letters that were arriving at the Catholic Worker from Merton
in those days. (Personally, they helped me form a determination that
soon led to my discharge from the Navy as a conscientious objector
and to my membership on the Catholic Worker staff.) Partly due to
Merton, the Catholic pacifist was to become far more common in the
years ahead and to receive open and unambiguous official support
from the highest levels of the Church. But at that time the Catholic
Worker was viewed with considerable suspicion for its talk of "the
works of mercy, not the works of war," though tolerated because of its
orthodoxy in other respects and its direct, simple, and unpretentious
commitment to the humanity of impoverished people who were
ignored by everyone else.

At this time, Merton was hardly a controversial figure. His books
were all over the place, in churches, drug stores, and bus terminals,
and each bore the *Imprimatur* ("let it be printed," a bishop's certificate
that the book was orthodox). Thousands owed their faith, and millions
its deepening, to the stimulus of Merton's writings: his continuing pilgrimage from non-belief to the depths of faith. His books were read by
the convinced and the unconvinced, from the pope's apartment in the
Vatican to prostitutes' apartments near New York's 42nd Street. His
writings had been published in more languages than we had staff
members in our Catholic Worker house of hospitality.

Yet here he was, often writing the Catholic Worker community,
taking our lives and vocations with utmost seriousness, and even
encouraging us in those aspects of our work which were the most controversial.

It was in these days of fallout shelters and air raid sirens that we
received Merton's first submission to the paper we published, the
Catholic Worker. It was an essay, "The Root of War Is Fear," that was
later to appear in *New Seeds of Contemplation*. The piece as a whole
had gone through the normal if often rigid channels of Trappist censorship, but Merton had tacked on a few prefatory paragraphs which
briefly expressed a message which eventually led to his silencing on
"political" issues:

The present war crisis is something we have made entirely for
and by ourselves. There is in reality not the slightest logical reason for war, and yet the whole world is plunging headlong into

frightful destruction, and doing so *with the purpose of avoiding war and preserving peace*! This is true war-madness, an illness of the mind and spirit that is spreading with a furious and subtle contagion all over the world. Of all the countries that are sick, America is perhaps the most grievously afflicted. . . .

What are we to do? The duty of the Christian, in this crisis, is to strive with all his power and intelligence, with his faith, his hope in Christ, and love for God and man, to do the one task which God has imposed upon us in the world today. That task is to work for the total abolition of war. There can be no question that unless war is abolished the world will remain constantly in a state of madness and desperation

During the next two years or more, censorship was often a subject in Merton's letters. It became increasingly difficult for him to get his peace-related articles in print as his Trappist superiors generally considered war an inappropriate subject.

It was in this area that his nonviolence was put to its hardest personal test. His nonviolence, like Gandhi's, implied enduring all things so that transformation might occur in which adversaries were convinced and won over rather than defeated but left unconvinced. Perhaps he recognized in the fears of his superiors the same fears that existed elsewhere in the world, the fears which give rise to war.

What would be the sense of calling others to patience in the labors of fostering life when he could not be patient with those close at hand? Certainly many others have stormed away from committed relationships, muttering about betrayal, the abuse of authority, the Inquisition, the death of God, the hypocrisy of this institution or that. The net result has been that the world was only a bit more fractured and embittered, all the more estranged from difficult truths in reaction to those who were so furious in their advocacy of truth.

Early in 1962 came a harder test. It was no longer a matter of enduring the delays of censorship, or the watering down and qualifying that might be involved. Now it was a matter of being silenced:

I have been trying to finish my book on peace [*Peace in the Post-Christian Era*], and have succeeded in time for the axe to fall. . . .

Now here is the axe. For a long time I have been anticipating trouble with the higher superiors and now I have it. The orders are, no more writing about peace. This is transparently arbitrary and uncomprehending, but doubtless I have to make the best of it . . . [In] substance I am being silenced on the subject of war and peace. This I know is not a very encouraging thing. It implies all sorts of very disheartening consequences as regards the whole cause of peace. It reflects an astounding incomprehension of the seriousness of the present crisis in its religious aspect. It reflects an insensitivity to Christian and Ecclesiastical values, and to the real sense of the monastic vocation. The reason given is that this is not the right kind of work for a monk, and that it "falsifies the monastic message." Imagine that: the thought that a monk might be deeply enough concerned with the issue of nuclear war to voice a protest against the arms race is supposed to bring the monastic life into *disrepute*. Man, I would think that it might just possibly salvage a last shred of repute for an institution that many consider to be dead on its feet. That is really the most absurd aspect of the whole situation, that these people insist on digging their own grave and erecting over it the most monumental kind of tombstone. . . .

Now you will ask me: how do I reconcile obedience, true obedience (which is synonymous with love) with a situation like this? Shouldn't I just blast the whole thing wide open, or walk out, or tell them to jump in the lake?

Let us suppose for the sake of argument that this was not completely excluded. Why would I do this? For the sake of the witness for peace? For the sake of witnessing to the truth of the Church, in its reality, as against this figment of the imagination? Simply for the sake of blasting off and getting rid of the tensions and frustrations in my own spirit, and feeling honest about it?

In my own particular case, every one of these would backfire and be fruitless. It would be taken as a witness *against* the peace movement and would confirm these people in all the depth of their prejudices and their self-complacency. It would reassure them in every possible way that they are incontrovertibly right and make it even more impossible for them ever to see any kind of new light on the subject. And in any case I am not merely looking for opportunities to blast off, I can get along without it.

I am where I am. I have freely chosen this state, and have freely chosen to stay in it when the question of a possible change arose. If I am a disturbing element, that is all right. I am not making a point of being that, but simply of saying what my conscience dictates and doing so without seeking my own interest. This means accepting such limitations as may be placed on me by authority, and not because I may or may not agree with the ostensible reasons why the limitations are imposed, but out of love for God who is using these things to attain ends which I myself cannot at the moment see or comprehend. I know He can and will in His own time take good care of the ones who impose limitations unjustly or unwisely. That is his affair and not mine. In this dimension I find no contradiction between love and obedience, and as a matter of fact it is the only sure way of transcending the limits and arbitrariness of ill-advised commands.

Very strong stuff. Very few in the peace movement then or now could understand or appreciate that kind of stubborn continuity. Marriages often end over much less. But it is the kind of decision that would be respected and valued by Francis of Assisi, or Gandhi, or Dorothy Day.

The "silenced" Merton wasn't altogether silent. The suppressed book was circulated in substantial numbers in a mimeographed form, not unlike the *samizdat* literary underground in the U.S.S.R.

In 1963, the Trappist freeze on his peace writing slowly began to thaw, at least in part, no doubt, because Pope John was saying in encyclical letters to the entire Church and world the kind of things Merton was, formerly in the *Catholic Worker* and, later, in *samizdat*. On occasion, he took pseudonyms: Benedict Monk was almost a give-away, but my favorite was Marco J. Frisbee. The pope having declared flatly in *Pacem in Terris* that war could no longer be considered "a fit instrument of justice," Merton wryly mentioned that he had just writ-ten the Order's Abbot General once again: "I said it was a good thing that Pope John didn't have to get his encyclical through our censors: and could I now start up again."

While the silencing order was not removed, some of Merton's peace concern began to reach at least fractions of the reading public again, and under his own name.

This same year he wrote a preface to the Japanese edition of *The Seven Storey Mountain*, in which he spoke of his present understand-ing of the monastic life:

> The monastery is not an "escape from the world." On the contrary, by being in the monastery I take my true part in all the struggles and sufferings of the world. To adopt a life that is essentially non-assertive, non-violent, a life of humility and peace, is in itself a statement of one's position. But each one in such a life can, by the personal modality of his decision, give his whole life a special orientation. It is my intention to make my entire life a rejection of, a protest against the crimes and injus-tices of war and political tyranny which threaten to destroy the whole race of man and the world with him. By my monastic life and vows I am saying *No* to all the concentration camps, the aer-ial bombardments, staged political trials, the judicial murders, the racial injustices, the economic tyrannies, and the whole socio-economic apparatus which seems geared for nothing but global destruction in spite of all its fair words in favor of peace. I make monastic silence a protest against the lies of politicians, propagandists, and agitators, and when I speak it is to deny that my faith and my Church can ever seriously be aligned with these forces of injustice and destruction.

No doubt Merton's silencing had been unjust and unwarranted, and something his Trappist superiors came deeply to regret, not simply because it came to be embarrassing, but because it was wrong. Yet the crisis it occasioned in Merton's life, if a friend dare make guesses about the "stranger" within his friend, more deeply purified his understanding and compassion, his vision of the Church and its mission, his sense of connection with all who suffer.

Merton did not view the peace movement through rose-colored glasses. He was, for example, painfully aware of how difficult it was for those in protest movements to grow in patience and compassion. He offered us his support, but it was a critical support that sought to prod us to become more sympathetic toward those who were threatened or antagonized by our efforts. Thus he noted "the tragedy" that the majority of people so crave undisturbed security that they are threatened by agitation even when it protests the national nuclear arsenal which is the real threat to their security. But it wouldn't help to get in a rage over this irony: "We have to have a deep patient compassion for the fears and irrational mania of those who hate us or condemn us."

On this crucial matter of managing patience while being aware of the desperate urgency of responding to immediate crises, he spoke of the special attitude we were going to depend on if we hoped to continue in such immensely difficult and frustrating work:

> We will never see the results in our time, even if we manage to get through the next five years without being incinerated. Really we have to pray for a total and profound change in the mentality of the whole world. . . .
>
> The whole problem is this inner change . . . [the need for] an application of spiritual force and not the use of merely political pressure. We all have the great duty to realize the deep need for purity of soul, that is the deep need to possess in us the Holy Spirit, to be possessed by Him. This has to take precedence over everything else. If He lives and works in us, then our activity will be true and our witness will generate love of truth, even though we may be persecuted and beaten down in apparent incomprehension.

He was worried we weren't seeing deeply enough into the subtle dangers that exist even in nonviolent action:

> One of the problematic questions about nonviolence is the inevitable involvement of hidden aggressions and provocations. I think this is especially true when there are a fair proportion of

nonreligious elements, or religious elements that are not spiritually developed. It is an enormously subtle question, but we have to consider the fact that, in its provocative aspect, nonviolence may tend to harden the opposition and to confirm people in their righteous blindness. It may even in some cases separate men out and drive them in the other direction, away from us and away from peace. This of course may be (as it was with the prophets) part of God's plan. A clear separation of antagonists. . . .

Even so, he went on, driving people in the opposite direction can never be seen as a goal of such actions:

[We must] always direct our action toward opening people's eyes to the truth, and if they are blinded, we must try to be sure we did nothing specifically to blind them. Yet there is that danger: the danger one observes subtly in tight groups like families and monastic communities, where the martyr for the right sometimes thrives on making his persecutors terribly and visibly wrong. He can drive them in desperation to be wrong, to seek refuge in the wrong, to seek refuge in violence.

We have got to be aware of the awful sharpness of the truth when it is used as a weapon, and since it can be the deadliest weapon, we must take care that we don't kill more than falsehood with it. In fact we must be careful how we "use" truth, for we are ideally the instruments of truth and not the other way round.

As the weeks and months went by, Merton often had reason to notice that very few peace activists were deeply attuned to some of these insights, and he expressed his anguish with the peace movement's "terrible superficiality," as he summed it up in a letter of August 27, 1962. Yet he was committed to his relationship with us, for all our immaturity and immense limitations, perhaps in a way analogous to his commitments to others in the monastic life and the wider Church who found some of his concerns so discordant and out of step.

The years 1963 and 1964 saw America's quiet war in Vietnam suddenly begin to bulge in size and devastation; these events helped prod the Catholic Peace Fellowship (CPF) into existence, first as a part-time officeless project initially involving Daniel Berrigan and myself with support from John Heidbrink of the Fellowship of Reconciliation (FOR), which Merton had joined formally.

Merton, while mentioning his increasing discomfort at being "a name," agreed to be one of the sponsors. The CPF, with roots both in the Catholic Worker and the Fellowship of Reconciliation, took an unequivocally pacifist stand, emphasizing on its membership brochure the sweeping rejections of war by Popes John and Paul.

In November 1964, several weeks before the CPF was to have an office and, in myself, a full-time staff person, a small group of CPF- and FOR-related individuals came together for a three-day retreat with Merton to consider, in Merton's phrase, "the spiritual roots of protest."

Merton's contribution at the retreat was to press on us, often more with questions than answers, that protest wasn't simply an almost casual human right, but rather a terribly dangerous calling that, if it lacked sufficient spiritual maturity, could contribute to making things worse.

All this time, however, the war was getting worse, and thus the pressures were on us to do more than hold seminars and counsel conscientious objectors. David Miller, of the Catholic Worker staff, unable to find words to adequately express his dismay with the war, its casualties, and the conscription of young Americans to fight in it without their consent or understanding, lifted up his draft card at a rally in front of Manhattan's military induction center and burned the card to an ash— an event on the front page of American newspapers the next morning.

A few months later, Tom Cornell of the CPF staff felt obliged to do the same, responding to a newly passed law that provided heavy fines and long jail terms for anyone mutilating or destroying these tiny forms that noted one's draft status. Tom reasoned it was an idolatrous law, making sacred a scrap of paper, and decided to burn his publicly as well. He did so at the beginning of November, the event occasioning substantial national attention.

A week later Roger LaPorte, a young volunteer and former Cistercian novice, burned not his draft card but himself. He sat before the U.S. Mission to the United Nations before dawn, poured gasoline on his body, and struck a match.

The events hit Merton like a bolt of lightning. On November 11, 1965, we received a telegram:

JUST HEARD ABOUT SUICIDE OF ROGER LAPORTE WHILE I DO NOT HOLD CATHOLIC PEACE FELLOWSHIP RESPONSIBLE FOR THIS TRAGEDY CURRENT DEVELOPMENTS IN PEACE MOVEMENT MAKE IT IMPOSSIBLE FOR ME TO CONTINUE AS SPONSOR OF FELLOWSHIP PLEASE REMOVE MY NAME FROM LIST OF SPONSORS LETTER FOLLOWS THOMAS MERTON

We were already in a state of shock, still trying to absorb the event of Roger's action. He was still alive, dying in Bellevue Hospital. Tom had been indicted and was awaiting a trial date. Merton's telegram, and the letter which arrived a few days later, added to a sense of exhaustion and despair.

In his letter he recognized that we were as shocked as he was by Roger's action. Such actions would harm rather than help the peace movement. So would draft card burnings, he went on. Such things were so disturbing, Merton said, that he was led to the "regretful decision that I cannot accept the present spirit of the movement as it presents itself to me."

In the exchange of letters that was to follow, however, as he heard details about what had happened and began to learn not only of the legal and political basis of Tom's action but more of the human dimensions of Roger LaPorte, he decided not to withdraw his CPF sponsorship after all.

John Heidbrink's letters to Merton at this time prompted a long reflection on the intersection of his redefined vocation (Merton had taken up full-time residence in a hermitage on the grounds of his monastery) with the recent events in New York:

Roger's immolation started off a deep process of examination and it will lead far. Wrong as I think his act was objectively, I believe it did not prejudice the purity of his heart and I never condemned him. What I condemned and . . . still . . . question is a pervasive "spirit" or something, a spirit of irrationality, of power seeking, of temptation to the wrong kind of refusal and impatience and to pseudo-charismatic witness which can be terribly, fatally destructive of all. . . . [There is] a spirit of madness and fanaticism [in the air] . . . and it summons me to a deep distrust of all my own acts and involvements in this public realm. . . .

The real road [for me] lies . . . with a real development in thought and work that will, if it is what it should be, be much more true and more valid for peace than any series of ephemeral gestures I might attempt to make. But anyway, now is a time for me of searching, digging, and if I mention *angst* it will not be to dramatize myself in any way but to assure you that I conceive my real and valid union with you all to make this form of silently getting ground up inside by the weights among which you are moving outside.

Merton changed his mind. This isn't a trait one takes for granted.

Paradoxically, the final effect of Merton's short-lived resignation from the CPF was that he decided to become more directly involved. He helped the CPF carefully define its "pastoral" work which, by December 29, 1965, he saw as being of immense importance. He offered to write a leaflet spelling out the Church's teaching on war. In time this emerged as a CPF booklet, *Blessed are the Meek*, not only presenting the Church's teaching but what nonviolence is all about: a meekness that has nothing to do with passivity, that involves selflessness and considerable risk, and which is liberating rather than murderous. "The chief difference between violence and nonviolence," he remarked, "is that violence depends entirely on its own calculations. Nonviolence depends entirely on God and His Word."

During the last years of correspondence, while there continued to be much that was of a practical nature relating to the work of the CPF and the FOR, there continued to be much that reminded me again that my first encounter with Merton was with a man of outrageous laughter.

I suspect his sense of humor had a great deal to do with his ability to persevere with his monastic community, but also with his peace community. If he spoke grumpily about his fellow monks, it tended to be in a way that occasioned at least a smile. When a friend designed a letterhead that featured the words "the monks are moving," he asked if I could send him some blank sheets for some of his own correspondence, then added:

> Only thing is I wonder if the monks are moving. Everything I do gives me scruples about being identified with this stupid rhinocerotic outfit that charges backward into the jungle with portentious snuffling and then bursts out of the canebrake with a roar in the most unlikely places.

With sweet irony he commented on a censorship of a very different kind, altogether unofficial and coming from the bottom of the ladder rather than the top: "Now I can't get secretarial help any more because my last available secretary is so pious that he thinks I am too wild and controversial."

When his old friend and mentor Dan Walsh was ordained in Louisville in 1967, Merton wrote of the celebration that followed afterward at the home of Tommy O'Callaghan:

> There was a lot of celebrating. In fact I celebrated on too much champagne, which is a thing a Trappist rarely gets to do, but I did a very thorough job. At one point in the afternoon I remember looking up and focussing rather uncertainly upon four faces of nuns sitting in a row looking at me in a state of complete scandal and shock. Another pillar of the Church had fallen.

Another letter arrived with a color snapshot of, Merton announced, "the only known photograph of God." In most respects it was just a view of the Kentucky hills, fold upon fold of green under a brilliant blue sky. But hanging down from the top, dominating the whole scene, was an immense sky hook, the kind used in construction for lifting substantial objects. It looked like an overgrown fishing hook.

If Leon Bloy was right when he said "Joy is the most infallible sign of the presence of God," then God was very present in Merton, for all his hard times in a hard century. That joy and laughter were a major element in what he had to say about peacemaking and many other things as well. He was at times a scandal to his brothers in the monastic life, and to pacifists too—the kind that can't admit a smile in These Difficult Times.

It was in that laughter that I best understood his seriousness. One discovered the connection that necessarily exists between a profound and attentive silence and words that have truth in them. A monk who could see God in a giant hook dangling above the Kentucky woods and who could roll on the floor with joy over the stench of unwashed feet was the same one who could consider war in its human dimension with all its agony and sense that God was obliging us not to make a peace with such peacelessness.

With prayer and with word, he was able to help others to do the same, to keep going when continuity seemed impossible. His letters did that for me on a number of occasions. But perhaps one letter was to you no less than me. It was written February 21, 1966:

Do not depend on the hope of results. When you are doing the sort of work you have taken on, essentially an apostolic work, you may have to face the fact that your work will be apparently worthless and even achieve no result at all, if not perhaps results opposite to what you expect. As you get used to this idea, you start more and more to concentrate not on the results but on the value, the rightness, the truth of the work itself. And there too a great deal has to be gone through, as gradually you struggle less and less for an idea and more and more for specific people. The range tends to narrow down, but it gets much more real. In the end, it is the reality of personal relationships that saves everything. . . .

The big results are not in your hands or mine, but they suddenly happen, and we can share in them; but there is no point in building our lives on this personal satisfaction, which may be denied us and which after all is not that important.

You are probably striving to build yourself an identity in your work, out of your work and your witness. You are using it, so to speak, to protect yourself against nothingness, annihilation. That is not the right use of your work. All the good that you will do will come not from you but from the fact that you have allowed yourself, in the obedience of faith, to be used by God's love. Think of this more and gradually you will be free from the need to prove yourself, and you can be more open to the power that will work through you without your knowing it.

. . . If you can get free from the domination of causes and just serve Christ's truth, you will be able to do more and will be less crushed by the inevitable disappointments. Because I see nothing whatever in sight but much disappointment, frustration, and confusion. . . .

The real hope, then, is not in something we think we can do, but in God who is making something good out of it in some way we cannot see. If we can do His will, we will be helping in this process. But we will not necessarily know all about it beforehand. . . .

Enough of this . . . it is at least a gesture. . . . I will keep you in my prayers.

All the best, in Christ,
Tom

VIII

BLESSED ARE THOSE WHO ARE PERSECUTED

Dietrich Bonhoeffer

Faith and Conviction

by Melanie Morrison

I remember a conversation that I had in America thirteen years ago with a young French pastor. We were asking ourselves quite simply what we wanted to do with our lives. He said he would like to become a saint (and I think it's quite likely that he did become one). At the time I was very impressed, but I disagreed with him, and said, in effect, that I should like to learn to have faith. For a long time I didn't realize the depth of the contrast. I thought I could acquire faith by trying to live a holy life, or something like it. I discovered later, and I'm still discovering right up to this moment, that it is only by living completely in this world that one learns to have faith. One must completely abandon any attempt to make something of oneself, whether it be a saint, or a converted sinner, or a churchman. . . . By this worldliness I mean living unreservedly in life's duties, problems, successes and failures, experiences and perplexities. In so doing we throw ourselves completely into the arms of God, taking seriously not our own sufferings, but those of God in the world—watching with Christ in Gethsemane. That, I think, is faith; that is metanoia.

Dietrich Bonhoeffer
Tegel prison, 1944

Melanie Morrison is co-director of The Leavon Center of Lyons, Michigan.

261

Dietrich Bonhoeffer was a German Christian who could not remain silent in the face of Hitler's fascism and genocide. He spoke out publicly from the pulpit, the classroom lectern, in ecumenical gatherings and in the printed word. In his last years he went underground, speaking by actions that were clandestine and covert. He joined the conspiracy to take Hitler's life. On April 5, 1943, Dietrich Bonhoeffer was arrested and interned in Tegel Prison. Two years later, April 9, 1945, he was hanged by the Gestapo twenty-one days before Hitler took his own life.

To come to the heart of Bonhoeffer's theological worldview and his reflections on Christian resistance, it might be best to focus on two critical junctures in his life when he struggled with what must be his response to Hitler. The first decisive turning point came during his visit to the United States in 1939. Bonhoeffer had accepted an invitation to teach at Union Seminary in New York because he wanted to avoid the draft, and he needed time to evaluate what he should do.

Bonhoeffer stayed in the United States only five weeks, although he had intended a much longer stay. He did not know until he left Germany that he belonged there. Coming to that realization was an agonizing struggle, and during those weeks of decision he kept a journal and wrote repeatedly to his close friend Eberhard Bethge. Here is his struggle in his own words:

> *26th June 1939:* It is for us as it is for soldiers who come home on leave from the front but who, in spite of all their expectations, long to be back at the front again. We cannot get away from it any more. Not because we are necessary, or because we are useful (to God?), but simply because that is where our life is, and because we leave our life behind, destroy it, if we cannot be in the midst of it again. It is nothing pious, more like some vital urge.

> *July 1939:* I have had time to think and to pray about my situation and that of my nation and to have God's will for me clarified. I have come to the conclusion that I have made a mistake in coming to America. I must live through this difficult period of our national history with the Christian people of Germany. I shall have no right to participate in the reconstruction of Christian life in Germany after the war if I do not share the trials of this time with my people.

Those five weeks in the United States were an intense personal struggle for Bonhoeffer. Yet his letters and journal are remarkably free of self-preoccupation. Struggling with the decision of whether to return to Germany, he did not have eyes that were riveted on his own soul. That soul's salvation or damnation, righteousness or unrighteousness was not the issue. He neither wanted to save his life by seeking safe refuge in the United States nor to lose it heroically in martyrdom. The decision was a lonely and solitary one to be sure, and yet the issue was not justification of self. His decision to return is grounded in corporate identification with his nation and his church: "It is nothing pious . . . not because we are necessary, or because we are useful, but simply because that is where our life is."

I think Bonhoeffer would have taken exception to the desire of some American peace activists to escape history's judgment of complicity, as he would have taken exception to the call to "come out of her, lest you partake of her sin," when that call is interpreted as separating oneself from identification with the people of one's nation. Bonhoeffer never denied his German citizenship in the name of a universal Christian citizenship, even as he worked for the demise and defeat of his nation. He did not return to Germany to escape the judgment of history, to flee complicity, or to justify himself in the eyes of God. Quite the opposite; he returned to actively share in the corporate guilt, judgment, and responsibility laid upon him as a German Christian. These were the people he belonged to, and he had to return to share their trials.

The second critical juncture for Bonhoeffer occurred shortly after he returned to Germany. He faced the decision of joining those actively engaged in conspiracy to take Hitler's life. This decision was not a sudden one; he had been moving in that direction over a period of years. Initially, Bonhoeffer had hoped that he could resist the course his nation was taking by speaking out as a member of the church. He hoped the Confessing Church would speak out boldly against anti-Semitism. He was disappointed in this hope.

Then Bonhoeffer considered resistance as a Christian pacifist, taking an individual stand as a matter of conscience. But this way proved unacceptable to him also in time. "Finally," says Eberhard Bethge, "he sacrificed himself quite differently, as a German, as a Christian, in order to pay the overdue price for the guilt of his class and his nation, without asking for any ecclesiastical protection any more." He chose to identify himself with the "secular" political resistance movement which involved him in a hidden witness.

Bonhoeffer's brother-in-law Hans Dohnanyi introduced Bonhoeffer to the narrower circle of conspirators. And it was Dohnanyi who one evening asked Bonhoeffer what he thought of the New Testament passage "All who take the sword will perish by the sword." Bonhoeffer responded that their circle conspiring to take up the sword against Hitler was not exempt from the judgment of this word. Its truth could not be suspended because of the extraordinarily evil circumstances. Yet, said Bonhoeffer, it was time that there be people willing to take that judgment upon themselves for the sake of others.

It is important to emphasize that Bonhoeffer never altered his conviction that violence was sin. He never sought to justify his decision to participate in the assassination plot on Hitler's life. Yet he also believed that he could not let others pull the trigger for him and thereby neatly protect his own righteousness.

For those who demand simple explanations, Bonhoeffer's decision to enter the political conspiracy under the guise of counterespionage will appear enigmatic and confounding. He had no illusions about his actions. He believed he was inviting the wrath of God. Resistance for Bonhoeffer was not a matter of fleeing complicity. It meant loving God and God's world enough to be willing to risk the sacrifice of his own salvation by complicity with the sin of killing:

> Who stands fast? Only the one whose final standard is not his reason, his principles, his conscience, his freedom or his virtue, but the one who is ready to sacrifice all this when he is called to obedient and responsible action in faith and in exclusive allegiance to God—the responsible person, who tries to make his whole life an answer to the question and call of God.
>
> *(Letters and Papers from Prison)*

Clear, principled martyrdom would have been easier for us to comprehend than the life Bonhoeffer chose when he went underground and joined this inner circle of conspirators. It might have been easier for Bonhoeffer as well. For the martyrdom he chose was fraught with unanswered questions and contradictions. But, as Eberhard Bethge has put it, "Bonhoeffer wanted to bear responsibility for himself and his time, leaving the justification to God." And bearing responsibility meant for Bonhoeffer bearing guilt. In prison Bonhoeffer wrote a confession of guilt for himself and his church. In this confession, he does not attempt to distance himself from the sins of his church. He writes as one who stands convicted along with the church.

This solidarity with guilt grows out of Bonhoeffer's incarnational theology. God, in Jesus Christ, spoke a yes to all creation, claiming the world for Christ. Thus, for Bonhoeffer, in the incarnation all dualism is overcome. There are not two spheres—one sacred and one profane—there is only Christ at the center of the world.

Throughout his life, Bonhoeffer struggled with and against the dualism inherent in Luther's formulation of the two kingdoms. Bonhoeffer was dismayed with a tendency in Luther's followers to proclaim a "cheap grace" that collapsed the rigorous demands of discipleship and thereby seemed to confer blessing on the world as it was.

Particularly toward the end of his life, Bonhoeffer grew equally uneasy with another formulation of the faith that called on Christians to separate from the world by trying to live a holy life. This was the disquiet he expressed about the French pastor's desire to be a saint. For Bonhoeffer, God is known not at the boundaries of life but at its center. And at the center, God does not speak a triumphant yes to godlessness, suffering, and oppression. God has, in Jesus Christ, entered into solidarity with those who suffer by standing with, and for, the weak, the outcast, the rejected. Indeed, this is who Jesus Christ is—a "man of sorrows, acquainted with grief," who died outside the city gates.

The Christian, according to Bonhoeffer, is not called to a life apart from, or over against, the world, even though the call be in the name of holiness and principle. The danger of this call is the Christian ghetto. Yet neither is the Christian called to condone and bless godlessness in the name of grace. The danger of this call is accommodation. In his own words, the calling of the Christian is "to plunge himself into the life of a godless world, without attempting to gloss over its ungodliness with a veneer of religion or trying to transfigure it. He must live a 'worldly' life and so participate in the suffering of God."

In the midst of the most apocalyptic times imaginable—in the midst of unspeakable human brutality—Bonhoeffer refused to abandon the world to darkness by speaking apocalyptically. In his last days, he was more firmly convinced than ever that the Christian must live a worldly life with all its "duties, problems, successes and failures, experiences and perplexities." Even as the signs indicate that we may live in the last days, God has not forsaken creation, and the only faithful question is still to ask how the coming generation is to live. We must always act on their behalf, that they may have a human world to inhabit.

Martin Niemoeller

A Confessional Courage

Martin Niemoeller, born in 1892 in the small Westphalian town of Lippstadt, spent his boyhood as the son of a Lutheran pastor in the industrial town of Elberfeld. At 18 he became a navy cadet, serving on U-boats during World War I, eventually as a commander. After leaving the navy, he followed up on a boyhood sense of vocation to the ministry. In 1920 Niemoeller and his wife, Else Bremer, moved to Muenster, where they stayed during the years of political and economic instability in which the Nazis first emerged. Young Niemoeller was a militant patriot and a leader in the Academic Defense Corps, an armed student nationalist organization which he helped found.

After his ordination, Niemoeller spent seven years as a church administrator. In July 1931, he accepted a call and moved with his wife and six children to the Dahlem parish in Berlin.

In the November 1932 Protestant Church elections, the Nazi-steered "German Christians" gained the majority, and in April

Nancy Lukens interviewed Martin Niemoeller in March 1981 in Wiesbaden, Germany, while she was in the country researching a book on resistance to Hitler.

1933, when Hitler's anti-Jewish laws began to eliminate Jews from all levels of society, the churches halfheartedly supported the move.

Although Niemoeller wanted to keep his church work separate from politics, he began to realize that Hitler, despite lavish religious rhetoric, intended to subjugate the official churches to totalitarian Nazi rule. When legislation was adopted by the Protestant Church to remove baptized Jews from the clergy, Niemoeller and a number of other pastors decided it was necessary to act to keep German Christians from adapting Christian doctrine to fit Nazi ideology.

Niemoeller sent a circular letter to all German pastors inviting them to join a "Pastors' Emergency League." This voluntary association of clergy intended to pool their spiritual and material resources to support those pastors, mostly of Jewish origin, who were being dismissed by the official church. By September 1933, there was a widespread response to this call, and almost overnight Niemoeller became the key spokesperson for the German churches' opposition to Hitler.

The Emergency League network eventually fed into the larger movement that in 1934 resulted in the formation of the Confessing Church. In opposition to the Nazi church policies and the official German Christians' church, the Confessing Church claimed sole authority as the Protestant church of Jesus Christ in Germany. Its theology was one of the cross and not of Germanic superiority.

The Confessing Church, however, did not oppose the Nazi state with political resistance. It was only after the war that Niemoeller pointed to his own and others' failure to oppose the regime's legalized atrocities in time, saying:

> When the Nazis came to get the Communists, I was silent. When they came to get the Socialists, I was silent. When they came to get the Catholics, I was silent. When they came to get the Jews, I was silent. And when they came to get me, there was no one left to speak.

But the illegal status and oppositional course of Confessing Church members did, by 1934, lead to clashes with the state over church issues. By the summer of 1939 most members were removed from the scene either through imprisonment or through the draft.

In 1937 Niemoeller was arrested and imprisoned in Berlin. When even the Nazi court that tried him the following

February on charges of breaching the peace could not bring itself to find evidence and impose a sentence, Hitler dismissed the judges and had Niemoeller taken to the Sachsenhausen concentration camp as his "personal prisoner." In July 1941, Niemoeller was moved to Dachau near Munich, where he was held for the duration of the war.

The story of Niemoeller's leadership in the postwar German church is one of constant alertness to the dangers of an established, self-interested church. Niemoeller had a major part in the formulation of the October 1945 "Stuttgart Declaration of Guilt," in which the Evangelical Church claimed its share of responsibility for the suffering brought by Germany on the world. He tried to make clear in countless speaking tours throughout Germany that no renewal was possible without recognition of the sins of the past.

Niemoeller and other Confessing Church pastors called on the German church to recognize the lesson of the Nazi catastrophe: The church becomes guilty toward humanity when it is concerned primarily for its own institutional well-being and the souls of its members. But it was an unpopular message, and the surviving leaders of the Confessing Church became more and more of a minority.

Meanwhile, reconstruction and the beginning economic boom in Germany had raised the issue of German rearmament and remilitarization. In the early 1950s, when anyone who dared to talk of a neutral Germany was called a traitor or a Communist, Niemoeller was among the most outspoken against German rearmament.

At the time of this interview, Niemoeller was 89 years old. He was still concerned with the issues of the church and its stance toward the state and war. Less than two months before, he had marched in Hamburg with more than 70,000 other Christians to protest the arms race.

Martin Niemoeller died in 1984.

Many people who are aware of the holocaust in Europe during World War II are increasingly concerned about developments which could mean nuclear holocaust in our generation. You have said that you see a similarity between the silence, apathy, and blindness of clergy and church—people in the Third Reich and that of Christians today in the face of the expanding arms race and the danger of nuclear war. Would you elaborate on this for us? In particular, could you help us understand the phenomenon of the church in Nazi Germany acquiescing to Hitler's foreign policies, which made a religion of German nationalism?

When the Lutheran church was formed at the time of the Reformation, the Lutherans placed themselves under the protection of the secular ruler and designated him as their highest lay member, and at the same time, as their bishop. In my own generation, few people realized that the king of Prussia was in fact also the supreme authority, the bishop, of our Protestant church in Prussia.

So your generation accepted this "throne and altar" connection?
We lived with that connection—until some of us saw that it had to lead to conflicts between what secular authority—the state—demanded and what the church teaches about what God asks of us. Then we began to make a separation between "throne" and "altar," in concept and in practice—one that still holds today.

Church authority and state authority are very different entities. The state, and the Christian within the state, can behave differently in the realm of politics than the gospel or conscience dictates. I once put it this way, and I've said it over and over in the last twenty years (although not until fifteen years after the end of World War II, I might add): "Bismarck was a good Christian. Not only did he want to *appear* to be one, but he sincerely wanted to *be* one. But on his office door, the same office in which I met Hitler in 1934, one could read an invisible sign: 'Jesus Christ not allowed to enter here.'"

That's what Bismarck's mentality said. Anyone could approach Hitler and Bismarck and all the figures in authority, but you had to leave Jesus Christ outside. There was no room there for the truth the church is called to preach: that Jesus is the Lord not only in heaven, in his kingdom, but here on earth in his church and in the world. According to the mentality behind Bismarck's invisible sign, there was a basic separation of one's existence as a citizen and one's life as a Christian.

But in 1933 it was different. Under Hitler, the church never tried to take over the role of the state. It was the other way around. When the state tried to dictate every detail of our life, including taking over the Protestant church, it should have been the urgent task of the church to shut its doors so that Mr. Hitler could not come in. But there was the whole business with the German Christians. Their belief degenerated into a heathen, and then a Germanic, religion.

For the individual, then, the question became: "What do I do when the state tells me something different than what Jesus Christ, or my Christian conscience, tells me is just?" In the face of this conflict, some gave the political demands of the day priority, and others said, "No, as a Christian I will not do that."

This was basically the conflict in the Third Reich. The issue was whether one saw Jesus as the highest authority, or Hitler. Few people understood this, and people today still have not caught on to the fact

that this was the real issue in the church struggle: the committed conscience of the Christian asking, "Lord, what would you have that I
do?" versus the obvious and all-pervading demands of Hitler's state.

To whom am I ultimately accountable? As a Christian, to Christ; as
idealist, to my ideal. Everyone has some higher authority. It is a grave
mistake today to think one can attain true ends without a true authority. Today, that is the ultimate question.

I have always said that a pious Christian can be essentially atheist
in ultimate commitment. The decisive factor is whether I live the consequences of my faith. Is God my authority? Which God?

As a Christian, I say that God comes to me in Jesus Christ and in
the spirit of love. That is the essence of the doctrine of the Trinity. I
cannot know God at all; rather, I have some idea or other about God.
But when I know Jesus, I no longer flounder with ideas about God, but
I ask Jesus—who tells me I can say "My Father," or "Our Father" to
God—I ask how Jesus relates to this Father and how I can know the
Father through Jesus. When I place myself under *this* authority, then
I can only act in the spirit of Jesus Christ.

I do not believe in any dogma; I can't any longer, because it is full
of expressions that must be understood and lived differently today
than when they were first formulated. For me, the authority of the living God is expressed in Jesus' teaching us to pray "Our Father." If I
live in this authority, I live in the Holy Spirit.

*And then you are free to live totally in the world, and there, too, God
is Lord.*
No, I don't live in the world; rather, I live as a Christian whose calling it is to live in the world. Of course, that means there is no area of
life where I could say, "This is where Jesus' authority stops." Jesus'
claim is, "*All* authority is given unto me in heaven and on earth." The
separation between politics on the one hand and being a Christian on
the other—there just cannot be such a separation.

*How did you get from this personal realization of the consequences
of Christian discipleship to your current involvements in the European
and worldwide peace movement? Last fall you joined a diverse spec-
trum of public figures in calling for resistance to new rounds of atomic weapons systems, especially to stationing American middle-range
nuclear missiles in West Germany by 1983. What is it about the argu-
ments for more and more armaments in the name of national security
that have appeal over the plea that you and others have formulated
again and again in recent years? Is it fear?*
I must make a personal confession on that point. I have often been
asked what one can do against fear. I have to say, "What is fear?" I

don't really know fear. We have been told, "Fear not—all the fear you conjure up in your minds I have been through for you and overcome."

It was in my encounter with Hitler in 1934 [Niemoeller was accused of criticizing the fuehrer in a tapped phone conversation] that this came over me: "Good grief, this man is scared!" He was much more scared than I was—that is what horrified me.

When he addressed me in front of all the others, I was the only ordinary pastor there among all the bishops that day. He thundered away at me, saying. "Every time I drive out of the gate of the Reich Chancellery, I have to be prepared in case somebody has a revolver and is planning to shoot me." At this point I was aware of being free of fear, and was glad. The fuehrer was more afraid than I was.

The fear I see in many Americans, including many Christians, is psychologically the same as what you saw in Hitler: the obsessive need for security, which eventually sees a potential enemy in everything that threatens our self-righteous interests. And the more we see this force at work, the more we become fearful.

Yes, certainly, if you put yourself in Christ's place and think you or your country must save the world—as if God weren't enough. For me it is sufficient that God gave his only son, in whom he was well pleased, and let him die, in order to show us what he meant: "Fear not death, but die. That is what life is." The cross and the resurrection go together, and that is the way of discipleship. What difference does it make how long I live or when I die—my life can be over at any moment.

My hope, the hope that has kept me going the past twenty years and for which I have taken a lot of beatings, is that there is always the next generation that has its own vision and goes on. The worst thing I see today is the loss of faith in the good news that we have to share with the world—that we are well taken care of in the hands of God, that he is our Father, that this fact redeems our human community and can be its security and its guideline, day by day; this is what history is about.

I have never hated anyone in my life. That is crucial. I can be very angry, and have I ever! With the Lutheran bishops during the church struggle, for example, when things got rough between 1935 and 1937. I could get abysmally angry at them.

Or in the concentration camp after 1937. But I am so glad that at the end of seven years I was not released from the camp but kept prisoner almost eight years—minus a week. For it wasn't until the last three months of my imprisonment that I began to understand what it means, existentially, to love one's enemy.

There were our SS-men in Dachau; they were the people who were hanging my fellow prisoners. We were forced to watch, and despised the whole mess, until it suddenly became clear: "These poor devils—how on earth can human beings become so depraved and sadistic? What have we come to? *These* are the people we should pray for, not only for the prisoners."

It is so easy to become cynical and forget the power of Christ's love. How can the church today rediscover the power of "love your enemies" in the face of potential nuclear holocaust?

They say there are now several tons of nuclear explosives for every human being alive on earth. A tiny bit sufficed to destroy the population of Hiroshima, and we now have many times that much for every man, woman, and child alive. How will we get rid of it, even if it were decided today to stop the arms race altogether and destroy all nuclear arms stockpiles? And yet more and more are produced.

I think the arms race on the level of nuclear weaponry is sheer insanity. I can only say, "Stop the insanity. But whether you stop or not, you have in effect laid the groundwork for your suicide."

I thank God every evening that the day has come and gone, and pray every morning that we might live another day.

How do we live? How can the church offer hope in the face of this impending second holocaust?

We live in faith. And faith can only be lived out of love and compassion. Sometimes that is expressed as faith, sometimes as hope.

By hope I mean avoiding despair. Faith is the same thing, except that it is only by faith, grounded in the knowledge of Jesus, that we have the chance to live in love, to look beyond ourselves to the welfare of others.

I remember a seminar of old Professor Smend in Muenster where I studied theology. One day he asked a rather sleepy fellow student of mine to recite the greatest commandment, whereupon the student rattled it off absentmindedly: "You shall love the Lord your God with all your heart, and with all your soul, and with all your mind, and your neighbor as yourself."

Smend responded, "Say it again!" So he did, after which Smend came down with his point: "Don't you ever say it that way again—as yourself!"

Today's translations make the commandment sound like a "fifty-fifty" proposition. Today's psychology (I started out studying psychology, by the way, until Barth came along, thank goodness!)—today's psychology makes us think as if we had to divide up the available love like a pie. Luther translated the Greek in one place in a way that makes sense for us today: Love your neighbor *in place of*, instead of, yourself. In other words, change places with your neighbor.

What does it imply in the Greek?

It's just as ambiguous there. It does not become unambiguous until we look at the cross. That's the point, isn't it? Not to think of yourself but of the other, of what is important for him or her. Let the other one enter the space where your love is, with all its inclinations, needs, desires. You show you care for a person by putting your life on the line, not by asking what will happen to you for defending the other person's interests.

Where there is no love of this kind there can't be any hope either. The anchorpoint of the Trinity is my fellow human being, whose well-being becomes my only point in living.

And what is the Christian church preaching, really? I mistrust churches today in what they claim to be preaching, and must say I prefer small groups of committed folks who try to live what the New Testament calls *agape*, which is centered in the person of Jesus.

Can you tell us more about how you became a pacifist?

I really haven't learned anything new in my understanding of Christian ethics since I was eight years old. My father was a pastor in the Prussian Church of the Union in Lippstadt, Westphalia. I started school at Easter-time, 1898, when Bismarck was still alive. I was the oldest of four after my older brother died; the fifth came along a year later, and all five of us are still alive, amazingly enough—God knows how often I've skated by the edge of death. We hope to celebrate my youngest sister's eightieth in November and my ninetieth two months later.

In any case, I was a schoolboy of eight when my father often took me along in the afternoons when he went around to visit the sick. One day we went to see a weaver who was dying of tuberculosis. Downstairs was his loom, and my father parked me there while he went upstairs to the sick man's bedroom. I took in the bare room with nothing but the loom and whitewashed walls.

In one corner, I noticed something framed and under glass which was embroidered in pearls—nothing but the question, "What would Jesus say?" I've never forgotten it—never. And that's the sum of Christian ethics.

Oscar Romero

A Shout of Victory

Archbishop Oscar Romero delivered his last homily in San Salvador cathedral on March 23, 1980. The next day, as Romero celebrated Mass in a small hospital chapel, a gunman stepped forward and shot him.

Romero had become increasingly vocal in his support for popular organizations and his denunciation of military repression in the weeks before he was killed. Many believe that this Lenten homily, which most directly addressed the immorality of the military's actions, brought on his assassination.

Before he died, Romero left a promise: "If I am killed, I will rise again in the people of El Salvador." His spirit and presence are celebrated throughout El Salvador, in all of Central America, and beyond—wherever people are working for justice.

The following excerpts from Romero's last homily, which appeared in the May 1980 issue of *Sojourners*, were translated by Nena Terrell and Sally Hanlon.

. . . Easter is a shout of victory. No one can extinguish that life which Christ revived. Not even death and hatred against him and against his

Church will be able to overcome. He is the victor!

As he will flourish in an Easter of unending resurrections, it is necessary to also accompany him in Lent, in a Holy Week that is cross, sacrifice, martyrdom; as he would say, "Happy are those who do not become offended by their cross!"

Lent is then a call to celebrate our redemption in that difficult complex of cross and victory. Our people are very qualified, all their surroundings preach to us of the cross; but all who have Christian faith and hope know that behind this Calvary of El Salvador is our Easter, our resurrection, and that is the hope of the Christian people. . . .

Today, as diverse historical projects emerge for our people, we can be sure that victory will be had by the one that best reflects the plan of God. And this is the mission of the Church. That is why, in the light of the divine Word that reveals the designs of God for the happiness of the peoples, we have the duty, dear brothers and sisters, to also point out the facts, to see how the plan of God is being reflected or disdained in our midst. Let no one take badly the fact that we illuminate the social, political, and economic truths by the light of the divine words that are read at our Mass, because not to do so would, for us, be un-Christian. . . .

I ask the Lord during the whole week as I go gathering up the clamor of the people and the aches of so much crime, the ignominy of so much violence, that he give me the suitable words to console, to denounce, to call for repentance; and even though I may continue to be a voice crying in the desert, I know that the Church is making the effort to fulfill its mission. . . .

The readings of Lent tell us how God applied his project in history in order to make the history of the peoples their history of salvation. And in the measure that those peoples reflect that project of God—to save us in Christ by conversion—in that measure the peoples are gaining salvation and are happy.

. . . Personal sin is the root of the great social sin: This we must be very clear on, beloved brothers and sisters, because today it is very easy to point out and beg justice for others; but how few cast a glance at their own conscience! How easy it is to denounce structural injustice, institutionalized violence, social sin! And it is true, this sin is everywhere, but where are the roots of this social sin? In the heart of every human being. Present-day society is a sort of anonymous world in which no one is willing to admit guilt and everyone is responsible. We are all sinners, and we have all contributed to this massive crime and violence in our country.

Because of this, salvation begins with the human person, with human dignity, with saving every person from sin. And in Lent this is God's call: Be converted! Individually there are among us here no two sinners alike. Each one has committed his or her own shameful deeds, and yet we want to cast our guilt on the other and hide our own sin. I must take off my mask; I, too, am one of them, and I need to beg God's pardon because I have offended God and society. This is the call of Christ: Before all else, the human person! . . .

Let us not try to call upon our country's constitution to defend our own personal selfishness, trying to use it for our own interests when it has been trampled upon everywhere. The law is for the benefit of the human person, not the person for the law. And so Jesus is the source of peace when he has thus given human dignity its rightful place. We feel that we count on Jesus, that we do not count on sin, that we must repent and return to Jesus with sincerity. This is the deepest joy that a human being can have. . . .

Our personal accounts with God, our individual relationship with him, set the stage for everything else. False liberators are those who hold their souls slaves to sin and because of this are many times so cruel because they do not know how either to love or respect the human person.

The second idea passes on from the individual to the communitarian. God desires to save people as a people. It is the whole population that God wants to save.

The famous songs of Isaiah present God speaking with a people. It is the dialogue of God with what the Scriptures call a "collective personality," as though he were speaking with one person. God speaks with a people and to that people. God makes them his people because he is going to entrust them with promises, revelations that soon will serve for all the rest of the peoples. . . .

This people of God exists throughout history. Did you notice what today's reading has said so beautifully? [Isaiah 43:16-21] "You glorify the first exodus when I took you out of Egypt, when you crossed the desert. What many wonders were made on that journey with Moses! But glory no longer in that past. That has already become history, I make things anew." What a beautiful phrase from God! It is God who makes the new; it is God who goes with history.

Now the exodus will be from another direction, from Babylon, from exile. The desert through which they are going to pass will flower like a garden, the waters will gush forth symbolizing the passing of God's pardon, the people reconciled with God on the way to Jerusalem. . . .

Today El Salvador is living its own exodus. Today we too are passing to our liberation through the desert, where cadavers, where anguished pain are devastating us, and where many suffer the temptation of those who were walking with Moses and who wanted to turn back. . . . God desires to save the people making a new history. . . .

What is not repeated in history are the circumstances, the opportunities to which we are witnesses in El Salvador. How dense is our history, how varied from one day to another! One leaves El Salvador and returns the following week, and it seems that history has changed so categorically. Let us not rest our stability on wanting to judge things as they were once judged. One thing, yes: May we have firmly anchored in the soul our faith in Jesus Christ, God of history. That does not change; but he has, as it were, the satisfaction of changing history playing with history: "I make things new."

The grace of the Christian, therefore, is to not be braced on traditions that can no longer sustain themselves, but to apply that eternal tradition of Christ to the present realities. . . .

This project God has for liberating his people is transcendent. I think that I may even repeat too often this idea, but I'll never tire of doing it because we run the risk often of wanting to get out of present situations with immediate resolutions, and we forget that haste makes waste, that quick answers are patches but not true solutions. The true solution has to fit into the definitive plan of God. Every solution we seek—a better land distribution, a better administration and distribution of wealth in El Salvador, a political organization structured around the common good of Salvadorans—these must be sought always within the context of the definitive liberation. . . .

Beautiful is the moment in which we understand that we are no more than an instrument of God; we live only as long as God wants us to live; we can do only as much as God makes us able to; we are only as intelligent as God would have us be. To place all these limitations in God's hands, to recognize that without God we can do nothing, is to have a sense, my beloved brothers and sisters, that a transcendent meaning of this time in El Salvador means to pray much, to be very united with God. . . .

We must continue to be mindful of how liberation must free us from sin. All evils have a common root, and it is sin. There are, in the human heart, egotisms, envies, idolatries, and it is from these that divisions and hoarding arise. As Christ said, "It is not what comes out from a man that defiles him, but rather what is in the human heart: evil thoughts." We must purify, then, this source of all slaveries. Why does slavery exist? Why is there margination? Why is illiteracy rampant? Why are there diseases? Why do people mourn in pain? All of these things are pointing out that sin does exist. . . .

That is why the transcendence of liberation lifts us from our sins, and the Church will always be preaching: Repent of your personal sins. And she will say as Christ did to the adulteress: I do not condemn you; you have repented, but do not sin again. How much I want to convince you, brothers and sisters, all those who see little importance in these intimate relations with God, that these things are important!

Without God, there can be no true concept of liberation. Temporary liberations, yes; but definitive, solid liberations—only people of faith can reach them. . . .

Paul says of Christ: "To know him and the strength of his resurrection and the communion with his sufferings, dying with his same death that I may arrive one day at the resurrection of the dead." Do you see how life recovers all of its meaning? And suffering then becomes a communion with Christ, the Christ that suffers, and death is a communion with the death that redeemed the world? Who can feel worthless before this treasure that one finds in Christ, that gives meaning to sickness, to pain, to oppression, to torture, to margination? No one is conquered, no one; even though they put you under the boot of oppression and of repression, whoever believes in Christ knows that he is a victor and that the definitive victory will be that of truth and justice!

In Aguilares we celebrated the third anniversary of Fr. Rutilio Grande's assassination. It is obvious that the repression is having its effects—there were few people present; there is fear. It is an area martyred in the extreme. The message was that Christ's messenger must always find what Fr. Grande found, if he would be faithful.

In Tejutla, in the village of Los Martinez, we celebrated the village feastday. And there they told me of a terrible violation of human rights: On March 7 about midnight a truck filled with military men in civilian dress and some in uniform opened doors, pulling people out in a violent way with kicks and blows from rifle butts; they raped four young women, beat up their parents savagely, and threatened them that if they said anything about it they would have to bear the consequences. We have learned the tragedy of these poor young girls.

[Archbishop Romero recounted the incidents of torture and repression throughout El Salvador for each day of the preceding week, listing the dead by name when possible, and concluding with a report on the severe violence of March 17 in response to a national strike, which made a strong statement against the military repression by paralyzing the economic activity of the country.]

. . . Beloved brothers and sisters, it would be interesting to analyze, but I don't want to abuse your time, what significance there is in these months of a new government that precisely wanted to draw us out of these horrible situations. And if what it wants to do is leave headless the organization of the people and obstruct the process that the people want, no other process can thrive. Without its roots in the people, no government can be effective—much less so when it seeks to impose itself by the force of bloodshed and pain.

I would like to appeal in a special way to the men of the army, and in particular to the troops of the National Guard, the Police, and the garrisons. Brothers, you belong to our own people. You kill your own brother peasants; and in the face of an order to kill that is given by a man, the law of God should prevail that says: Do not kill! No soldier is obliged to obey an order counter to the law of God. No one has to comply with an immoral law. It is time now that you recover your conscience and obey its dictates rather than the command of sin. The Church, defender of the rights of God, of the law of God, of the dignity of the human person, cannot remain silent before so much abomination.

We want the government to seriously consider that reforms mean nothing when they come bathed in so much blood. Therefore, in the name of God, and in the name of this longsuffering people, whose laments rise to heaven every day more tumultuous, I beseech you, I beg you, I command you in the name of God: stop the repression!

The Church preaches your liberation just as we studied it today in the Holy Bible. A liberation that holds, above all, respect for human dignity, the salvation of the common good of the people, and the transcendence that looks above all else to God, and from God alone derives its hope and its strength.

Let us now proclaim our faith in this truth.

Edicio de la Torre

Like Dove and Serpent

Edicio de la Torre, a Catholic priest in the Philippines, spent nine years in prison under the regime of Ferdinand Marcos. He was released after the government of President Corazon Aquino came to power in February 1986. De la Torre founded a movement called Christians for National Liberation, and was active for years in the struggle for democracy and justice in the Philippines. The following interview took place in Manila only days after his release from prison. It was conducted by Earl Martin, Dave Schrock-Shenk, and Brenda Stoltzfus of the Mennonite Central Committee. De la Torre subsequently left the priesthood and continued his human rights work.

How did you survive being imprisoned for nine years under former President Ferdinand Marcos, and how did your faith help you?

It's always difficult to talk of one's faith and how one survives. As you say, I survived, and people immediately hasten to say, "It must be his faith." I guess it must be too. But if you ask me right now, I'm not quite sure what precisely made me survive.

Was I specifically faithful and religious during all those years in prison? I think so, but not only so. At various times in your life, in prison or in the struggle, when you cannot hold fast to any other person, thing, movement, or fact, but just yourself, you stand up and ask yourself, "Do you know what you are, and is this worth it?" If you believe in the life beyond physical death, you ask, is it something that you can look to with some joy and some quiet pride? If you relate those feelings to faith, which I think we should, then it was faith and religion that helped me survive.

For me, the privilege of being in prison and my survival of that experience were related to the fact that, compared to many other prisoners, I never lacked friends. I was always aware that there were a lot of people who knew I was in prison, who were waiting for me to get out, who were working to get me out, and who, even when I was inside, were giving me a lot of work to do—which is good for one's sense of self-worth. Whether it's giving inspiration or counsel or even technical advice, it's good when someone asks something of you and you can give. I never felt that I was out of the living movement. It just was a different assignment.

All situations have their limitations, and all situations have their possibilities. What matters is that you have a sense that you are not isolated from all the rest. If you are part of a movement, each one does his or her thing and the whole thing builds up to something. So long as you can relate to that and you know that the others relate to you, the meaning of your life is not reduced to what you personally do, or what you personally see, but what the whole group is aware of. That, I think, is the most succinct and most adequate explanation of being and believing and surviving for me. I've never felt alone.

Do you see a need for reconciliation in Philippine society, and what is necessary for reconciliation now that Marcos has fallen?

Ah, reconciliation. This is a big problem. The concept is good—reconciliation with justice—but justice has an element, or undercurrent, of vengeance. Reconciliation, especially with the late-comers who want things to be normal again without a settling of accounts, means a kind of "forgive and forget" attitude.

How do we handle reconciliation and justice simultaneously? First, let's consider if someone you know has committed an injustice and has sinned, comes to you and says, "I'm sorry, I recognize I did something wrong. I'm asking you for forgiveness. Will you forgive me?" At that moment the challenge is for us to be able to find that grace, which is divine, to forgive, prior to the settling of the grievances. By definition, forgiveness is given beforehand. All it asks for is a confession of guilt and a call for forgiveness.

Second, I feel that forgiveness is the privilege of the victim. We will not forgive for someone. Let us say that someone in the reform movement of the military comes and says, "I joined the reform movement because at a certain point in my life I had followed orders too faithfully and too often and 'salvaged' [killed] a lot of people." He will not say that for public consumption, but he will admit that he killed certain people. And he says at a certain point, "*Sobra na, tama na*"—"It's too much, and I refuse to follow the next order." So I say, "Brother, you are safe."

But what happens now to the family of those he has killed? I cannot forgive him for them. But I can help set up a meeting between them. Let us pray and hope that those families who have the right and privilege to forgive will find the grace to forgive him. Then, if these people are genuinely repentant, they will use the grace given them from that forgiveness to make restitution and offer penance.

That is the only way to approach a just reconciliation, safeguarding mental, human, and Christian values and, at the same time, acknowledging the realities of human wickedness and folly and deviousness. This is the mixture that I call biblical politics, reflecting a simplicity of heart, like a dove, and assessing the deviousness and labyrinthine ways of the human mind, like a serpent. To be both as simple and forgiving as one is given the grace to do and to be at the same time politically clever and cautious as we have to be to live within a historical world—that is the problem of any movement for reconciliation.

People ask me, "Fr. Ed, how will you bring back your nine years in jail?" Well, those nine years were not lost; but still there were some losses. I remember Gandhi facing, I believe, a Hindu, an Indian who had killed a Muslim in a riot, who said, "I set fire to a Muslim house and I know I roasted them alive. But now I know I have done wrong. I ask your forgiveness." Gandhi said, "Obviously, I can forgive you, but how do we now make an effort of restoring your sense of wholeness and being saved?" Eventually they found a Muslim orphan baby, and Gandhi said to the man, "Raise him as your child. Raise him as a Muslim. Maybe that way you can recover your wholeness."

I think something like that would have to be worked out in the Philippines. That's possible, perhaps, to do on an individual basis. Can you imagine it on a societal, massive level? But that kind of ministry is possible and needed. A lot of those in the struggle, who perhaps are not as tempered through the process of suffering and thought and life, might not find it easy to do that.

People say to me, "Fr. Ed, to forgive is divine. God is lavish, forgiving everyone. If God discriminates, God wouldn't be God." But why are people in hell? They can't accept the forgiveness. They can't forgive themselves. So the very punishment is precisely that: They cannot believe in their hearts that they can be forgiven. They hate themselves so much and do not believe that someone can be so good as to accept them even after all they've done.

It's a very deep question, but it's part of the reality we have to live with. It's hard enough at the personal level. It's also hard on the social and political level.

In my case prison was not really that draining or negative. But I remember there was a forum where I was with many detainees, less-known people, heavily tortured. When they were discussing this, I was close to crying. And then I said, "I can laugh and even casually converse with some soldiers; but, my God, this worker whose brother was killed, this one whose wife is missing . . . who am I to talk to them of reconciliation?"

This big project of kingdom and social transformation is part of our reality, but there is also the intense and smaller drama of human lives relating to each other. And the trick is not to separate the two, but to interrelate them, giving them their proper time and method.

It's a very challenging and difficult job, and we haven't even discussed these matters with all the ex-detainees. I know a lot of them are in more difficult circumstances than I am. They're unemployed; no one is going to give them a job soon. Their families are still in shambles. They have missing people, and they know that some of their torturers and captors are now riding high on a new popularity in the "new" military.

How can you have a genuine reconciliation, and yet avoid having premature and unnecessary conflicts within this fragile coalition that could very well be in danger of some *"contras"* loyal to Marcos from Hawaii? That is the difficult field of politics. A moral training for that must be more sophisticated, more long term, and yet more intense, because it is much harder than the already hard job of forming personal consciences for interpersonal ministry.

What reflections would you offer on liberation and the movement for democracy in the Philippines, after spending nine years in prison and much work in the movement?

It's very hard. Sometimes I tell myself I should not have learned all these things. Before, it was so simple. I thought liberation was simply this: The world is sinful, it's been redeemed, and God has promised the kingdom. And the people will make history, and that's it!

But in fact it's very complicated. You become more modest and less dogmatic. You realize there's no one person who can be in charge of all these things, so we need to work together. Each one has something to contribute, some more dramatic, some less dramatic.

The challenge is to grasp the complexity and richness of all this, and at the same time, realize two things: first, the need for a more conscious relatedness among us, so that we know that the advance here, the advance there, the setback here, are all part of one movement internationally. Certainly frontiers, whether political, national, or cultural, are present. But they are ultimately secondary to the basic oneness of our common struggle to create a better world, a better earth, including our clashes and quarrels over what, in fact, constitutes that better world.

Second, the challenge is to become clearer at every moment of one's life, as a person and as part of a group, about where we can maximize our contribution at each stage. All of us can sit back and dream the big visions and fantasize about our moment of glory at center stage, but one has little control over that. What matters is that you understand yourself at a given moment, with your resources, skills, weaknesses, and strengths and say, "This is the historical moment. This is where I am. This is where I am rooted. This is where I am assigned. This is what I either chose or have been sent to. What can I do best at this point, given this larger picture?" Then pour yourself there. And after a moment, you sum up, and then you reaffirm yourself.

It's like pronouncing vows in the religious order. You have a novitiate—you think of yourself, you assess yourself, and then you try to gather yourself as much as you can, so that when you commit yourself you are not just committing a part of you, but all of you. Then after a while, you review and reaffirm your vows. And then you reaffirm them again.

Sometimes you can change, just as, in a sense, I have been changing my vocation. I don't see myself anymore in traditional, institutional ministry. So many things have changed in my life. I see more meaning and more need for me here in this people's movement.

You can accept the less visible tasks as long as you have no illusions about yourself and therefore have no false need for heroism or things that are more personally satisfying. That's the discipline of being part of a historical, popular movement toward the coming of the kingdom.

Four U.S. Martyrs

A Journey of More Than Miles

by Joyce Hollyday

Dorothy Kazel

"We talked quite a bit today about what happens if something begins. And most of us feel we would want to stay here. Now this depends on what happens—if there is a way we can help—like run a refugee center or something. We wouldn't want to just run out on the people. . . . I thought I should say this to you— because I don't want to say it to anyone else—because I don't think they would understand. Anyway, my beloved friend, just know how I feel and 'treasure it in your heart.' If a day comes when others will have to understand, please explain it for me. . . ."

— Dorothy Kazel
Letter to a friend,
October 3, 1979

Thirty-six hours after Dorothy Kazel, Jean Donovan, Maura Clarke, and Ita Ford had disappeared in El Salvador, a Salvadoran priest handed a scrap of paper to a worried U.S. visitor. The message, scrawled in Spanish with a pencil, read simply: "The bodies of four women wearing sandals have been found."

When the visitor asked what the message meant, the priest answered, "It means that these are probably your friends." He explained that very few Salvadoran women can afford a pair of sandals. Another friend remembered, upon hearing the news, that she had planned to tease Dorothy about wearing sandals to the U.S. Embassy.

Dorothy Kazel, an Ursuline sister who had spent six years in El Salvador, and Jean Donovan, a lay volunteer who had been in the country for eighteen months, were widely known as "The Rescue Squad" by other U.S. missionaries. From their base in La Libertad, the energetic and dauntless pair traveled the countryside in a white Toyota van, picking up supplies, transporting refugees, accompanying grief-stricken families in search of disappeared loved ones. As North Americans—both blonde and blue-eyed—Jean and Dorothy were considered the "last best protection" for anyone in trouble.

Father Paul Schindler, head of the Cleveland diocese's mission team in El Salvador, assumed that the two women were spending the night at one of the team's other two bases, as they often did, when they didn't return on December 2, 1980. The evening before, the three of them had shared dinner at the U.S. Embassy. The conversation with Ambassador Robert White and his wife, Maryanne, had gone late into the night, and the couple had insisted that the three missionaries stay with them to avoid the dangerous road home after the 9 o'clock curfew.

In the morning Paul had plans to visit friends in San Salvador. Jean and Dorothy were headed off to do some shopping for a new children's refugee center, and then on to the airport to meet four friends. Before they parted, Jean—always ready for a party—leaned out of the window of the van and called to Paul, "Don't be too late tonight! We'll have a party with the Maryknollers to celebrate their return!"

Jean Donovan

Jean and Dorothy expected to meet four Maryknoll Sisters returning from a regional conference in Nicaragua at 3 o'clock that afternoon. But Maura Clarke and Ita Ford had been unable to book reservations on the plane with the other two. Dorothy and Jean returned to the airport to meet their flight at 6 o'clock.

The next morning, concern was high as the members of the mission team gathered for a weekly staff meeting and Jean and Dorothy were unaccounted for. The morning's business was canceled. Paul began making phone calls, and two sisters from the Cleveland team drove from La Libertad to the airport, looking for clues. They found an unforgettable one: the white van, now a stripped and burned-out shell, abandoned at the side of the road.

The trail of tragedy that wound for a time over the roads around the San Salvador airport on the night of December 2, 1980, began more than three years before on a country road in Aguilares. In this valley 30 miles north of San Salvador, 30,000 desperate *campesinos* fought for survival, farming tiny, steep plots of rocky, barren soil, watching their children die of malnutrition while a handful of landowners grew wealthy from exporting the sugar that dominated the fertile land.

Father Rutilio Grande was a Jesuit priest who took seriously the Catholic Church's embrace of the poor at its Medellín Conference in 1968. In Aguilares, he fostered the formation of base Christian communities, which upheld the dignity of the peasants and encouraged them to organize toward the promises of justice they read daily in the Bible.

The priest's brand of faith spread like wildfire through the valley, and eventually through all of El Salvador. The landowners soon recognized that the wealth and privileges ensured by their feudal system were threatened by this hope. On March 12, 1977, Rutilio Grande and two friends were riddled with government-issue bullets while riding in a jeep on their way to celebrate evening Mass.

In one of his last sermons, Grande had preached:

Soon, the Bible and the gospel won't be allowed to cross our borders. We will get only the bindings, because all of the pages are subversive. And I think that if Jesus himself came across the border, . . . they would not let him in. They would accuse [him] of being a rabble-rouser, a foreign Jew, one who confused the people with exotic and foreign ideas, ideas against democracy—that is, against the wealthy minority. . . . Brothers and sisters, there is no doubt, they would crucify him again.

The weapon that cut down Rutilio Grande was the starting gun in a marathon of murder. Soon the path of death branched out over El Salvador, sweeping up a dozen more Jesuit priests, hundreds of base community "delegates of the Word," thousands of community organizers and students and workers.

Targeted was a widening circle of opposition to the country's brutal injustice. But at the center of the bull's-eye was the church. Bumper stickers appeared in San Salvador: "Be a patriot—kill a priest." Full-page ads in the government-controlled newspapers accused the Jesuits and other church workers of "inciting, directing and supporting the vandalous hordes in a plan to create a climate of terror and violence."

But of course it was the government, the military, and the wealthy elites of El Salvador who controlled the climate. In the wake of Grande's death emerged the first of the organized right-wing death squads. That year the number of people "disappeared" doubled, prosecution of "subversives" tripled, and political assassinations increased tenfold. By March 1980 an archbishop was among those who had been gunned down.

Dorothy Kazel, Jean Donovan, Ita Ford, and Maura Clarke were far from naive about the mad violence engulfing El Salvador. Ita and her closest friend, Maryknoll Sister Carla Piette, left eight years of work in Chile to respond to an urgent call for more U.S. missionaries in El Salvador, to try to help stay the tide of brutality after Archbishop Oscar Romero's death.

Ita wrote to her younger sister, "You say you don't want anything to happen to me. I'd prefer it that way myself—but I don't see that we have control over the forces of madness. And if you choose to enter into other peoples' suffering, to love others, you at least have to consent in some way to the possible consequences."

But among those consequences Ita had not imagined the tragedy that struck on August 23, 1980, a month after they had arrived in El Salvador. While Carla was driving them in a jeep across a riverbed

Ita Ford

that evening, a flash flood sent a wall of water over them, turning the jeep on its side. Carla's last act was to push Ita through a half-open window to save her life.

Ita recounted later that, as she was being swept down the river, "I just said to myself, 'You won't make it'—so I said, 'Receive me Lord.' . . . I really wasn't afraid. I never said 'Help,' it never occurred to me to say 'Save me'. . . . I just said 'Receive me, I'm coming.'"

Ita was saved by the root of a tree. Jean found Carla's body the next morning, nine miles downstream. The following days were marked by extreme grief for Ita. But something profound had happened in her: She had faced her own death and found peace about it. That peace was something that for Ita and the others was at times strong, and at times elusive.

Jean had written to a friend that she had seen so many bodies horribly tortured and mutilated that she prayed that, if she were killed, she would be killed instantly. Then she added, "I am a coward. I don't want to die."

Facing death was inevitable in El Salvador. It wasn't possible to spend every day looking for the disappeared, drying the tears of the orphans and the refugees, and putting back together for burial the dismembered bodies—left by the death squads to the dogs and the vultures—without inviting a face-off with death.

There were moments of doubt, bouts with depression, and thoughts about returning home. Family members seemed far away, and communication was often difficult. Jean wrestled intensely with the choice between marriage and her ministry in El Salvador. In a letter, she spoke of the struggle to remain:

> I think that the hardship one endures maybe is God's way of taking you out into the desert, to prepare you to meet and love him more fully. . . . Several times I have decided to leave El Salvador. I almost could except for the children, the poor, bruised victims of this insanity. Who would care for them? Whose heart could be so staunch as to favor the reasonable thing in a sea of their tears and helplessness? Not mine, dear friend, not mine.

The fears and questions, large and small, voiced and recorded in diaries and letters, show a picture of four women who were, above all, human. Their courage was remarkable. But perhaps more astounding was their joy.

Jean, who serenaded her friends with Irish folk ballads on her guitar, gave children frequent rides on her motorcycle, and baked chocolate chip cookies every week for Archbishop Romero while he was alive, was dubbed "St. Jean the Playful." Ita was described this way by Maryknoll friends: "Her twinkling eyes and elfin grin would surface irrepressibly even in the midst of poverty and sorrow." And Dorothy, quoting St. Augustine, said she wanted to live as "an alleluia head to foot."

Maura, who had spent many years in Nicaragua and was known there as "the angel of our land," was chosen by the Maryknoll Sisters to carry on Carla's work after her death. Ita described Maura to her mother before Maura's arrival in El Salvador as "very Irish," with "a huge, loving, warm heart." Ita had also added, "For all these people who come in who are traumatized, or who have been hiding, scared for their lives—I just think Maura's going to be God's gift to them."

Indeed, the description was more than appropriate. The same could be said of Ita herself—and of Jean and Dorothy. Above all, they were gifts from God.

In early November 1980 a crude sign appeared on the door of the parish house where Ita lived. It depicted a bloody human head, with a knife embedded in it, and the words, "This is what will happen to anyone who comes to this house because the priests and nuns are communists." By the middle of the month, the church in the province of Chalatenango, where Maura and Ita lived and ministered, was virtually occupied by the army.

On Thursday, November 27, six of the most prominent leaders of the opposition Democratic Revolutionary Front (FDR) were brutally assassinated. It was Thanksgiving Day for the U.S. community, and at an ecumenical service that evening Jean and Dorothy first met Ambassador White.

Just one week later, the day after the funeral for the opposition leaders, Robert White stood over a shallow grave near the remote village of Santiago Nonualco. A man delivering milk had come upon the bodies in a cow pasture.

With ropes, local *campesinos* pulled the bodies out. Jean and Ita were very badly bruised, and Jean's face had been crushed by the impact of the bullet that killed her. Dorothy's jeans were on backward; a *campesino* explained that the women had been found without their jeans on, and those who found them had, for reasons of dignity, tried to dress them. At least two of the women had been raped.

At the graveside, Robert White questioned the local justice of the peace, demanding to know why the deaths hadn't been reported. The man's answer was simple: "This happens all the time."

The 1980s began in El Salvador with the murder of an archbishop. The decade ended with the killings of six Jesuit priests and two women at San Salvador's University of Central America in November 1989. In the years in between—and the months before and since—75,000 anonymous Salvadorans have joined the rolls of the martyrs. It is for them that the others died.

Ten years ago, upon hearing of the murder of the four church women, the Carter administration suspended $25 million in U.S. military aid to El Salvador. That immediate instinct was the correct one. The scandal was that the 9,000 other killings in El Salvador up to that point had not prompted such action.

But within two weeks the aid had been reinstated. Ronald Reagan took over the reins of government and made a consistent sham of the previous administration's effort to tie U.S. aid to progress in the investigation of the murders of the four women. And as 1990 comes to a close, the United States is sending $1.5 million every day to the lethal government of El Salvador. The deaths continue to mount.

We have learned many things from the loss of Maura, Dorothy, Ita, and Jean. They reminded us in a dramatic way of both the vulnerability of women and the power of the religious community. They showed us the faith that is born of sorrow. But, perhaps most of all, they forced us to look again at the thousands of others who have made a similar sacrifice.

Maura Clarke

Maura and Ita were buried, in keeping with Maryknoll tradition, in a small country cemetery in Chalatenango in El Salvador. A funeral Mass was held in La Libertad after an all-night wake for Dorothy and Jean.

As dawn appeared, and their co-workers prepared to carry their caskets from the church, Salvadorans moved in front of the others. They passed the caskets through the crowd, from shoulder to shoulder, as triumphant applause spread from the church to the throng waiting outside in the square and along the route leading to the airport. It was the first Friday in December, when Jean and Dorothy would have taken the white van and gone up and down the hillsides of El Salvador, picking up the suffering ones and bringing them to a special annual Mass for the Anointing of the Sick.

Two were buried in the United States, two in El Salvador, signifying a journey that had been made from one world to another. It was a journey of more than miles.

The night before she was murdered, at the closing liturgy of the Maryknoll conference in Nicaragua, Ita Ford read a passage from one of Archbishop Oscar Romero's last homilies:

Christ invites us not to fear persecution because, believe me, brothers and sisters, the one who is committed to the poor must share the same fate as the poor. And in El Salvador we know what the fate of the poor signifies: to disappear, to be tortured, to be held captive, and to be found dead by the side of the road.

That same night, miles away at the U.S. Embassy in San Salvador, Jean Donovan asked of Robert White, "What do you do when even to help the poor, to take care of the orphans, is considered an act of subversion by the government?" Without words, she answered her own question. What you do is continue—even in the face of death.

Ultimately, it was Matthew 25 that got these four women killed. It was that simple mandate to love the poor: to feed the hungry, clothe the naked, visit the sick and imprisoned, and shelter the refugees. And, in El Salvador, more and more it meant comforting the tortured and burying the dead.

But Dorothy, Jean, Maura, and Ita did more than love the poor. They became like them. They carried the burden of injustice, learned the grace of simplicity, and grew to embrace their powerlessness—and to trust God's sufficient power.

There is no way to explain it to the world's satisfaction. Blank stares, confused questions, and even manufactured lies were the responses dished out to friends and relatives of the women who tried to explain it to the media, to Congress and the State Department. The language of faith is not comfortable in the halls of power and persuasion.

In the end, it was a pair of sandals that distinguished these four women. This—their concession to North American feet lacking the callouses of the poor—was their luxury.

We must be cut to the heart and shaken to the core once again by these deaths; because these women of God knew something of that which we still do not know. And if we cannot learn it, there is little hope for us. We will simply be doomed to repeat again and again our war against the poor, which—like a metastasized global cancer—has spread from the jungles of Southeast Asia to the ravines of Central America to the sands of the Middle East. It shows no signs of remission; and our nation, no signs of remorse.

Jesus showed us another way. About a decade ago he crossed over the border into El Salvador—and met himself among the faithful poor. He was wearing sandals. And he was crucified again.

But we know that death is not the last word. The witness continues. We "treasure it in our hearts." And, to the extent that we try to follow the example set before us a decade ago, we honor the Christ who comes to us in many forms.

Further Reading about this "Cloud of Witnesses" from Orbis Books

Love Is the Measure
A Biography of Dorothy Day
Jim Forest
ISBN 0-88344-042-0

Witnesses to the Kingdom
The Martyrs of El Salvador and the Crucified Peoples
Jon Sobrino
ISBN 1-57075-468-3

The Blindfold's Eyes
My Journey from Torture to Truth
Sister Dianna Ortiz with Patricia Davis
ISBN 1-57075-563-0

Clarence Jordan
Essential Writings
Edited with an Introduction by Joyce Hollyday
ISBN 1-57075-497-7

God's Beloved
A Spiritual Biography of Henri Nouwen
Michael O'Laughlin
ISBN 1-57075-561-2

Martin Luther King
The Inconvenient Hero
Vincent Harding
ISBN 1-57075-064-5

Pedro Arrupe
Essential Writings
Selected with an Introduction by Kevin Burke
ISBN 1-57075-546-9

Further Reading about this "Cloud of Witnesses" from Orbis Books

Spiritual Questions for the Twenty-First Century
Essays in Honor of Joan D. Chittister
Edited by Mary Hembrow Snyder
ISBN 1-57075-369-5

Testimony
The Word Made Fresh
Daniel Berrigan
ISBN 1-57075-545-0

Living with Wisdom
A Life of Thomas Merton
Jim Forest
ISBN 0-88344-755-X

Dietrich Bonhoeffer
Writings Selected with an Introduction
by Robert Coles
ISBN 1-57075-194-3

Oscar Romero
Reflections on His Life and Writings by
Marie Dennis, Renny Golden, Scott Wright
ISBN 1-57075-309-1

Please support your local bookstore or call 1-800-258-5838

For a free catalog, please write us at
Orbis Books, Box 308
Maryknoll, NY 10545-0308
or visit our website at www.orbisbooks.com

For more information about Sojourners magazine, write
Sojourners, 2401 15th St. NW, Washington, DC 20009
or visit their website at www.sojo.net